We Too

In 2007 I published a book dealing with sexual abuse and entitled *Confronting Power and Sex in the Catholic Church*. The book *We Too: The Laity Speaks* shows us that, even after the Royal Commission, power and sex are still the two realities that most need to be confronted. The twelve contributors each approach the subject from a different angle, but they all emphasise change in these two fields.

If the Church does not do so, there will be a severe price to be paid, for there will be a continuing loss of the lifeblood of the Church in this country. We cannot change the promise of Jesus to be with his Church forever into a promise that he will save the Catholic Church in Australia despite its strenuous efforts to destroy itself through a continuing failure to confront power and sex. If you want proof of this, just watch the continuing disappearance of young people from our churches as they reach their teenage years.

The Plenary Council has quickly become a crisis moment, a last chance to rectify a desperate situation. My greatest fear has always been that the people with the greatest power would be continually looking over their shoulders at what the Vatican might think and would be afraid to make the changes necessary. They would be afraid to actually confront power and sex rather than merely try to manage them. May this book help to wake us up to reality.

Bishop Emeritus Geoffrey Robinson

The Laity Speaks!

We too

EDITED BY
BERISE HEASLY & JOHN D'ARCY MAY

COVENTRY
PRESS

Published in Australia by
Coventry Press
33 Scoresby Road
Bayswater Vic. 3153
Australia

ISBN 9780648861201

Compilation copyright © Berise Heasly and John D'Arcy May 2020
Copyright of individual chapters remains with the authors.

All rights reserved. Other than for the purposes and subject to the conditions prescribed under the *Copyright Act*, no part of this publication may be reproduced, stored in a retrieval system, or transmitted in any form or by any means, electronic, mechanical, photocopying, recording or otherwise, without the prior permission of the publisher.

Scripture quotations are from the *New Revised Standard Version Bible*, copyright 1989, Division of Christian Education of the National Council of the Churches of Christ in the United States of America. Used by permission. All rights reserved.

Cataloguing-in-Publication entry is available from the National Library of Australia http://catalogue.nla.gov.au/.

Cover design by Ian James - www.jgd.com.au
Text design by Megan Low (Film Shot Graphics FSG)
Set in Vollkorn

Printed in Australia

Contents

Acknowledgments 5

Gospel Reflection 6

Introduction 8
        Berise Heasly and John D'Arcy May

Part I
Experience Speaks

Chapter 1
    Dying To Self: The Evolution Of Identity 18
    Hugh McGinlay

Chapter 2
    God's Mission Has A Church 39
    Sue Phillips

Chapter 3
    Full Equality For All In The Catholic Church 62
    Marilyn Hatton

Chapter 4
    The Church As We Know It Is Broken 92
    Eleanor Flynn

Chapter 5
    Suffer The Little Children 107
    Judy Benson

Chapter 6
    Julian: A Mystic For Today 128
    Janette Elliott

Part II
Theology Responds

Chapter 7
    Clericalism, Women And The Family Of Jesus
        In The New Testament..........................156
    Constant J. Mews

Chapter 8
    Rediscovering Jesus: Reimagining Church........187
    Ian Hamilton

Chapter 9
    Clericalism And Reforming The Church In
        History..217
    Constant J. Mews

Chapter 10
    Evangelisation, Ecology and Australian
        Catholicism...................................239
    Paul Collins

Chapter 11
    Interreligious Relations in Multicultural
        Australia 265
    John D'Arcy May

Conclusion
    From Clericalism And Hierarchicalism
        Towards Regeneration And Reform............291
    Berise Heasly

Epilogue... 320
    Berise Heasly

Contributors......................................325

Acknowledgments

The editors would like to express our special appreciation to Michael Elligate PP, AM, Hugh McGinlay, Denis Heasly and Morag Fraser AM, for editorial, philosophical, theological and technological support as we negotiated our way through this project.

Finally, we congratulate the authors of all the papers in this volume and thank them sincerely for their deliberations and discernment.

Gospel Reflection

Then he put them all outside, and took the child's father and mother and those who were with him, and went in where the child was. He took her by the hand and said to her: *Talitha cum*! And immediately the girl got up and began to walk about (she was twelve years of age). At this, they were overcome with amazement.

Mark 5:40-42

Dear Mark,
You have the gift of imagination.
You got it!
You set up the first Gospel.

Was it a last ditch attempt to save
A panic-stricken community?
We don't like crowds, mobs...
Things can quickly go wrong,
Turn violent, nasty and demanding.

The crush of that jostling crowd,
Curious, desperate, irreverent,
One never forgets this fear of being crushed
And trampled underfoot.

Followers of your community were restless, jumpy
Seeing hidden danger and the chance of abandonment
   everywhere...

Storms on the lake, upturned boats, and drowned people,
> old and young.

Smiling excited crowds followed him everywhere,
Some desperate to link up,
Others just after a handout.

Your image of a young woman, fresh and innocent,
Restored to life.

His presence makes us lose our fears and begin to hope.
> Hope that will
Always take us forward.

The Daughter of Jairus

Michael Elligate, PP, AM
St Carthage's University Parish
Parkville

Introduction

Berise Heasly and John D'Arcy May

'We' are the laity responding to the call of Pope Francis and to the command of Pope John XXIII to read the 'signs of the times'. In the spirit of Vatican Council II, we are responding to the call of *aggiornamento*: to open the windows of our church and learn from what exists in the world, where the 'People in the Pews'* live out their daily lives. We are responding to a perceived need for an authentic, faithful message from the laity, whose lived experience can add another dimension and perspective to existing and emerging theologies. We bring an awareness of the human and ecological challenges – including the pandemic currently sweeping our world – that confront us as people who wish to live the message of Jesus in this twenty-first century.

We offer our knowledge, expertise and personal faith as an adjunct to the various preparations being made for the Australian Plenary Council (whenever it is convened – and a substitute date has been established in October 2021, with open and careful attention to accurate access to content submitted but not manipulated within this extended time period). We are mindful of papal documents and current developments in church governance, synodality, philosophical, ethical and theological thinking; together these point to the urgent need for development of methodologies relevant to faith and *sustainability* for our twenty-first-century church.

We are aware of the response-ability *and* the responsibility, inherent in the call of Jesus to Jairus' daughter:

Talitha cum – to awaken, to arise (Mark 5:41-43), echoing the touch of Jesus when he restored a son to the Widow of Nain (Luke 7:14). We, too, must arise and be awake. We must seek, authentically and autonomously, the message of Jesus as the 'People in the Pews'; we must fuse secular and sacred elements of life into a balanced and evolving experience of faith in our Trinitarian God of the Cosmos in relationship with twenty-first-century humankind.

We explore what Pope Francis has called a change of era, by attempting to address an authentic paradigm change without blurring, redesigning, manipulating or deserting the message of Jesus. This new paradigm needs to be fostered carefully, freed of clericalism and hierarchicalism; it requires subtle understanding and compassionate response so it can become a re-foundation of faith in our Cosmic Creator, our loving Cosmic Christ, our Cosmic Sophia-Spirit. The changed paradigm will focus on the One God who asks us, in this third millennium, to be co-creators of the next stages of humankind's evolving journey towards eternity, infinity and love.

We, the authors whose writing appears in this volume, each identify an issue that needs development, research, enrichment and explanation in ways that identify the concerns of many of the 'People in the Pews'. We have striven for coherence, depth, subtlety of insight, and painstaking analysis, so that no false discernment stains the message of Jesus. It will be important that we don't give in to selective memory loss when regulations for living are loosened and community life begins again. We can't collapse into the old ways because the message of Jesus needs our twenty-first-century lived experience, expertise, wisdom and clarity of discernment. We must look forward, not back.

We remember the isolation that confronted us when we realised that Easter 2020 would be experienced in our homes, with digital connections only. That in itself was another form of wake-up call. Timothy Radcliffe reminded us recently of the abandonment felt by Jesus in the Garden of Gethsemane, writing that 'isolation can be more terrible than death'. Pope Francis, however, offered hope when he urged those at the thirty-fifth Youth Day (2020) to realise their calling to awaken. He reminded them of his words after the 2018 Synod: 'these words also speak of resurrection, of awakening to new life'. Pope Francis' biographer, Austin Ivereigh, interprets Francis' response at the 2019 Amazonia Synod (*The Tablet*, 22/2/20) as a clarification of how 'we begin to love, not use; value, not exploit; serve, not dominate'.

We are indebted to three eminent Victorian scholars for the analytical precision of their comments on the encyclical *Laudato Si'* (*Vox* 2, October 2015). Professor Mark Brett notes that 'Many Christians have lost a sacramental understanding of the interconnectedness of creation', and further, 'The political and economic realities of Aboriginal Australia are well known, but Francis also provokes us to reflect further on the theological significance of caring for ancestral lands and waters'. Rev. Dr Bruce Duncan adds: 'Pope Francis locates the key issues of climate change, economics, inequality and poverty in a moral framework which is deeply Christian, but in a language which communicates not just with Catholics, or even other Christians, but people of other religious traditions, and even atheists and agnostics'. Finally, Dr Deborah Guess states: 'Unlike theologies which focus primarily on a two-dimensional relationship between God and humankind, *Laudato Si'* takes for granted that there exists a three-way interrelationship between God, humanity and Earth'.

We must also heed the research of scholars and writers like Gerald Arbuckle, Chris Geraghty, Uta Ranke-Heinemann, Frederic Martel, Christos Tsiolkas and Gianluigi Nuzzi. They help us to identify the tangled threads of logic, interpretation, experience and belief that have marked every century since Paul began his journeys around the Mediterranean coast. Change was a constant: traditions were ruptured; power and control were ruthlessly manipulated, in ways altogether antithetical to the original message of Jesus – then as now. So history and our present experience prompts 'People in the Pews' to identify where they stand in relationship to the message of Jesus, and to offer their knowledge and expertise to us in this volume.

We are fortunate in having been able to assemble a group of committed lay Catholics, 'People in the Pews', who, despite everything, still have an attachment to what is, after all, *their* Church. Their voices are sometimes critical but always affirming. This is not an exercise in anti-clericalism; indeed, it is led off by a biblical reflection from **Father Michael Elligate**, pastor of St Carthage's university church in Parkville, Melbourne. Michael's theme is summed up in the words Jesus spoke to the young girl whose family believed she had died: *Talitha cum*, 'Young girl, get up!' (or in another translation, 'wake up!'), surely a striking metaphor for what is now being asked of the battered and humiliated Catholic Church.

The book is divided into two parts: in Part I, Catholics with many years of experience working in a variety of ministries tell their stories of struggle against an often uncooperative institution. Two important topics are missing from this section. We approached two Indigenous women who had worked with Catholic Aboriginal ministries, but each independently said that the experience had been so painful they could not bring themselves to revisit it. Their reason for declining our invitation is itself a telling example of what we are calling 'clericalism', that is, the rigidity of institutional structures whose main purpose is to shore up the institution itself.

To our great regret, the person we had earmarked to contribute a chapter on the Catholic Church's role in the ecumenical movement in Australia, someone with long experience in the teaching and practice of ecumenism, was unable to contribute in the time available. We suspect that similar institutional constraints would have come to light here. Finally, prominent lay leader Peter Johnstone regards it as 'supremely ironic' that the report of a Governance Review Project Team set up by the bishops and religious orders to respond to the Royal Commission into the Institutional Responses to Child Sexual Abuse (2013-2017), which recommends a review of governance in the local church with greater lay involvement, is now being withheld for consideration by the bishops – without involving the laity (*The Age*, 22/5/2020; see Massimo Faggioli, *National Catholic Reporter*, 19/5/2020).

The stories in Part I provide ample evidence of the indifference, misgivings or even frustrations that critical Catholics experience as they engage with their church, but also of the possibilities their skills can offer. **Hugh McGinlay** sketches a long journey from an Irish Catholic milieu in staunchly Protestant Scotland to the new horizons opened up by biblical studies and progressive religious education, to eventually becoming a religious publisher with wide sympathies (he is the publisher of this volume). Along the way, however, he has become estranged from many aspects of traditional Catholicism, yet he feels a painful sense of loss. **Sue Phillips** tells how as a religious sister she was immeasurably enriched by her years spent among Muslims in Morocco, only to be confronted with the reality of clericalism when she was appointed to her Order's leadership team in Rome. As a committed Catholic laywoman, **Marilyn Hatton** has invested much time and energy in promoting reform in the Church, moving from advocacy of women's ordination to the broader question of equality of women and men in all areas of the Church's life. Medical graduate and educator **Eleanor Flynn** offers a feminist critique of a conference in preparation for the Plenary Council, which confirmed her conviction that our Church is broken. Barrister and former editor **Judy Benson** is intimately acquainted with family violence and particularly the abuse of children from her work with the Children's Court and the Family Court, and she locates the by now well-known saga of clerical sexual abuse in this wider context. Finally, there is such a thing as 'mystical experience', and **Janette Elliott** offers a study of the mediaeval mystic Julian of Norwich, whose response to the signs of *her* times can be an inspiration to us as we try to do the same in *our* times.

In Part II, we move to the ways in which Catholic theology tries to come to terms with the present situation. **Constant Mews,** in a remarkable piece of research into the first followers of Jesus, their family relationships and rivalries, reflects on the impact these had on the widely differing ways in which the early church was structured. **Ian Hamilton** delves into the contested area of historical Jesus scholarship to show that it has important implications for the way we conceive of the church and its leadership. **Constant Mews** complements his family relationship study with an additional chapter, giving an account of how structures inherited from these early developments became corrupted and perverted by the power struggles of those competing for influence in the mediaeval church, leading to opposition by the monastic orders and reform movements within them. If evangelisation is to be to the fore in getting the church 'back on mission', **Paul Collins** asks challenging questions about evangelisation's purpose and context, stressing the centrality of the ecological crisis in the thinking of Pope Francis. Finally, **John D'Arcy May** explores the profound but largely overlooked theological issues raised by the Second Vatican Council's documents on relations with the Jews, inter-religious dialogue and religious liberty, asking whether these have been acknowledged by the Australian church. **Berise Heasly**, the initiator of this project, uses her hard-hitting Conclusion to challenge those preparing the Plenary Council of the Catholic Church in Australia to take full account of the issues raised in this book. Does a church tightly structured by a hierarchy trapped in a clericalist mindset fully appreciate the pressure for reform coming from an increasingly frustrated and alienated laity? She sees in the strength of this lay movement not just a potential for reform, but a source of *regeneration* for a church hesitating on the threshold of reinventing itself for the twenty-first century.

The Epilogue brings together final elements, pointing forward, focusing on Jesus.

Berise Heasly and John D'Arcy May
Melbourne, Easter 2020

*The 'People in the Pews', a phrase used throughout this book, is a coinage taken from Berise Therese Heasly's, *Call No One Father*, Coventry Press 2019.

Part I

Experience Speaks

Chapter 1

Dying To Self: The Evolution Of Identity

Hugh McGinlay

Preamble

Unless a grain of wheat falls into the earth and dies, it remains a single grain; but if it dies, it bears much fruit. (John 12:24)

In his recent book *Mass Exodus: Catholic Disaffiliation in Britain and America since Vatican II* (OUP, 2019), Stephen Bullivant traces the gradual (and in recent times, substantial) decline in Mass attendance in those major English-speaking countries. Bullivant asserts that in the US, only fifteen per cent of born Catholics attend Mass on a weekly basis and that thirty-five per cent no longer tick 'Catholic' in formal surveys. The UK statistics are even more startling: only thirteen per cent of people who were raised as Catholic attend Sunday Mass, and a staggering thirty-seven per cent say they have 'no religion'. The decline in Mass attendance among Catholics in Australia is well documented in the research of Bob Dixon, and probably reflects the statistics that are at the heart of Bullivant's work.

In a review of *Mass Exodus* in the Jesuit magazine *America* (February 2020), Timothy P. O'Malley comments that 'disaffiliation is rarely a single moment in the life of a Catholic. Instead, it is a *process* in which one no longer identifies as a Catholic'. For me, this all raises issues surrounding identity, and particularly my own sense of identity within the Catholic tradition – how it began, how it evolved, what it means today and in the future.

Immersion

In his 2017 book *The Tempest-Tossed Church: Being a Catholic Today* (NewSouth Publishing), Gerard Windsor reminds us that 'From the beginning, my religious adherence was an immersion'. I don't think Windsor is specifically referring to Baptism – although the allusion is clear – but an immersion in a culture, a tradition, a way of being and thinking and relating and behaving. It is certainly my experience and memory. When my father and mother married in 1939, the families of each traced their ancestry for generations back to Ireland and Scotland. For reasons entirely of geography and isolation, their families had been Catholic Christian probably for 1500 years. My father's people came from the remote parts of Donegal in Ulster; my mother's people on her father's side were from the island of Barra in the Western Isles of Scotland, an island so remote in the sixteenth century that the Reformers who swept the rest of Scotland failed to reach it and, in any case, it was already receiving missionaries from Ireland to sustain the ancient Catholic faith. So, for whatever reason, the Catholic tradition on both sides remained intact, even if they rarely – if ever – reflected on it. That was left to me!

This was the faith in which I was immersed. Formally, by Baptism in the Church of St Quivox in Prestwick in Ayrshire in 1940; less formally, into a way of being Catholic in a Scottish culture that was generally hostile to Rome except in those areas where Irish and Highland emigrants had established themselves as Scottish and Catholic in a country that was traditionally suspicious of the connection.

The immersion was complete and all-embracing. But you have to have been there to understand the complete dominance of the reformed tradition in Scotland. The Reformers had abolished the ancient Catholic seasons and liturgies, including Christmas Day, which was a working day in Scotland until 1958, (and also explains the significance of New Year in the Scottish calendar, as well as such secular festivals as Burns Day in late January). It also explains the great sense of division between Catholics and Protestants. Even in sport: the rivalry of Celtic (Catholic) and Rangers (Protestant) football teams; the annual Orange Walks (an importation from Ulster that recalled the 1690 victory of the forces of Protestant King William over the Catholic Stuart pretender at the battle of the Boyne); the great sense of identity of (most) Scottish Catholics with their fellow Catholics in Ireland; the fact that many Catholics preferred to listen to Radio Eireann rather than the BBC.

I suspect that the Second World War had softened many of those prejudices but they were still around in my childhood. I remember clearly the first time I was called a papist. Admittedly, it was when I was on holiday as a child in an area far from my home village. This was a time when the greatest fear among Catholics (and perhaps some Protestants) was 'mixed marriages'. *Ne Temere* was a decree issued by Rome in 1907 whereby – for the first time in post Reformation history

– marriages of Catholics were only valid when they took place in the presence of a priest. Clearly, among Catholics, this resulted in the expectation that Catholics would marry within the tradition; and to a renewed emphasis in preaching and teaching about the evils and dangers of mixed marriages.

Catholics were expected to marry Catholics, and it was a source of disgrace within the community to be courting someone not of the faith. When one of my cousins married a Protestant in a non-Catholic setting, none of my family attended the marriage or acknowledged it; and her mother practically excluded her from the family for many, many years. Ironically, my uncle, her husband, was a Protestant but they had married presumably with the usual dispensation, which was not always granted, and required strict understanding that any children born of the marriage would be brought up as Catholic. The strongest and saddest example of such attitudes in my family occurred during the war. A cousin of my father was a sailor in the Royal Navy in the Atlantic convoys. His ship was torpedoed and he was lost at sea. His mother – my great aunt – experienced some consolation at his death because he had been going out with a Protestant girl and his death put an end to the possible disgrace of it all!

Catholic Primary school

Immersion was also into a Catholic school culture. Scotland is unique, I think, in that Catholic schools are State schools. In 1918, the Scottish bishops were persuaded to sell the Catholic schools to the Government in return for the guarantee that the Government would take responsibility for all aspects of Catholic education – building and maintenance of buildings, training of teachers, standards of education.

The Church retained some control over senior appointments but it meant in effect that there was no cost to Catholics to manage a separate school system. This meant that, especially in industrial areas, all Catholic children attended Catholic schools. I don't recall any Catholic child who attended a State school, which, in any case, were normally (if wrongly) called Protestant schools.

Religious education was central: catechism, sacramental preparation, learning prayers and hymns, going to Mass in church, calls from the clergy, annual visits from diocesan examiners, celebrations of the major feasts and seasons. Attendance at Sunday Mass was regarded as compulsory. There was a designated Children's Sunday Mass, with class teachers scheduled to attend and expected to supervise; and often on Mondays, the public shaming of those children who had not been to Mass the previous day. Preparation for First Confession involved vague (it seemed) instructions from the priest about the serious sin of doing 'dirty things' with one another – my first and only introduction to Catholic sex education; and at my first Communion, I remember the taint of nicotine on the priest's fingers as he placed the host in my mouth.

Catholic Secondary school

The immersion continued at Secondary school except that we were no longer associated with a single parish. But religion was central. Assembly with prayers each day, followed by a short RE class; two formal classes of RE each week; prayers at the end of each morning and at the end of each day; an entire week of formal retreat each year, given by various religious– usually Jesuits. I remember a Jesuit who taught us the Masonic handshake, another not too subtle reminder that Catholics were different and threatened by forces we did not yet understand.

One teacher (a stalwart in his local parish) would physically punish students if they came to class without their catechism or rosary beads, which led to a considerable number of pages being ripped from catechisms and rosary beads torn apart so that each student could pretend to have both for presentation to his teacher. 'His' because it was, of course, a boys' school. The girls were educated separately at the convent school. In my final year, there was a suggestion that the senior pupils from both schools have a formal dance event – strictly supervised. Vetoed by the local parish priest.

Beyond school, the Catholic culture dominated. Catholic Youth Groups, Catholic Cubs and Scouts, Catholic choirs, Catholic film nights; and we were learning the importance of Catholic Social Clubs where young people came together to meet one another and learn formal dancing. No Protestants allowed. At the door, you were asked your parish, and could be required to name a priest, recite the *Hail Mary*, or the topic of last week's sermon. I think that's where my parents met, so the outcomes were not all bad! In addition, in the parish, there were regular door-to-door collections for various church charities; and once a year the Church Workers Social where everyone involved in parish life – pass keepers, collectors, altar boys, choir and musicians, cleaners, teachers – gathered for a meal and entertainment, hosted by the parish. The sense of Catholic identity was not only experienced but celebrated.

Seminary education

In those days, there were four seminaries in Scotland (plus one in Spain and one in Rome). All were full. For young men like me, with a strong sense of the importance of clergy as well as an overwhelming awareness of Catholic identity, seminary training was an almost inevitable next step. I had been accepted for undergraduate studies at the University of Glasgow but postponed them for the time being. I began studies towards a D.Phil. at the University many years later.

I had studied Spanish at school and half expected to be sent to Valladolid but because my stepmother was now a widow, it was decided that I would study at the local seminary near Glasgow.

The immersion continued, reinforced by the increasingly clerical culture of the place and the times. The major emphasis was on Dogmatic and Moral Theology whose content had not changed in centuries. An awareness of specialness and otherness was subtly introduced while the piety and spirituality were preparing us for life in parishes, under obedience to parish priests and the company of other clergy. Parishes were booming; priests were plentiful. As well, there was a sense that we knew all the answers to every moral or theological issue raised either within the seminary or in the parishes we visited as part of our formation. Infallibility was built into our training and education.

I don't, however, recall a single sermon, lecture or address where celibacy was mentioned or explained, nor any investigation as to how we would cope with the demands of such a lifestyle. Perhaps it was too difficult; perhaps it was assumed that we would learn on the job; perhaps it was assumed that the Moral Theology we were taught would simply reinforce that first lesson I recall at my First Confession – about avoiding 'dirty things' – and be enough to enable us to live as sexless human beings.

And yet... even then, things were beginning to crumble at the edges. In 1943, Pius XII's encyclical *Divino Afflante Spiritu* had encouraged new translations of the Bible, approving the hitherto condemned approach of textual criticism and the historical-critical method of interpreting the texts. After the Second World War, more and more Professors of Scripture, graduates of the Biblical Institute in Rome, were beginning to teach in seminaries, and gradually we were becoming aware of the shallowness of the biblical foundations of many of the assertions of traditional Dogmatic Theology lectures and the absurdity of their claims.

In addition, reform was in the air. Pius XII had died and the new Pope John XXIII had summoned a great council to read the signs of the times in which the church had to live and proclaim the message of the gospel. New, exciting authors were writing about renewal. Hans Küng, especially, had a way of challenging former assumptions, encouraging us to ask questions about the tradition, suggesting new ways of being church in our time, promoting a great sense of hope and confidence in the council that was already meeting in Rome. The enthusiasm about the council was palpable. There was such an increase in vocations that Glasgow decided to construct a huge new seminary building at great expense. (Within a few years, it became a white elephant, and a huge drain on diocesan funding to this day because it is a listed building that cannot be knocked down. It stands unused, decaying – a memorial of a time that has gone, a culture changed forever.)

The beginning of wisdom; the end of certainty

Being in Rome, studying in Rome was a different kind of immersion. The pool was wider, deeper, invigorating, liberating. Meeting and mingling and studying with students from all over the world offered experiences of being Catholic that challenged old certainties and identities. Here were men (all men at that time) from Europe and South America, whose Catholic lineage was longer than mine and less of an issue; men from Africa and India with a sympathy for the beliefs of others that threatened and overcame (to some extent) the prejudices of my own narrower understanding. These were men with a startling variety of pieties and spiritualities and traditions – Jesuits and Franciscans, Dominicans and Passionists – in their habits, proclaiming their particular understandings of and contributions to the richness of the Catholic tradition. Men with first languages that reflected the universalism of the church, all worshipping in the as yet unchanged Latin of the liturgy; all studying through the medium of Latin lectures offered by professors from all over the world.

And in the background, the Second Vatican Council at work, producing texts, promoting discussion, encouraging new ways of interpreting the ancient Catholic tradition. And discussions and presentations not only by bishops but by the many *periti* (advisors) who offered insights and advice not only to the bishops but to any who attended their discussion sessions: John Courtney Murray, Henri de Lubac, Yves Congar, Hans Küng, Joseph Ratzinger, Karl Rahner and others; and, surprisingly, the presence of non-Catholic Christian leaders– a challenge to someone brought up to regard such people as misguided in their opinions and misled in their Reformed origins.

An aside: the Scottish bishops attended the four sessions of the Council but did not speak even once during the Council. Probably because they had nothing to contribute and, like many (I suspect), were anxious for the whole thing to be over so that they could get back to the real business of being bishops in their dioceses.

At the university, progress in theology was tentative but at the Biblicum, there was a sense of renewal and excitement among professors and students, especially with the anticipation of the dogmatic constitution *Dei Verbum* which had had a troubled beginning in the Council and became one of the key areas of dissent and reform. And after Rome, a semester in Jerusalem. A different kind of immersion in what is sometimes called the Fifth Gospel.

Changing an identity culture in Religious Education

Bishops all over the world in the late 1960s and early 1970s were establishing new Centres of Religious Education to create programs and resources for educating Catholic students and adults about the teachings of the Council. It was a formidable task to create new senses of identity after centuries of entrenched attitudes and expectations. Those in need of education included clergy, of course, and the new centres and their staff quickly became objects of suspicion, heresy and deep disquiet.

In preparation for undertaking leadership in this area, I completed a Diploma of Religious Education at Dundalk in Ireland. Corpus Christi College in London had fallen foul of the hierarchy in England and Wales, especially following the published opinions of key staff members on *Humanae Vitae;* and Ireland seemed a safer bet for orthodoxy. Actually it was Corpus Christi with Irish accents. Seven years as Director of the Religious Education Centre resulted in completely rewritten programs for primary and secondary schools, annual conferences for teachers and interested adults, appointment of school chaplains, creation of resources for liturgy and sacramental programs, conferences in adult faith development and meetings for clergy and religious.

It was an exciting time; and frustrating too. Many teachers, parents and clergy were reluctant to accept the new emphases and liturgical changes. Instinctively, I think, they appreciated – perhaps more than I did – the demands that were being made on them in terms of their understanding of what it meant to be Catholic.

Opportunities for change; extending borders; changing identities

After seven years, for me, it was time to change and I sought employment in publishing. For more than forty years, I have worked in Christian publishing, in the UK and in Australia. Secular employment freed me from the constraints of any narrow Catholicism that might have lingered, and working with authors from various Christian Churches expanded my ideas about belonging and identity. In particular, I worked for twenty years with the Joint Board of Christian Education in Melbourne.

Formed in 1914, it was originally a union of Presbyterian and Methodist Boards of Education in Australia and New Zealand, and over the years had become the largest independent Christian publishing house in the southern hemisphere. Its focus was on Religious Education, providing resources for Sunday schools and adult faith education. When I joined the staff, it had become the publishing agency for the recently formed Uniting Church in Australia and there was a great sense of renewal and purpose. My function was to write adult faith materials, based in Scripture, of course, as well as editing their general Christian publication list from denominations that also included Churches of Christ and Anglicans.

This was a huge learning curve for me: to re-focus attention from official Roman teaching and worship and tradition to live and work within the tradition of the reformed churches. It was, of course, a two-way situation. My expertise in Scripture and education was respected and valued; and once the need for new liturgical resources was acknowledged, I began to work with their own specialists in liturgy to produce texts that were seminal in the life of the new denomination. It was also broadening and changing my sense of identity as Catholic and Christian. This was an extraordinary opportunity to value the richness of the Reformed tradition, to explore the historic documents that emerged from the sixteenth century, and to appreciate the theological and biblical insights that had coloured the faith journey of millions of my fellow Christians since that time.

It also provided new ways of talking about church. The foundation document of the Uniting Church is called the *Basis of Union*. Finally approved in the mid-1970s, it followed years of negotiation among the various churches as they planned for union. Various models were explored, including that of the Church of South India which had opted for a hierarchical model that included bishops. This was too much, of course, for the Presbyterians especially, with their inbuilt historic prejudice against such an idea. Originally, the efforts of those involved was to find a common denominator of belief and worship among the churches and find some way of accommodating those traditions within a statement that would lead to union.

The head of the Presbyterian theological hall at Ormond College in Melbourne was Dr Davis McCaughey (who later was Governor of Victoria). He is credited with the idea that, instead of looking backwards, they should look forwards towards the kind of church to which God was calling God's people. Here was an inspired way forward; and the *Basis of Union* reflects that approach – full of faith and hope for the future – and trying to describe a new way of being the Church of God in Australia. It was also a new way for me to think of being Catholic! To honour the tradition, to value the ancient creeds, to acknowledge the structures and yet to be open to new ways of interpreting – if possible – the purposes of God for the people of God.

There was a fatal flaw in the entire justification for the Joint Board of Christian Education – its assumption, based on nearly a hundred years – that Sunday school was an integral part of the Australian Protestant way of life and would continue to be so into the future. But already there was substantial evidence – especially from the UK after World War II – that Sunday schools were in decline (like church attendance) and that, sooner or later, this would affect Australian society. It is also claimed that the increasing availability of motor cars gave families other ways of spending family time on Sundays. Whatever the reason, Sunday schools in Australia collapsed rapidly, especially in the 1980s and '90s, and the Joint Board, after many attempts to re-badge it, simply ceased to exist.

Fortunately, I had been able to find other employment in distribution of Christian publications, working for Rainbow Book Agencies, at that time the largest distributor of Christian publications in Australia. My job was to focus on theological titles and promote them within the various theological libraries in Australia. And not only Catholic authors but representing the broadest range of informed theological opinion in the churches worldwide. Here was another gift – to read and promote a wide range of theological and biblical books. The identity was ready for a new phase, and, curiously, one related to my interest in the Bible.

New insights into the formation and interpretation of Scripture

Fresh approaches to interpreting the Bible were emerging at this time. Other voices were beginning to appear in the area of theology and Scripture: feminist theology, queer theology, third world theology; informed and insightful Jewish scholarship in New Testament studies. All of these brought their own significance and unique insights into how the Bible was formed, established, interpreted and – in many cases – imposed as the eternal, unchangeable Word of God, fixed forever – with implications for Catholic and Christian and religious identity. And a special problem for those Christians whose recent origins are in the sixteenth-century Reformation with its claim that only the Bible is the authoritative source for knowing God's will. What happens when new ways of understanding the Bible clash with the expectation that the Bible gives clear unambiguous teaching, especially in ethics and morals?

Contributing to the dilemmas this brings is a forthcoming book by a Uniting Church minister who is also a zoologist. He writes about the development of sex in our cosmic and human species: when did it become a function of more than a single cell?; what happened when it became pleasurable?; when did it become a source of commitment and community as well as procreation? The author is particularly suspicious of those who say: 'Let's go back to the Bible to find definitive answers to it all'. He reminds us that the Bible's teaching on marriage and sexuality is more about power than respect, especially for women; about patriarchy rather than inclusion; about ownership rather than partnership; about women as property. (Incidentally, why do so many women not notice the patriarchal, offensive and exclusive language of the Bible? Is it, as someone has suggested, that women have been conditioned to read the Bible as if they were men?)

Contributing to fresh ways of approaching the Bible, involving the evolution of identity and culture, two other recent books were significant for me. In the excellent series 'Lives of Great Religious Books' published by Princeton University Press, Joel Baden's *The Book of Exodus – a biography* was published in 2019. Baden, a Jewish scholar of both Old and New Testaments, shows how the influence of this second book of the Bible affected the rest of the Bible, especially its key theme of Passover, key to both Jewish and Christian understanding of God's purposes for God's people. Central and recurring also in developing attitudes – within and beyond the text – to slavery, oppression and freedom, whether expressed by the Maccabees, the Reformers, the Pilgrim Fathers, in the American War of Independence, the

American Civil War; or inspiring and sustaining universal civil rights and liberation theology.

Like most contemporary scholars, Baden is not concerned about the dubious origins of Exodus (little or no evidence from any contemporary sources – literary, historical or archaeological); rather, he focuses on the fact that by ritualising the memory of the events – escape from captivity, promised land, giving of Torah – the celebration became one of *identity* – a commanded remembering of God's choosing of this people for God's purposes. What is evident from the book is how the Exodus tradition unfolded and developed over the centuries, with a variety of emphases, memories, rituals, practices and teachings.

The Exodus is *living* tradition that is still evolving. For example, in some contemporary Jewish Passover celebrations – Seder – there is an orange on the table to remind those gathered that the gay and lesbian Jewish community belongs within this tradition, to be remembered, honoured and celebrated. Obviously, there is no mention of oranges in any biblical or liturgical texts but the community that 'owns' the tradition is comfortable enough to allow this evolution and development. Interesting too that after the Exile, Seder and Passover became a family-centred meal, no longer owned and controlled by the Temple, whereas in the Christian development of Eucharist, the opposite happened. The clergy took it back!

An earlier book (2017) is *Crucible of Faith* by Philip Jenkins (Basic Books). The subtitle is 'The ancient revolution that made our modern religious world' and the focus of the book is the period of around three hundred years before the Christian era, significant for the emergence of Christianity. This was a period of intense struggle within Judaism as it found itself increasingly influenced by ideas and teachings whose origins were not within traditional Judaism and the Hebrew Bible but coming from the developing Hellenisation of those Jews who had left the lands of Israel and formed their own communities in Greece, Egypt and throughout Asia Minor. This was the period of the origins of the Greek translations of the Old Testament (Septuagint) and the gradual growth of influence within Judaism (at home as well as abroad) of new emphases, new developments, new ideas.

Central were new ideas about life after death, the tentative seeking for concepts and words to describe ideas about personal survival after death, body/soul philosophies, resurrection. It was also a time when apocalyptic ideas were developing: the emerging importance of angels and demons, heaven and hell, the nature of God, the meaning of the Fall and the power of the devil. As the author suggests: ideas that might once have been considered bizarre became normalised and thus passed on to Christianity and later to Islam.

We recognise many of these emphases and terminologies and theologies in the New Testament and in the teaching and ministry of Jesus. They colour so much of his teaching, his parables, the controversies of his time and the background to much of the early church. They established boundaries of identity, of how to be Christian, of creedal statements, of structural development; they led to primitive fears, superstitions, catechisms, binary ways of thinking and ultimately to the kind of conditions into which many of us were immersed, religiously and culturally.

Cosmic awarenesses; the limitations of knowledge

Catholic Christianity was born in a time and place that had little or no appreciation of the vastness of the cosmos or the evolution of species or the connection of humans to the rest of creation. But we contemporary Catholics do have those insights; how do we make sense of our faith in such a context, when creeds, teachings, ethical principles have their origins in philosophies – and are expressed in language – that is so utterly different from our own? What does it mean that the central teachings of the Gospel, for example, reflect a time of growing emphasis on apocalyptic language, other worldly expectations and divine interventions? Pope Francis in his *Laudato Sí* encyclical does acknowledge the intimate connection between ourselves and our cosmos; theologians like Teilhard de Chardin (and our own Denis Edwards) have tentatively explored the opportunities of marrying the faith tradition with contemporary science. Surely this is the challenge of our time.

Conclusion

From the Charlie Brown series of cartoons: Snoopy, on top of his kennel, is typing a manuscript.

> *Charlie Brown*: 'What are you doing, Snoopy?'
> *Snoopy*: 'Writing a book about theology.'
> *Charlie Brown*: 'Good grief. What's its title?'
> *Snoopy* (thoughtfully): 'Have You Ever Considered You Might Be Wrong?'

Have I ever considered that I might be wrong? And if so, can I live with that? Can faith coexist with the possibility that I might be wrong – about God, about the Bible, about Jesus, about the church, about resurrection? And, if so, can I still claim to be Catholic, and what does Catholic identity then mean for me?

I am comforted and encouraged by the statement of American Cistercian priest Thomas Keating who writes in his book *Invitation to Love: the way of Christian contemplation* (Bloomsbury Academic, 1994) that 'Silence is God's first language; everything else is a poor translation'. Silence is – for me – an attractive metaphor to associate with the mystery we call God. Within the vastness of the universe, the millions of years of the evolving cosmos, the struggle to grasp concepts of eternity, creation and purpose, silence would seem to be the appropriate response.

Not just the silence of God, but my own; the realisation of my utter and ultimate insignificance within whatever is the meaning of life.

Elizabeth Kübler-Ross' five stages of grief (denial, anger, bargaining, depression and acceptance) presumably apply in some way to dying to self, the topic of this recollection. It is different from the physical processes of dying and I find that over the years, I have consciously contributed to it, sometimes less willingly than others. I have enthused about the influences – people, experiences, study, books, authors – that have been part of the long, on-going journey.

But it comes at a cost. I remember the piety of my parents; I acknowledge that the faith of our ancestors sustained them over many centuries, often in times of persecution, certainly through periods of hardship and poverty; I regret that, in some sense, that ancient, focused tradition ends with me. But

I have to live with that, and perhaps die with that. I gladly admit that others within the tradition and in the church still identify with familiar structures, teachings and spiritualities and find within them sources of strength, faith and identity. I recognise that the path on which I find myself is mine alone... no, not alone but in the company of the faithful in every generation.

At the Easter Vigil liturgy each year, the part that moves me most is the sung litany of the saints. I experience deeply at that moment the company of the great cloud of witnesses who from the beginnings of the Jesus story have tried to live his message in their own time and in their own circumstances. The identity of each of them has been shaped – and limited – by how they understood themselves as created in God's image, their insights into the language and teaching and formation of the Bible, their understanding of the creation and the cosmos, their awareness of the vastness of our universes and of their place within the evolution of it all. And each of them faithful in their own unique way.

So, within that ancient company of faithful people, my conclusion to reflections on the evolution of my own identity calls for humility, seeking, exploring, uncertainty, acceptance of the limitations of knowledge. I am a Catholic Christian. Within the limitations of it all, I believe that the way of Jesus is an authentic and reliable translation of God's silence and that his interpretation of that silence gives meaning and purpose and shape to my life. And I accept my need for an ongoing community called church, people who share commitment to the gospel of Jesus Christ and who sustain one another in this particular way of translating and interpreting and celebrating the silence of God.

And at the end of it all? A submission to the silence of God: 'Into your hands I commend my spirit'.

Chapter 2

God's Mission Has A Church

Sue Phillips

My journey

A cradle Catholic, educated in a Catholic girls' college, I worked for seven years in the corporate world, before joining the Franciscan Missionaries of Mary (FMM), an international missionary congregation, forty years ago. I completed social welfare studies and for several years was involved in ministries with disabled children, children at risk, as well as with refugees from Central and Latin America, before spending nine years in Morocco and living the dialogue of daily life with Muslims. At various times after my return to Australia, I accompanied women in street prostitution, coordinated an inner-city parish[1] with a significant LGBTIQ+ population, and established a welcome agency for refugees released from Immigration detention. I then spent twelve years based in Rome on our international Leadership Team. In this position I was responsible for over seven thousand women in seventy-four countries, visiting and encouraging their amazing ministry efforts in sometimes extremely delicate political situations. My present involvements focus on the place of women in the church, and being part of a chaplaincy team at a men's prison.

Such a life trajectory has granted me the incredible privilege of walking with people on the margins of society. My experiences have helped me understand the incarnation of God and God's boundless and unconditional love. These transforming insights stood in sharp contrast to the stultifying centre of ecclesial power I experienced in the Eternal City. It is through these eyes that I reflect upon my understanding of Church and the ecclesial administrative realities that so often define and shape its presence.

God's mission has a Church

This declaration is frequently on the lips of missiologists in our days, helping us to regain the correct focus on how we need to be as church in our modern world. Internationally renowned missiologist and author, Anthony Gittins, says the church has been at its best historically when it has listened to God's mission, and at its worst when it thinks it *is* the mission! Vatican II clearly defined Church as the People of God (Flannery, 1975, 28.2). Yet we all know that any human organisation needs a certain structure to animate its life and vision, a structure that is at the service of the organisation, unlike the present situation where many of the privileged, ordained single males called to servant leadership could be aptly defined as temple police.

'God's mission has a Church' signifies that the official Church is secondary, not primary to the mission of God. Fortunately, this radical break with the traditional model is manifest most clearly in the vision and direction of our current Pope, Francis. On repeated occasions since the beginning of his pontificate, Francis has referred to his vision of the church as a 'field hospital after battle' – a church that heals wounds and warms the hearts of the faithful. Francis explains that it is useless to ask a seriously injured person if they have high cholesterol and about the level of their blood sugars! The aim is to heal wounds (Spadaro, 2013). Yet the contrast between this vision for the church and the findings of the Royal Commission into Institutional Responses to Child Sexual Abuse (RCIRCSA) could not be starker. The Royal Commission's final report clearly stated the devastating impact of clerical sexual abuse perpetrated on many thousands of vulnerable young children. And this was just in Australia! Similar investigations targeting the church were also carried out in countries such as Ireland, UK, Germany, Chile, Canada and USA, all with equally destructive and damaging findings.

The primary mission of the clerical leadership in the church is to empower, not disempower; to call all to a common humanity, not to divide and discriminate; to assist in discerning the life-giving work of the Spirit in our times, not to allow fear of change to control and stifle.

To empower, not disempower

Those of us old enough can remember the rigid, sacramental focus of earlier years – being taught the prayers to say and to pray, without assistance in developing a personal relationship with the God of our lives. We were taught to imagine God as a presence way beyond us in Heaven. This God was distant from us, judging our every move. Such images of a remote and impassive God went after the changes of Vatican II, but the emphasis on sacramental attendance, exclusive and alienating language, on who is worthy and who is not, perpetuates such alienating imagery. The importance of community, of inclusivity, of healthy images of God and inspirational liturgical language do not seem to be on the official radar.

It was when I was missioned to Morocco, and being immersed daily in the all-encompassing presence of another world religion, that I was challenged to plumb the depths of what it was that I really believed as a Christian. I met some of the most amazingly hospitable and generous people in that country, so charity and love could not be the defining factor of my faith. I eventually discovered that the key to it all was the Christian belief in the Incarnation, the Jesus event in our world, our God Emmanuel, God with us and in us, in the Spirit abiding in our hearts. Not distant, not remote, not untouchable, but intimate, vulnerable and tangible through Word and Sacrament. This is the God I came to believe in. The spirituality of Francis of Assisi helped me to understand this God of Jesus, the God of utmost humility, manifest in the crib, the cross and the Eucharist. Unbelievable really, that it took a Muslim country to help me to understand what the Church had never managed to convey to me.

In 2019, Australian Jesuit Michael Kelly wrote of the power of such faith encounters: 'Being an Australian Catholic hasn't been a lot of help either. It was tribal and ritualistic in my formative years and hardly prepared us to deepen the interior life that is indispensable for a growth and deepening of faith as life's ambiguities and paradoxes unfold.'[2]

How do we become a Church that helps us deepen the interior life that is indispensable? Maybe this point could be taken up by the postponed Plenary Council. We have an incredible treasure lying within the earthen vessels that we are (2 Corinthians 4:7), as well as in our rich mystical tradition. The human journey into union with this incredible treasure has been elaborated for us in the writings of many mystics throughout the centuries, Hildegard of Bingen, Francis of Assisi, Julian of Norwich and John of the Cross, to name but a few. Unfortunately, this precious heritage has been pushed to the margins by an over-emphasis on the sacramental life of the Church. Ordination has been only for the performance of ritual, not for the accompanying of the faithful in the development of spirituality.

The attitude of the official church in Australia – more concerned for the survival of the institution than to the mission of Jesus – is typified, I believe, in a story that has stayed with me for many years. It concerns my own religious congregation. During the 1930s the Franciscan Friars, among others, had made several requests for the FMM, already present in Asia, Europe, Africa and the Americas, to open a foundation in Australia, and work with women by running retreat houses and boarding hostels. Contact had already been made with Archbishop Mannix, who was keen on the idea. The opportunity only came in 1941 when the bishops asked the Apostolic Delegate, Giovanni Panico, to invite a community of religious sisters to provide for the domestic care of the new regional Pius XII Seminary, Banyo, Queensland.

Panico knew of the FMM from his days in Colombia and Argentina. In writing to the Superior General in Rome, he said that if the FMM did not seize the opportunity to go to the seminary, he feared that it would be difficult for them to enter at a later date (Scanlon, 2012, p. 29). This implied that if the sisters wanted to come to Australia, they had to accept the condition of working in the seminary even though such work was definitely not a priority for them. Due to the danger of wartime travel from Europe, the first three sisters, all Europeans, journeyed from FMM communities in southern China.

The sisters cooked and served three meals each day. In addition, they were also responsible for the washing and ironing for the rector, several priests and four Christian Brothers on staff, as well as the fifty-seven new seminarians. Plainly this was a huge task for the three women. On several occasions the sister-in-charge was obliged to approach the rector about the heavy work expected of the sisters, the small stipend paid to each and even the lack of necessary food for the community (Scanlon, p. 31). From 1944, the arrival of more sisters, this time from the USA, meant that the FMM were able to take on ministries much more in keeping with their Franciscan spirit. Service to the Aboriginal people at the leprosarium on Fantome Island was then followed by the Palm Island Mission, as well as a Retreat House for women in Melbourne and care of elderly/poor women in Sydney. The FMM left Banyo Seminary in 1975, by which time they had established a residential centre for children of families in crisis in Canberra, a hospital for disabled children in Brisbane and retreat houses in Sydney, Brisbane and Perth. Also included were hostels for Aboriginal girls in Townsville and Mt Isa, schools for girls in Melbourne and Sydney, plus response to the medical and educational needs of six different missions in PNG.

Yet a further example of the mission outreach of the sisters being subject to ecclesial authority occurred in 1963. The FMM vision had been to do social work with needy children and families in Canberra. Their entry into the diocese was only approved by Archbishop O'Brien on the condition that the FMM provide two teachers for his new diocesan girls' high school. Two sisters were sent from the USA. Even in our times, women still have to 'work around' the unbridled power and authority of local bishops.

Acknowledgment needs to be made that the establishment of these FMM services, and I am sure those of other religious congregations, could never have happened without the overwhelming generosity and hospitality of the 'People in the Pews' (Heasly, 2019). Fun runs, fêtes, fundraising dinners, donations, determination and dedication of lay people giving life to services to help the disadvantaged of our society, incarnating the mission of Jesus.

The four Gospels provide us with a very clear understanding of God's mission as revealed in the person of Jesus – most explicitly in Luke's reference to Isaiah, about bringing good news to the poor, setting prisoners free, to the blind new sight, and to the oppressed freedom (Luke 4:18). We know to whom he ministered: the marginalised; and who he challenged: the temple authorities for their rigidity (Matthew 21:31-32, 43-45). This work of supporting society's most vulnerable people is commonly referred to as the social service arm of the Church. In current times our bishops have frequently referred to it when they wish to publicly acknowledge their pride in all the good that the Church is doing. Could this be in order to detract from the darkness and shame of the horrors of child sexual abuse perpetrated by the clergy?

I have never, *ever* heard any of the bishops acknowledge the fact that most of these social services were originally established through the energy, vision, hard work, poverty and dedication of women religious; women, who had the foresight and sense, in the face of their own diminishment, to actively engage the commitment and service of their lay collaborators to continue their vision. These collaborators have so eagerly grasped the task, responding with creativity and expertise, to expand and promote the flourishing of these institutions, offering an enormous contribution to the social welfare needs of vulnerable Australians. Each of these institutions, except the St Vincent de Paul Society, is under the collective umbrella of Catholic Social Services Australia (CSSA) and the authority of the Australian Catholic Bishops Conference (ACBC). The bishops have every right to be proud – if they give credit where credit is due. It is a dismal fact that the expertise and giftedness of all women and lay men is locked out of any decision-making process in the clerical system that governs the church.

I must mention here that the St Vincent de Paul Society (commonly referred to as Vinnies) was founded in 1833 by now Blessed Frederic Ozanam, a French layman, to serve the needs of the poor in Paris following a cholera epidemic. According to a former CEO of CSSA, Frederic never wanted the Society to be affiliated with bishops and wished for it to remain an entirely lay Catholic organisation. It remains to this day an undisputedly recognised Catholic charity in Australia and acknowledged as such by recently being included as one of the four major charities officially promoted by the government to receive donations for Bushfire Relief. Maybe there is a connection there? Could it be that this kind of organisational model, independent of the authority of the bishops, run entirely by lay people, is what has made the St Vincent de Paul Society an undisputed Catholic charity?

As a Church, it is imperative that we are close to all our vulnerable, poor and marginalised sisters and brothers. We are fortunate to have so many dedicated lay women and men who now continue this essential mission of the Church. Their work is not just an off-centre-stage effort to implement Catholic Social Teaching, something so clearly stated by Pope Leo XIII (1891, 55): it is the heart of what we are about as followers of Jesus. Yet one infamous local archbishop was heard to say 'social justice poisons the wells of faith'!

To include, not exclude

The letter to the Colossians tells us that 'Jesus is the image of the invisible God' (Colossians 1:15). The Gospels show us a Jesus whose understanding of God's mission was to find himself always acting to bring justice for those on the margins of society and challenging those who put obstacles in their way or laid heavy burdens upon them (Matthew 23:1-10). How did we get it so wrong? The burdens and the obstacles continue: labelling some as 'intrinsically disordered' and denying their love choices a sacramental blessing; casting judgment on the worthiness of the divorced and re-married to receive the Eucharist; excluding women from any rightful place as an equal among the baptised when it is impossible to believe that God's call is gender-biased; denying Eucharist to so many, because single male celibacy is deemed to be of greater value and women's ordination seems to be so incomprehensible. Why did we get it so wrong? But more importantly, why do the ordained, the only ones who have the canonical authority to rectify these injustices, refuse to listen and lack the courage to act? The clarity of Jesus' mission has become seriously blurred and manifestly impeded.

God created us all as equal (Genesis 1:27), all one in Christ Jesus (Galatians 3:28). Jesus helped us to understand that we are all children of God, sisters and brothers together; and the author of Acts has told us that God shows no partiality (Acts 10:34). This equality is reflected in being baptised into this community we call Church. Each one of us at our Baptism was anointed, like Jesus, priest, prophet and king. All of us, as daughters and sons of God, share in the priesthood of Jesus. The ordained priest is the one who presides only, when the 'priesthood of the faithful' gathers in community. We are all equal, each with our own unique story, God's story of our lives, living in a society that reinforces status, power, wealth and privilege at every turn. As followers of Jesus, we are all called to show to society that we *are* all sisters and brothers, all equal in God's sight; called to continue that mission and vision of Jesus.

So why then as an ecclesial body do we allow ordination to the clerical state to continue to bestow status, power, wealth and privilege, and insist on titles and places of honour? The invention of ascending titles of honour is enough to confuse anyone who is not part of the exclusive men's club, namely: reverend, right reverend, very right reverend, monsignor, my lord, your grace, your eminence, your excellency, your holiness! And considering themselves to have been raised above the rest of humanity, by being 'ontologically changed'! How did we get it so wrong? Heasly in her book *Call No One Father* (2019) has valuable insight on strategies for countering clericalism in our tradition.

A personal anecdote illustrates the point of ordination conferring status and privilege. In October 2012, in my responsibility as our international leader, I was one of five women religious invited to be an auditor at the Bishops' Synod for New Evangelisation. As a woman I had no right to speak formally at that gathering, even though in my role I had already visited fifty-five of the seventy-four countries where our sisters are present, hence having some idea of the wider Church and maybe something to contribute. My only duty was to listen silently, day after day, to the ordained voices of the more than three hundred bishops and cardinals assembled in the Synod Hall, who considered themselves the only acceptable representatives of our universal Church. The token women silenced! Not even the women who had dedicated their lives to ministry and service for the good of the Church and God's people were deemed worthy to contribute.

One morning during the Synod, whilst walking from the train station to the Vatican, I engaged in conversation with a bishop from Canada. Our conversation continued as we approached the entrance to the Synod Hall and joined the queue to pass through one of the three security machines. As I laid my possessions on the conveyor belt, the attendant told me to remove them because this was the security machine for the bishops and that I needed to join another queue! A token woman demeaned! Some days later, I was diagnosed with a serious illness that entailed hospital admission and a justifiable absence from the remainder of the Synod. The body holds its own wisdom!

Living in Rome, one could never imagine that in the rest of the world there may be a shortage of priests. So many are working in office jobs in the Vatican, and have been there for a considerable number of years. We all know that the Eucharist is so important for our life of faith, and yet the system insists on restricting its priesthood to the selection of single men, leaving thousands of the faithful deprived of the sacraments in so many parts of the world.

The importance of the Eucharist, for those on the margins of society, came home to me powerfully when I was working with refugees being released from an immigration detention centre. We had a celebration of the Eucharist every week in that detention centre and the people were so appreciative. It seemed to give them the hope that God truly was with them, and it privileged the rest of us, as Australian witnesses who did care about their situation. It is so important for the Church to be present in all those places where hope is fragile and easily extinguished.

In the early 2000s, the plight of refugees in our onshore centres was just as desperate as it is today for those offshore. So much so that, at one time, a group of men in the centre I visited had literally stitched their lips shut – a visible sign of their being rendered voiceless and impotent – in their utter frustration and sense of powerlessness at being trapped in our immigration system. During our Eucharistic celebration this day, I noticed one man, an Iraqi Christian who after receiving Communion broke the host into tiny pieces so he could push them through the narrow openings in his sewn lips. The sight of it plunged a knife into my heart. I felt the tears of God. Thankfully, the compassionate priest had not asked him if he were divorced or re-married! How can our shortage of male priests deprive so many desperate people around our world of the opportunity to participate in the Eucharist?

Why do our ordained leaders consider the ordination of women and married men as being a problem and not as part of a solution? Why are they so fixated on who is worthy or not worthy to celebrate and to receive? What do their actions and priorities tell us about Jesus' ministry? What is being ignored or sacrificed because the bishops have other priorities? This loss of focus can be seen most clearly in our day with the official statements in response to the Seal of Confession. Why has the Seal of Confession been seen as more important than reporting the abuse of children? Recently, the then President of the ACBC, Archbishop Mark Coleridge, responded to mandatory reporting laws introduced by our various Australian states by saying that the laws would 'limit and unjustly interfere' with the human rights of Catholics, and that clergy had died 'because they have refused to submit to the claims of the state and preferred to defend the rights of the penitent before God' (2020).

Yes, in some dictatorial regimes clergy have died, but in Australia? How can the rights of a penitent paedophile be more important than the rights of a child? Furthermore, one could argue that the Church, in denying the sacramental blessing for same-sex couples, interferes with the human rights of Catholics! I can only concur with Francis Sullivan: 'Why do we have to be publicly associated with inane, even incompetent, statements from Church officials and spokespeople, that fuel the flames of social division, demonise particular social groups, and present our Catholicism as just another socially conservative reactionary grouping?'(2020).

We are all familiar with the cliché, the 'Canberra bubble', meaning those in leadership who are removed from daily realities by being closeted in a sub-culture. I would suggest that there is also such a thing as the Vatican bubble, and in my years of living in Eternal City I have personally witnessed the phenomenon of a continuing slide into another reality.

One Sunday afternoon in Rome, I received a phone call from one of our province leaders in Asia. She was distraught.

For many years their country had suffered from a violent civil war. The Church was the only institution in the country whose members were from both warring factions. The sisters had been working for years to bring together widows from both sides to try to build peace and reconciliation. There were also other Church agencies involved with similar efforts.

The archbishop had recently retired, and his replacement was a fellow countryman who had spent several years in Rome working in Vatican offices. He returned to his country, was installed as the new archbishop, and on the following Sunday, he circulated his first pastoral letter to the people. It was this letter that caused the distress of the sister. It comprised several pages, all devoted to detailing the eligibility criteria for Eucharistic ministers. If the priest needed help it was to be from a deacon; if no deacon were present then a religious brother; if no brother were present, then it was to be a religious sister; if no sister then a layman, and on and on. It also specified the type of clothing that was appropriate for the occasion! The parishioners were outraged and turned to the sisters for explanation. The sisters then found themselves caught in a cultural bind, between deference to the hierarchy and solidarity with the people. It was obvious the bishop was still in his Vatican bubble, but pastorally it was not good enough, and why *should* such nonsense be inflicted upon people who have already suffered so much?

Fortunately, we now have a Pope who is trying to reverse this trend; but unfortunately, there are still many bubblers who are resistant to change. Much energy is still being wasted on non-essentials (deckchairs on the Titanic) because the fearful opposers are protecting the ideologies that have scaffolded their worlds. So much for the message of Jesus! Such emphasis on irrelevance has only served to alienate many and dissuade them from entering the doors of a Church.

One day, when I was involved in a ministry assisting women in street prostitution, I was sitting on the front veranda of the agency drinking coffee and chatting with one of the clients. During the conversation she looked across the rooftops of the neighbouring houses and noticed the spire of the local Catholic Church. She then told me that she had attended church as a child, and had often walked by that church on her rounds and was desirous to know what it was like inside. I suggested that she should just walk in one day and see for herself, as it was usually open during daylight hours, adding that it was a lovely place to just sit and feel the peace and quiet. She immediately shook her head and shuddered. She couldn't do that, she said. Didn't she like being inside unfamiliar buildings? I enquired. No, it was not that, she said; it was because she worked the streets now and couldn't possibly be good enough to enter a church! I felt those tears of God again in my heart. I recounted the story of Jesus telling the chief priests that tax collectors and prostitutes would make their way into God's kingdom before them (Matthew 21:31); that it is all about believing in God's unconditional love for us, nothing more. Her face lightened, and a faraway look and gentle smile showed themselves. She would think about going into that church one day, she said. Such a tragedy that the rules have made so many people feel unworthy. Being inside a bubble can only blur the focus.

Many men, registered as Catholic, who I encounter in the prison have a similar reaction: they hesitate to attend our weekly Eucharist, celebrated in a large room, not a chapel. They experience a sense of unworthiness, guilt for not practising, the shame of being a public sinner, unease in no longer remembering how to say the prayers, to follow the ritual, the negative God images that feed their anxiety, and the many other blocks and obstacles that add more layers of stress to their already complicated circumstances.

Yet prison really is a time of potential retreat, a time when they can seriously reflect and attend to connecting with the God of unconditional and unbounded love, present in the hearts of each one. This is the place where we really try to be the 'field hospital' that Pope Francis refers to, accepting, encouraging, supporting, welcoming all who come, no questions asked, no distinctions made, all equal, all brothers and sisters on this journey of discovery into the God of our lives. The vulnerability, being stripped of wealth, status, power and prestige becomes an energy for authenticity, shared humanity, compassion and healing. These are privileged places for me, where we touch the very heart of our faith and belief, devoid of all the trappings that differentiate and discriminate – a privileged place of encounter. During my ministry, offering pastoral support without discrimination to all the men I meet, there have been among them clergy perpetrators of child sexual abuse. Yet there is no official pastoral outreach to the survivors of these crimes, despite the twenty-five years of advocacy by one Melbourne diocesan priest. This gaping omission needs addressing. It is the consequence of yet another distortion from the 'bubble view'!

The Church is not the mission of God, but God's mission has a Church, and we have lost our way. How do we reclaim the primacy of the people of God and not that of the institution? How do we become a Church that serves the needs of the people, not one that decides who is worthy or not worthy to receive what the institution chooses to bestow?

We need urgently to adjust our focus, honestly accepting that the institutional Church has become woefully distorted. We must courageously condemn the 'bubble view'. The recently launched compendium of Catholics for Renewal (2019) has many ideas to help us move forward.

To cultivate life, not stifle

There is much work to be done to bring the governing body of the Church to grasp the urgency of our times and re-align the distorted lens and focus that has betrayed the vision of Jesus and his mission. The Final Report of the RCIRCSA (2017, p. 36) states that there are 'catastrophic failures of leadership of Catholic Church authorities over many decades', resulting in what Gerald Arbuckle claims (citing an Irish author): that 'most church-going Catholics have given up on the bishops, who blissfully confuse apathy with acceptance' (Arbuckle, 2019, p. 114).

Inertia has often been the default position for bishops – 'don't do anything and hopefully it might go away'. This is no longer an acceptable position for those of us in the pew. It is urgent that we claim our voices as equal members of the community of the baptised, with equal responsibility for safeguarding the integrity of the Gospel and faithfulness to the vision of Jesus: God's mission. We need to recognise that the hierarchical structure of our institution, which only bestows governing powers on the ordained, with no accountability to the people in the pews, is no longer tenable. Lack of accountability has been a major factor in the catastrophic failure in leadership. Accountability, transparency and inclusivity are now considered indispensable for good governance. We must hold our leaders to account.

The mission of Jesus not only means right action and good governance. Most importantly, it means giving attention to discerning the movement of the Holy Spirit in our times. We must not allow the fear of change to control and stifle. I am in firm agreement with Arbuckle that 'it is impossible for one leader, particularly in the contemporary turmoil of the church, to lead effectively alone' (p. 123). My own experience in international leadership affirms this. I could never have imagined that my own limited experience and personal giftedness would have been sufficient to address, adequately and appropriately, the many governance issues that crossed my desk, or discern – so important in a faith community – where the Spirit may be leading our congregation at that point in its history. It defies belief that a bishop alone could accomplish both of those tasks for a diocese. The RCIRCSA Final Report (2017, p. 44) made clear the failures of diocesan governance when it stated '[t]here has been no requirement for their decisions to be made transparent or subject to due process'.

All leaders in religious congregations require the assistance of a leadership team, officially known as a council, that is either elected or nominated. The Code of Canon Law (1983) Canon 627.1 states that superiors of religious institutes are to have their own council, and they *must* make use of it in the exercise of their office. The matters a leader alone can decide are very limited; most require either the advice of, or the consensus of the team/council. This is clearly stated in their own constitutions. At our international level, we were a team of ten members from nine nationalities, working in several languages. Ours is not an easy task, I agree. It takes formation, time and effort, using the facilitation skills of external professionals. But my twelve years of experience have convinced me, before God, that such consultation is the only way to make the best decisions for the on-going life and vitality of the congregation.

When positions of power and authority come your way, there is a great temptation for the ego to consider oneself as superior in intellect and wisdom. But only teamwork can multiply the gifts and experience needed to achieve the best outcome. Teamwork also allows for openness to the surprises that the Spirit brings, for example, in arriving at consensus on an idea, position or judgment that no single individual had suggested, yet all could support with enthusiasm. Here too is a call to our theologians to address the under-developed Pneumatology[3] of the Church, to assist all believers to understand more fully the action of the Spirit incarnate in our lives and times.

Vatican Council II stated, 'it was highly desirable that in every diocese a special pastoral council be established... and laity specially chosen for the purpose will participate' (Flannery, 1975, 28.27). Yet Canon Law (1983) took a step back on this. Canon 129.1 states that only those who are in sacred orders are capable of the power of governance, and 129.2 adds that lay members of Christ's faithful *can* cooperate in the exercise of this same power. Women and lay men can participate in church governance, yet everything depends on whether those in sacred orders invite them to do so! This disinclination or inability of our leaders to issue such an invitation is no longer acceptable. They must be held to account; otherwise everything will continue to be business as usual. I have heard it said that there are only seven out of Australia's thirty-five dioceses that have diocesan councils, and then only with a consultative vote. It needs to be a deliberative one. Maybe the Plenary Council, whenever it reconvenes, could look at this as a priority, and thereby help facilitate the necessary changes, insisting that every diocese has a pastoral council that is inclusive, transparent and accountable.

At the time of writing, the Novel Corona Virus COVID-19 has forced the closure of churches and largely prevented reception of sacraments. This extraordinary circumstance obliges us all to reflect on the essentials of our faith understanding and expression. It also provides a perfect opportunity to focus on the development of one's personal relationship with God, the mystery of Love who dwells within; a moment to move us to a more interior and introspective way of living our Christian faith. Pope Francis launched such an invitation seven years ago when he said that '[n]o one should think that this invitation is not for him or her' (*Evangelii Gaudium*, 2013, 3). 'Everyone needs to be touched by the comfort and attraction of God's saving love, which is mysteriously at work in each person, above and beyond their faults and failings' (44).

Ritual and sacrament are there to nourish and nurture that primary relationship in community; without it ritual becomes meaningless practice. No wonder so many no longer darken the door of the church. I hope this stay-at-home experience will give added impetus to the Plenary Council deliberations and sharpen its determination to bring urgent reform to a dysfunctional system.

I conclude with the words of Pope Francis: 'I hope that all communities will devote the necessary effort to advancing along the path of a pastoral and missionary conversion which cannot leave things as they presently are. "Mere administration" can no longer be enough. Throughout the world, let us be "permanently in a state of mission" '(25).

REFERENCE LIST

Arbuckle, Gerald A., *Abuse and Cover-Up: Refounding the Catholic Church in Trauma* (Maryknoll: Orbis Books, 2019)

The Canon Law Society Trust, *The Code of Canon Law – in English translation* (London: Collins, 1983)

Catholics for Renewal, *Getting Back On Mission: Reforming Our Church Together* (Mulgrave: Garratt Publishing, 2019)

Coleridge, Archbishop Mark, 'Revealing confessions "won't make kids safer"', online *CathNews: A Service of the Australian Catholic Bishops Conference*, 15 January 2020, https://cathnews.com/cathnews/169-draft-8/36973-revealing-confessions-won-t-make-kids-safer, accessed 28 March 2020

Flannery, Austin OP, General Editor, *Vatican Council II, The Conciliar and Post Conciliar Documents* (New York: Costello Publishing Company, 1975)
28. Decree on the Pastoral Office of Bishops in the Church, *Christus Dominus*
45. Dogmatic Constitution on the Church, *Lumen Gentium*

Gittins, Anthony J., *The Way of Discipleship: Women and Men and Today's Call to Mission* (Collegeville, Minn.: Liturgical Press, 2016)

Heasly, Berise, *Call No One Father: Countering Clericalism in the Catholic Tradition* (Bayswater: Coventry Press, 2019)

Kelly, Michael, 'What is to become of us?', https://international.la-croix.com/news/what-is-to-become-of-us/11317 (2019), accessed 28 March 2020

Francis, Pope, *Evangelii Gaudium* (Strathfield: St Pauls Publications, 2013)

Leo XIII, Pope, *Rerum Novarum* (1891),Vatican Press online version, https://vatican.va/content/leo-xiii/en/encyclicals/documents/hf_l-xiii_enc15051891_rerum-novarum.html, accessed 25 March 2020

Royal Commission into Institutional Responses to Child Sexual Abuse, *Final Report: Volume 16 – Religious Institutions Book 1* (2017),online version, https://childabuseroyalcommission.gov.au/sites/default/files/final_report_-_volume_16_religious_institutions_book_1.pdf accessed 28 March 2020

Scanlon, Kerry, *The Franciscan Missionaries of Mary in Australia and Papua New Guinea, Volume One – 1941-1984* (Sydney: Printed Matter, 2012)

Spadaro, Antonio SJ, *A Big Heart Open to God: An interview with Pope Francis* (2013),https://americamagazine.org/faith/2013/09/30/big-heart-open-god-interview-pope-francis, accessed 31 March 2020

Sullivan, Francis, 'New Wine, New Wine Skins' (2020), https://johnmenadue.com/francis-Sullivan-new-wine-new-wine-skins/ accessed 28 February 2020

Endnotes

1. This was a pilot project of the missionary congregation that had the care of the parish. They foresaw the need to appoint lay co-ordinators to take the pastoral and administrative responsibility of the parish, with priests only involved in sacramental ministry because of other congregational commitments. When the new Archbishop was appointed, this project ended as he considered this role was not that of a lay person! There are only two classifications in Canon Law, a cleric (an ordained member) or a lay person. Women religious are lay people.
2. Michael Kelly is an Australian Jesuit, a journalist and former director of Jesuit Publications and publisher of *Eureka Street*, former CEO of UCAN Asia-based Catholic News Agency, currently English edition editor of *La Croix International* and *La Civiltà Cattolica*.
3. The branch of Christian theology concerned with the Holy Spirit.

Chapter 3

Full Equality For All In The Catholic Church

Marilyn Hatton

I am a woman of faith who unintentionally started the journey for equality in the Australian church in the 1960s. The progress of this journey has been constant and has ebbed and flowed. What I want to capture is one woman's experience of the relentless energy and commitment demanded of women and men, and some of the flash points on this journey from the 1960s until now as we approach the 2021 Plenary Council.

Having been nurtured by a loving and erratic extended Catholic family, and educated by the Ursulines, a gift of powerful messages is imprinted in my consciousness, and daily they contest and influence my actions. These messages are that God is ever present; her/his touch is as gentle as silence; you must do unto others as you would have them do to you; recognise that you have free will and understanding; keep an informed conscience and let it be your guide; never be afraid to say you don't know and to question and seek understanding. The messages I carry are supported by a practice of faith, regular Eucharist and collective worship, guided by the gospels and the discerning support of family, friends and faith communities.

I imagine that many others of our era of faith, or no faith, also carry these simple messages, though I doubt that future generations will. That is not to say that they are not impressively fine young people. They are, and I learn from them constantly, but I do wonder what my messages translate to in their world. This is a world in which we are increasingly challenged by our market driven, individualistic society, where 'fake news' rules and where, in Waleed Aly's words, 'we are all becoming ever more connected, but less social', a world in which loneliness, mental health problems and domestic violence are continually increasing.[1]

As a young woman, I was pretty self-satisfied and unquestioning of my Catholic practice of faith, until I was stopped in my tracks by real life events. These burst my comfortable cocoon and had me in complete dissonance, questioning the Catholic Church's stance on issues like normal sexual activity, reproductive health, and access to life-giving Eucharist for divorced and remarried and gay and lesbian people.

In retrospect, this questioning was the start of my unintentional journey for renewal to an inclusive lay-led practice of faith, one in which all are held equal in Jesus Christ, consistent with St Paul's message to the Galatians: 'There is neither Jew nor Greek, there is no longer slave or free, there is no longer male and female, for all are one in Christ Jesus' (3:8). I recognise now that my faith is as important to my identity as my gender, as Senator Kristina Keneally said recently. It rings true for so many Catholic women of the sixties.

Graduating in 1964 as a registered nurse from St Vincent's Hospital, in Sydney, I had the privilege of interacting with the many people in my care. They were often at their most vulnerable, sometimes in joy, but too often in difficult and tragic circumstances and this gave me a great affinity for humanity in all its frailty and strength. So it is not surprising that I found that aspects of my Catholic faith produced dissonance for me in my professional work as a nurse, and subsequent work developing government social policy related to both women's health and the status of women in society.

Many young women in the sixties and on into the eighties, striving for understanding and authenticity, experienced dissonance between changing societal mores and aspects of their faith. This was the 'Age of Aquarius', during which women moved from the private sphere to the public sphere of life, the contraceptive pill became available, women now had control of their fertility and this meant economic independence. In Australia, for a short period, university education was free, so women in their droves stepped up to the challenge, fulfilling their dreams of advanced education across disciplines.

Women had always been in the workforce, but now they were moving into senior positions of responsibility and seeking equal recognition. They were also able to claim their sexuality in a way that they hadn't previously. Sexuality came into the language; we could talk more openly about the preciousness of attraction, seduction, the joy and awkwardness of intimacy, love and unity. Women's identity shifted; they were lovers, wives, mothers, students and responsible professionals, all in the space of ten years.

There was tremendous energy in this change, a real sense of freedom and wholeness, particularly for women, but also for men. Many men embraced added family responsibilities; they shared the process of parenting and being the breadwinner. But many, of course, did not, and tensions were constantly negotiated. These changes were supported by radically progressive government policies. The learning curve was enormous for all, both in the privacy of the home and in the public sphere of the workplace. Australia was developing as a multicultural society and our Indigenous peoples were recognised as the original owners of the land and were rightly gaining their place as equals in our society.

The sanctions of an authoritarian church did not help Catholic women and men. More and more Catholics questioned the authoritarian aspects of the faith. Unplanned pregnancies impacted on women's health and family economies. People were torn between their practice of faith and a normal sexually active life. This caused even greater demands on women's health and on marriages.

Church leadership failed to recognise the signs of the times, as democracies around the world were acknowledging women's contribution and place in the public sphere and in decision-making. Increasingly, inclusive language was being adopted. Meanwhile, our church's practices were becoming less and less acceptable to many who felt that Jesus would not impose such sanctions: he was a radical social reformer who particularly supported women. Many priests and nuns also were starting to challenge multiple aspects of old-style Catholicism.

Pope John XXIII opened the Second Vatican Council in 1962. Interim reports brought hope of a less authoritarian and more contemporary practice of faith, ensuring Christ's message of love and justice for future generations. Vatican II swept through the Church in 1965, and priests, religious and faithful were inspired with the possibilities. It called for the Church to eliminate discrimination against 'the other' as contrary to God's intent, and embraced a vision that called for the fundamental rights of the person. In the pews people were taking notice of Church governance in a way we hadn't before. Here was a blue print for the Church of the future and generations to come.

My parents and other families were being exposed to novels like Thomas Keneally's *Three Cheers for the Paraclete* (1968) and Morris West's Vatican series *The Devil's Advocate* (1959) and *The Shoes of the Fisherman* (1963). These books and others like them across the world raised awareness in the public sphere about the Catholic Church.

Sadly though, for priests and people alike, the enormous potential of Vatican II was not realised, and after John XXIII's transforming work, church culture seemed to become more authoritarian and clericalised. The energy of Vatican II started to dissipate. Then, in 1968, to shock and disappointment, *Humanae Vitae* was released, rejecting reliable birth control for Catholic couples. The Commission advising Pope Paul VI voted in favour of the moral use of contraception. However, at the last minute, the pope did not follow their advice. People were devastated.

This was a wake-up call for so many of the faithful and progressive nuns and priests. Many felt that *Humanae Vitae* represented an abandoning of the spirit of Vatican II and a failure to acknowledge the pastoral reality of married couples. After 1968, many abandoned Catholicism itself, and among those who remained, many searched for a way to live the Vatican II practice of faith for which they yearned.

Many of us turned to reform and renewal groups. These had begun in Europe following the Second World War. From the late 1970s on, more groups started to emerge nationally and internationally. These groups functioned in various ways and addressed specific issues. For example, my husband and I joined an international group, *Équipes de Notre Dame* (Teams of Our Lady), established in 1947 in Paris and nationally in Australia around the mid 1970s to encourage spirituality in marriage. The Teams met once a month in family homes for a simple meal, discussion and Eucharist, presided over by a priest.

In Canberra, the chaplains for our groups were frequently Missionaries of the Sacred Heart from Daramalan College, which was also the college attended by many of our children. In other parts of Australia, diocesan priests and other order priests became chaplains. The Teams discussion format exposed us to the works of Edward Schillebeeckx, Karl Rahner, Pierre Teilhard de Chardin and many others. There were many parallel groups in Australia and overseas.

Also, in the late 1970s, men and women religious and other non-ordained people, responding to the vision of Vatican II, began to be formally engaged in parish ministry as Pastoral Associates. Accreditation standards were gradually developed. Pastoral Associates are paid employees who still work in parishes today. Since the latest accreditation standards of 2014, Senior Pastoral Associates and Pastoral Workers had also become part of the Melbourne picture. The situation though has now changed, affecting the face and experience of pastoral leadership in the Archdiocese.

More and more priests, if they employ pastoral personnel, prefer Pastoral Workers. Diminishing finances are one factor in this choice, but many overseas priests and a significant number of those ordained in the last ten years prefer a clerical model of church, in which the non-ordained and especially women, are considered subservient. Pastoral Associates recognise that the leadership, to which they have been called and formed, is threatened because it is not compatible with a clerical church. This group, who are at the centre of non-ordained pastoral care, ministry and new ecclesiologies, have much to contribute to reform thinking.

As the long papacy of John Paul II wore on through the 1980s and 1990s, new and more activist groups emerged overseas, including the European-based international movement 'We Are Church', led by Martha Heizer, and 'Future Church USA', led by Sister Christine Schenk and now Deborah Rose-Milavec. All supported and advocated for a Vatican II practice of Catholic faith. Others, like Sister Jeanne Gramick, worked to meet the needs of marginalised LGBTI people. All these groups monitored and responded publicly to Vatican pronouncements and actions and worked to build relationships with local bishops – even with Vatican cardinals – to advocate for a changed practice of faith.

This was the time when many popular books by priests, nuns, and women theologians were published reflecting the spirit of Vatican II. People like Timothy Radcliffe, Richard Rohr, Elizabeth Johnston, Sister Joan Chittister, Elizabeth Schüssler-Fiorenza and Rosemary Radford Reuther published widely and gave us hope.

Through a friend I was invited in the mid-1980s to attend a meeting of Women and the Australian Church (WATAC), a national group under the dedicated and creative leadership of Sister Bernice Moore. It was first established in 1984 as a means of changing the understanding of the role of women in the Australian church and in society. It was initiated by women religious and was supported ideologically – and to some extent financially – by the religious orders of both men and women. It has developed into a network of local and regional groups in various Australian states. Men are included in the membership. Although Catholic by origin, it encourages membership from other denominations. WATAC aims to raise the consciousness of women on Christian feminist issues. It has a membership of approximately 2000.

WATAC is committed to 'a participative, inclusive model of church which commits women to work towards new forms of partnership with men and with each other in the church', and to encourage 'the emergence of the feminine as intrinsic to an understanding of God, to human wholeness and thereby to church renewal'.[2] The name WATAC emerged from the ideas of the founding committee members, who wanted to include all women regardless of whether they were active members of an institutional church or not.

WATAC continues today and has provided hope, information and education to thousands of women, men and young people through their excellent newsletter and monthly chapter groups, which are spread across Australia and meet for liturgy, prayer, discussion and meditation. In addition, they hold two annual events in NSW Parliament House to which they invite senior students from Catholic colleges. Their conferences attract overseas speakers like the Benedictine Sister Joan Chittister and the Roman Catholic Women Priests' Bishop Patricia Fresen, as well as prominent bishops including Bishops Pat Power and Bill Morris, and public figures including young female indigenous lawyers and ABC broadcaster Rachael Kohn. WATAC members had read the signs of the times and were working for equality by informing the baptised of our Catholic theology, exploring other models of Catholic practice, and presenting other images of God.

The other influential organisation was Ordination for Catholic Women Inc. (OCW), founded in 1992 by Dr Marie Louise Uhr, a biochemist and activist with a degree in theology. OCW advocated for the ordination of women into a 'renewed ordained ministry' at the same time calling out the inbred 'clericalism' in our church. I became an active member of OCW, while having responsibility for status of women and women's health policies in government in my professional life and at the same time undertaking a post-graduate degree in Gender Studies at the Australian National University History Faculty.

Marie Louise applied her scholarship to explain how clericalism played out to diminish and discriminate against women, and demonstrated how some of the Church's authoritarian practices marginalised women, alienating them from their practice of faith and the Eucharist. She made clear that this was not Christ's intent. She drew on the work of many of the theologians previously mentioned to develop, explore and explain what a 'renewed priestly ministry' might look like. Importantly, as well, she built relationships across the world with others in the renewal movement who were also challenging the seventeenth-century *Persona Christi* model of priesthood that excluded women from full equality in the Catholic Church.

Marie Louise was an eloquent and intelligent spokesperson, and under her leadership OCW became an internationally respected ginger group. It established strong contacts internationally with groups such as Women's Ordination Conference USA (WOC) and Women's Ordination Worldwide (WOW). OCW members like Dr Marie Joyce attended and presented papers at their meetings and conferences in Canada, UK and Europe. OCW also built a close relationship with The Wijngaards Research Institute, established in 1983 as Housetop Centre for Adult Faith Formation (Housetop).

A series of pamphlets on renewed priestly ministry were produced by OCW. They outlined the key arguments for a renewed ministry that included women in priesthood. They remain an excellent resource. OCW's newsletters, authored by Ann Nugent, attracted an extensive overseas and national readership for many years. They are now archived in the National Library. OCW also hosted a number of conferences in Melbourne, Sydney, Hobart and Canberra.

On 22 May 1994, advocates for the role of women in the church were shocked and disappointed when the Apostolic Letter *Ordinatio Sacerdotalis* (Priestly Ordination) was issued. The pope declared that the Catholic Church's position requires 'the reservation of priestly ordination to men alone', and stated that 'the church has no authority whatsoever to confer priestly ordination on women'. This action seemed like another retrograde step for progressive Catholics, and it mobilised the laity to become more informed and pro-active about Church governance. It remains the church's official position.

The release of *Ordinatio Sacerdotalis* lead the Wijngaards Institute to decide that its focus would be on women's equality in the church, and specifically on research into the ordination of women, including the development of a website to present the academic evidence for and against. The website has grown to be the largest internet resource on women and holy orders, with extensive documentation in twenty-six languages.

In Australia, following the release of *Ordinatio Sacerdotalis*, OCW tried to build relationships with church leadership by writing to each of the forty-three bishops. Initially, OCW received a few responses but they persisted and in subsequent years received many more. Some reflected empathy for our position but all said that their hands were tied by Rome. These were our shepherds who we expected to intervene on our behalf. We are more than half the church! One very pastoral bishop heart-warmingly sent us a hundred dollars. I still have a letter from another bishop in response to an OCW request to meet with him, which says 'Wrong Way Go Back!' He 'God blessed us', and went on to say he would meet with OCW, but could not discuss the ordination of women.

The renewal movement gained a new lease of life when ten Catholics met over lunch in July 1994 in a private house in Sydney. The discussion continued and by the end of the year Catalyst for Renewal was born. The members described themselves as 'believers who are attempting to establish a forum for conversation within the Catholic Church of Australia.' And they added, 'Our aim is to prompt open exchanges among the community of believers, mindful of the diversity of expressions of faith in contemporary Australia'.[3] This springs explicitly from the spirit of John XXIII and Vatican II: 'Let there be unity in what is necessary, freedom in what is unsettled, and charity in any case' (*Gaudium et Spes*, 92). This is the group that still organises Spirituality in the Pub on a regular basis.

Australian Reforming Catholics is another group that first came together in 1997 and produced a charter that reflected the passionate resolve of many for reform in the church. This group was formed 'to think through together moral and logical principles and practices in [the] church, drawing deeply on the gospel and in the light of contemporary knowledge, while at the same time applying steady pressure for change in the church'.[4] They organise events, produce a newsletter that attracts overseas readership, and are involved in preparation for the 2021 Plenary Council.[5]

Meanwhile, overseas in July 1996, nine members of the Women's Ordination Conference USA attended the first European Women's Synod in Gmunden, Austria. They went hoping to forge an international strategy network to promote women's ordination in Catholicism. They weren't disappointed. At the outset, fourteen countries joined the budding international coalition, including Germany, Austria, Spain, Netherlands, UK, Ireland, France, US, South Africa, Canada, Australia, New Zealand, Japan, and the Philippines. They named the network WOW — Women's Ordination Worldwide! Today, sixteen organisations from eleven different countries are represented. The mission of WOW is 'to promote worldwide the ordination of Roman Catholic women to a renewed priestly ministry in a democratic church, and to stand in solidarity with women who are ordained in the ongoing renewal of the church.'[6]

Although WOW is, at present, predominantly Catholic, it does not exclude other religions working for the same aim, for example, the Orthodox churches and those Protestant traditions where women are not yet ordained. Australia was there at the beginning and has maintained its representation on WOW through OCW, Catholics Speak Out and WATAC.

The focus on women's ordination in the Church was beginning to gain momentum, despite the fact that discussion of women's ordination was forbidden on church property. Nevertheless, the Australian Catholic Bishops Conference (ACBC) commissioned research into the participation of women in the church. This research included consultation across the country in rural and urban areas and, at the time, was one the most extensive pieces of social research undertaken nationally. The excellent report *Woman and man, one in Christ Jesus* was published in 1999.

Outside Australia, women were taking matters into their own hands. In June 2002, seven Catholic women with ministerial training were ordained to the priesthood on a boat on the Danube River by a bishop whose ordination was considered valid but illicit by the Catholic Church. The Vatican moved swiftly to excommunicate these women. However, inspired by these ordinations, a group was formed called Roman Catholic Women Priests (RCWP) – 'Roman' because they followed the Roman Catholic rite adapted for an inclusive practice of faith. Shortly after these ordinations, a South African Dominican nun, Sister Patricia Fresen, was also ordained, and two years later was persuaded by a Catholic bishop in good standing to be ordained to the episcopate. This ceremony was celebrated in secret. RCWP Eucharistic faith communities now number 130 across Europe, USA and Canada.

Back in Australia, Catholics for Ministry was established in 2003 by Frank Purcell, Anne O'Brien and Paul Collins. This group emerged out of desperation and lack of confidence in church leadership. Mass attendance numbers were dropping, destructive clericalism was increasing, and the shocking child abuse crisis was being exposed in the USA together with associated lack of appropriate governance. The faithful felt the Church had broken people's trust. In 2007, one of

Catholics for Ministry's major initiatives was to survey Mass going Catholics in over one hundred parishes across Australia about an inclusive practice of faith. They received almost 17,000 responses, including from senior priests and religious, all supporting reform and dialogue on the ordination of Catholic women and optional celibacy.

Reform groups were now effectively working as ginger groups, responding to papal and bishops' announcements and making visible the silent, dark, dismissive culture that is now known as clericalism, while advocating for a Vatican II practice of faith. The international renewal movement generously shared their ever-increasing intellectual resources. Being able to participate in their meetings and conferences gave a great insight into ways of expanding the reform movement in Australia. Around this time, historian Gary Macy published *The Hidden History of Women's Ordination* (2008), in which he explains the interface between history and theology and traces the ordination of women for the first twelve hundred years of Christianity.[7]

In the early 2000s, European renewal groups and those from Ireland, UK, and USA started meeting more regularly in Rome for events like papal elections and synods. These groups contacted one another on arrival in Rome and where possible worked together supporting, each other's specific efforts. This created a great sense of common purpose and forged strong links that resourced renewal work back home.

In 2004, I was privileged to attend a WOW meeting in Paris. It was a very special occasion for me, not only because it was my first meeting with this crucial group, but because I coincidently met RCWP bishop Sister Patricia Fresen who had flown in from Cape Town en route to Zurich. Patricia was the first woman Catholic bishop.

As Australia's representative on WOW, I also participated in a number of these gatherings in Rome. They seldom occurred without resistance from the Vatican and Italian authorities. Women's Ordination Worldwide have persisted in taking opportunities to get their message out to the world for the ordination of women, despite sometimes having their passports confiscated and on one occasion being detained by Italian police. In Rome, public demonstrations were always challenged by the authorities.

OCW had a similar challenge during Pope Benedict's visit to Australia in 2008 when we demonstrated using tea towels printed with 'Ordain Women Now NIHIL OBSTAT', which we wore like sandwich boards. We were constantly shifted around Sydney's Hyde Park by the host organisers and NSW police to keep us out of view. However, young back packers who wanted to support us pinned the tea towels on their backpacks and followed Pope Benedict wherever he went. The Holy Spirit was with us! If Pope Benedict did not get the message in English he might, we hoped, at least understand the Latin. In 2010 in the UK, the organisation Catholic Women's Ordination scooped the pool with 'Pope Benedict Ordain Women Now' signage on the London buses during the pope's visit to the UK. No one could say the women of the world have not tried to communicate our message to our leaders.

One of the latest new groups, Catholics for Renewal, was established in Melbourne in 2011 by Peter Johnstone and Peter Wilkinson. This group has worked tirelessly from its inception to research and develop data relevant to reform. They have presented submissions, press releases and open letters to bishops, supported by media interviews. They have worked relentlessly to reveal and counter the sexual abuse of children, and have been key drivers for the renewal movement in recent years. The national online petition they organised attracted 8000 responses.

In 2012, Prime Minister Julia Gillard established a Royal Commission into Institutional Responses to Child Sexual Abuse. To co-ordinate the church's response, the ACBC appointed Francis Sullivan as the CEO of the newly established Truth, Justice and Healing Council. He fulfilled this task with courage, integrity and diligence. His truth, skill and compassion made him almost the only credible face of the church at times. One can't help but think that if ordained women and biological fathers had been in positions of authority in the Catholic Church, many individuals and families would not have experienced the horror of child abuse. Some sense of conscience might have prevailed and trust might not have been abused and broken in such a shocking manner. The church's credibility might still be intact.

As the extent of child abuse within the church emerged, the idea arose of forming the Australian Catholic Coalition of Church Reform (ACCCR). At a meeting in Melbourne in December 2011, hosted by Catholics for Renewal with the already established renewal groups (Catholics for Ministry – now Catholics Speak Out, WATAC and Inclusive Catholics) tried to work out how they might engage with the bishops to assist them to address church reform. The question was: how could we penetrate the hierarchy's continued silence on crucial reform in the church? As a starter, we believed that coming together on common causes would strengthen our voice for renewal with the bishops. Significantly, the meeting drew up a call statement that all member groups accepted.

Since then, fifteen groups have joined ACCCR. A facilitated national workshop was held at the Australian National University in 2013, attended by fifty representatives from across Australia. It set priorities for renewal addressing governance and structural change in the church. Other major ACCCR initiatives included correspondence and several formal meetings of representatives of ACCCR with bishops in Sydney, Canberra, Darwin and Melbourne. These meetings were always courteous, but obtaining responses that reflected thoughtful understanding of the urgent need for renewal was difficult. Our efforts were often rejected.

ACCCR, through the efforts of Catholics for Renewal and Catholics Speak Out, forwarded comprehensive submissions to the Royal Commission and attended hearings. Peter Johnstone of Catholics for Renewal presented a strong case for reform at the Royal Commission hearings. Peter Wilkinson provided extensive and excellent research to inform ACCCR member groups and the Royal Commission itself.

In early 2013, Pope Benedict resigned, and as the cardinals gathered for the conclave, international renewal groups swung into action. It was raining lightly in Rome. Martha Heizer (IMWAC Europe), and my husband, Paul Collins, who was covering the election for ABC and Channel 7, and I were sitting in a café at the edge of the Vatican about to order a meal when Christian Wiesner of IMWAC rang Paul to say 'We have white smoke'. Paul hurriedly left to join Channel 7, and Martha and I found ourselves running with thousands of Italians into the Piazza of St Peter's. Pope Francis signalled a new era the minute he said 'good evening' and asked the thousands gathered in the Piazza to pray with him. You could hear a pin drop; he is so recognisably a man of

Christ's humanity. Martha and I looked at each other teary-eyed and speechless; it was such a sacred moment.

Earlier that week, we had joined WOW in the Piazza Garibaldi, releasing 'Pink smoke over the Vatican' in a demonstration organised by the WOC USA team. Visually stunning, the demonstration was covered by TV news broadcasts across the world. Miriam Duignan's CWO UK declared that 'Catholic women want our Catholic Church to be a healthy and vibrant place, with equality, with both men and women called to priesthood. Jesus did not exclude women. Jesus encouraged women and actively included them.'[8] The demonstration was attended by groups from USA, UK, Canada, Austria, and Australia.

Pope Francis set the theme for his Papacy in the exhortation *Evangelii Gaudium* (2013). Released so soon after his election, it gave heart to all in the renewal movement. His emphasis on equality and change, reflecting Christ's gospel message of love and justice, helped renewal movements across the world to accelerate their efforts to rid our church of crippling clericalism and to work towards the radical reform Pope Francis articulated.

ACCCR responded to the pope's call for renewal during the two sessions of the family Synod (2014-2015). We set up a liaison with all renewal groups, the ACBC, the Papal Nuncio and especially with Australia's episcopal representatives to the Synod, Bishop Eugene Hurley and Archbishop Mark Coleridge. This exercise required great persistence, and the idea of the laity being involved in it was a steep learning curve for all. Dr Maria Harries, a respected lay woman, and Drs Ron and Mavis Pirola accompanied our bishops to Rome for the Synod on the family.

In 2014, as part of the WOW leadership team for the 2015 Gender, Gospel and Global Justice Conference in Philadelphia, I contacted Senator Kristina Keneally and the Australian National University's Professor Hilary Charlesworth to speak at a fundraiser held in Canberra to bring women from developing countries to the Philadelphia Conference. Together with contributions from WATAC, we raised three thousand dollars. Kristina also chaired a panel and attended the full conference in Philadelphia.

ACCCR and its member groups have followed Pope Francis' lead for a synodal church, highlighting governance, accountability, transparency and inclusiveness. It has emphasised the inclusion of women at all levels of decision-making and ministry as a key governance issue. Over this period, we were strongly supported by the National Council of Priests (NCP), who published many of our articles in their quarterly magazine *The Swag*. Others who have firmly supported the renewal movement are Bishops Pat Power, Bill Morris, Vincent Long, Father Frank Brennan SJ and Sister Clare Condon.

Parallel with this, in 2013, national priests' councils from around the world who were keen to support Pope Francis met in Bregenz, Austria. Their aim was to establish an international network of priests' groups, to build alliances with other reform groups and to learn and reflect together. I was invited by this network to represent ACCCR at its second meeting in Limerick in 2015. This brought together over thirty Catholic priests and renewal group members from Ireland, Austria, Australia, Germany, India, Italy, Slovakia, Switzerland, the UK and the US. Also representing Australia were Fr Ian McGinnity (NCP), David Timbs (Catholics for Renewal) and Paul Collins (Catholics Speak Out).

A key objective was to devolve authority away from the Vatican to local churches. Connected to this was the need to enhance the authority of the local church, especially parishes. The meeting was an exceptional experience for me, as for others who attended. We worked together over four days and nights with two facilitators in open, authentic and respectful discernment and discussion, 'as equal in Christ'.

Fr Tony Flannery described the meeting in the *Irish Times*: 'Participants focused on several topics affecting the life of the Church. Central to the discussion was the role and full equality of women in church life. During a very open and honest discussion, it became clear that there is much pain concerning the exclusion of women from governance, leadership and ordained ministry – and how that causes division and affects the entire life of our Church.'[9] Frustration mounted – even to the point of tears, because, while people thought women should not be excluded from presiding at Eucharist, the priests present knew that they would be immediately removed from office if they participated in this celebration. The honesty and emotional rawness of this experience will stay with me forever. I was struck, as were others, by the power and value of the baptised and the ordained being able to discern together.

Later at the Philadelphia Gender, Gospel and Global Justice Conference where I participated with six hundred others at wonderful early morning Eucharists with women presiding, had me questioning where best to direct my efforts for this inclusive practice of faith so urgently needed in our church. I was still a member of the WOW leadership team; I decided that, despite the essential work on women's ordination WOW and other relevant groups were doing, there was a way in which they could be sidelined. It seemed important to me to mainstream the idea of women's ordination. We needed a critical mass of women and men arguing for equality for all in our church. From then on, I decided to focus my energy on the grass roots in Australia and try to build and mainstream the idea of equality for all in our church.

Then, in 2016, the priests' groups held their third meeting in Chicago. I again attended and argued the case for equality for women. The whole meeting is best summed up by Fr Tony Flannery's press release, which captures the division caused by women not being able to preside at Eucharist: 'Some, and not all of them men, believed that pushing for ordination at this stage was not helpful, because it only served to make dialogue with church authorities impossible. Instead they argued that a better policy was to work for "full equality for women in decision making in the Church". Others were more passionate about the ordination question, and believed that full equality was not possible without ordination. The celebration of the Eucharist, as in the previous conference in Limerick, posed complex and emotional questions. Some said there could not be a Eucharist among us without a specific ordained priest presiding. Others, mostly, though not all, women, believed that that was yet again highlighting the inequality of the church, and not acceptable. In the end the Eucharist was celebrated, though not with everyone present.'[10]

My position was that arguing for equality was consistent with our theology of all being equal in Christ, and that whatever the model of priesthood, it should be the same for women and men. So I hadn't abandoned ordination of women, but saw the equality argument as a way of opening the dialogue and progressing the process for equality by working to include the baptised as well as the ordained in decision-making. I believed this would be a step towards equality.

The group, including myself, that opted to work for equality for women arising from this discussion developed the 'Listening to Women' package, which we completed on Skype and launched in May 2018. Listening to Women is sponsored by the Association of U.S. Catholic Priests, the Australian Catholic Coalition for Church Renewal, DignityUSA, FutureChurch, RAPPORT (Renewing a Priestly People, Ordination Reconsidered Today) and the Women's Ordination Conference. It is running as a five-year project in the USA and could be easily adapted for Australia.

In Australia, Concerned Catholics came onto the renewal scene with a bang in April 2016, hosting an event in Canberra with Professor John Warhurst as chair and Francis Sullivan, Senator Kristina Keneally and myself as speakers. Concerned Catholics have made an enormous impact on renewal in the church in a very short space of time. John Warhurst has provided outstanding leadership and has developed important relationships with the episcopate and the Plenary Council. Concerned Catholics have hosted numerous public events with speakers including Robert Fitzgerald, Bishop Vincent Long, Francis Sullivan, Sister Clare Condon, Fr Peter Day and Senator Kristina Keneally. Their regular press releases in response to Vatican and Plenary Council statements have encouraged individual members to speak out on Catholic current affairs in the press and on-line media. In 2019, they facilitated Concerned Catholic groups in Tasmania and Wagga diocese.

Concerned Catholics also hosted a national gathering of ACCCR groups in March 2018 at the Australian Centre for Christianity and Culture in Canberra to assist in implementing the Royal Commission recommendations and give clear priorities for the 2021 Plenary Council. The gathering produced a communiqué that was distributed to the national press and all bishops. (The group had planned to meet in April 2020 but the event was rain-checked due to COVID-19).

Following the gathering, ACCCR representatives (Trish Hindmarsh, Peter Johnstone, John Warhurst and myself) met in Melbourne with Archbishop Mark Coleridge and Lana Turvey-Collins. At this meeting, we outlined key structural issues arising from the March gathering, particularly the importance of women in decision-making. We offered to help the ACBC in the lead-up to the Plenary Council. In one of the best meetings the renewal movement has had, ACCCR set up an agenda with them and agreed on a process that allowed us to discern and listen as equal in Christ. However, when asked to consider a greater role and representation for the renewal movement in the Plenary Council process, they essentially said thank you, but no thank you. We reiterated that as the baptised, we are the church and are equal and as committed to its survival as the ordained. We noted that we have also held positions of responsibility in public life and have skills and time to contribute.

Another significant, recently developed international network with outreach and social media in fifteen countries, including Australia, is Voices of Faith. It is an initiative that hosts events, media outreach and international network groups to empower Catholic women into decision-making roles at local and global levels in the church. Voices of Faith usually host their annual conference in the Vatican on International Women's Day. Mary McAleese, former President of Ireland, was to speak at their 2018 conference, however a senior Vatican official, the conservative, Irish-born US cardinal, Kevin Farrell, banned her from taking part. Rather than cancel the conference, Voices of Faith moved it to another location in Rome – outside the Vatican walls. Given Mary McAleese's credentials – she is an award-winning Catholic academic and author who holds a licentiate and doctorate in Canon Law – one can only conclude that systemic clericalism still rules.

The 2021 Plenary Council is the most significant opportunity for renewal ever presented in the Australian church. It has the potential to position Australia to lead a radical shift to the synodal church that Pope Francis and so many of us have worked towards with such dedication. If we are concerned about renewal, we have to support and influence any moves towards change that can be made during the Plenary process. Late last year, Catholics for Renewal published *Getting Back on Mission: Reforming Our Church Together*.[11] The publication is a comprehensive and clear guide for all involved in reform and the Plenary Council.

But despite the push toward renewal, many in the Catholic community are doubtful the Plenary Council will achieve its reform potential. The steps along the way have not met expectations. They have not demonstrated that the pleas of the baptised – and many of the ordained – have been heeded. Little regard has been given to openness and transparency, particularly regarding a female co-chair, access to the thousands of submissions, and representation of the baptised at the Plenary itself.

Jesuit George Wilson's book, *Clericalism: The Death of Priesthood* (2008), argues that the whole church is responsible for the clerical culture, and that we all unintentionally contribute to it and collude with it. He highlights the damage the baptised do when they don't call out banal and inauthentic communication; he insists we must pursue honest and authentic communication as equals in Christ.[12]

The Plenary Council team must be aware of the urgency to bridge the void between the baptised and the ordained. I had hoped that the six writing groups for the Plenary Council might have achieved the level of discernment I had experienced at both Limerick and Chicago. However, when the void between the baptised and the ordained is as great as it is at present, bridging it requires a skilled facilitator to develop authentic discernment, communication and trust. The writing groups did not have facilitators, so we still await the outcomes.

A further reason for concern about the Plenary is the list of delegates released in late-March 2020. Taking the Canberra-Goulburn archdiocese as an example: here four men (a bishop, two priests and a respected layman) and a young woman have been appointed to the Plenary. We know that all those appointed are good people, but the background story leaves a sour taste. Two mature women with excellent credentials who have dedicatedly worked in the lead-up to the Plenary were nominated, but passed over. We understand there are constraints on numbers attending, but we expected our archbishop to have stood up and argued for an additional number to ensure fair representation of women. In addition to the compulsory three ordained attendees, there should have been three members of the laity. This number could have included the existing male and female appointees, whom we welcome, plus an additional mature and experienced female from the two nominated women representatives.

What has happened is disrespectful and dismissive of the hundreds of women in our archdiocese who have given time and effort, attending consultations both in the city and across rural deaneries, to support the success of the Plenary. It demonstrates a dismissiveness, a lack of discernment and transparency. At a recent family gathering, one of our Loreto-educated nieces (a graduate) was asked what she thought about the lack of young women attending church. Her response was 'Well, when the church recognises women, women will recognise the church'.

This brings us to Pope Francis and women. There is no doubt that Pope Francis has been one of our best and most exceptional popes, promoting equality, and care for the most vulnerable, the poor and concern for our environment. However, he does not conceive of women as intelligent, clever, competent, equal creations in Christ. He seems to have an ideological understanding of women that sometimes leads to the stereotyped, dismissive and offensive comments he makes. It is understandable as a cultural trait, but not acceptable.

In contrast to the hope that the Amazonia Synod brought to the world, the release of Pope Francis' *Querida Amazonia* was met with bitter disappointment from many, including women. I can applaud the Pope's emphasis on the environment, but for him to deny Amazonia married priests after listening to the words of its men and women – and after getting a two-thirds majority vote to act – suggests that he doesn't understand how introducing married priests would allow life-giving Eucharist to many more in a culture where the people of God crave such support in their lives. To have done so would also have been a step towards breaking clericalism and correcting the gender imbalance in our church. It seems he doesn't realise that both of these issues need urgent attention. Surely, he could have done both? The impact would have increased the benefits for the environment not detracted from them.

Some say Pope Francis has left the door open for these issues. Well, we will push that door wide open. Equality for all has greater prominence than ever now and the urgency to make it a reality has never been greater. Women are united in the belief that there can be no justice in a church that does not treat all its members as equal. If our church recognised equality for women, there would be pressure to raise the status of women in countries where human rights are not respected. There is an accountability and justice issue here for the church. On International Women's Day 2020, baptised women and men, lay and religious, representing countries from across the world, made sure they were visible and their voices heard by demonstrating outside churches, including Australia, under the banner of 'Dignity and Equality, the time for change is now'.

The plethora of work outlined here is a snapshot of one woman's experience of efforts towards reform in the Catholic Church. But it represents the tip of the iceberg when one considers the amount of work in progress by the baptised and the ordained across the country and across the world.

Finally, turning to the 2021 Plenary, and to implementation of the recommendations of the Royal Commission: it will be crucial to network with those attending the Plenary to ensure that, after all the time and money spent, we have effective outcomes. Pope Francis' synodal approach is one path to an inclusive church. But it is an approach that will only succeed if there is less episcopal control. This would entail changing Canon law so that deliberative and consultative voting is equal between the baptised and the ordained. Secondly, women and men must be included in all decision-making; and thirdly, in Sister Clare Condon's words, 'recognition of different images of God is essential or else we will be patriarchal forever'.

Someone who has thought carefully about the Plenary is Andrea Dean, former director of the ACBC Office of Participation of Women and newly elected President of WATAC. She suggests that all dioceses establish diocesan pastoral councils; that there be a national council for the laity with responsibility for the Catholic Church in partnership with the ACBC; that there be disciplinary measures for priests who limit women's involvement at parish level (for example, in parishes where women are no longer 'allowed' on the sanctuary, or in rural parishes where Eucharistic liturgies are limited); that every diocese have a women's council whose voices are heard through two representatives on the diocesan pastoral council; and finally, that inclusive language be adopted as recommended in the ACBC Research *Woman and Man: one in Christ Jesus* (1999). A recommendation that has still not been realised.

Francis Sullivan, former CEO of the Catholic Church's Truth, Justice and Healing Council, commenting on the gospel passage where Jesus calls for 'New wine in new skins' (Matthew 9:17) issues this challenge: 'Let's shape a Church that constantly asks whether it is fit for purpose. Flexible, adaptive, attractive to the young and inquisitive. That develops ministers, pastors, deacons and priests that we can relate to, aspire to be and select from within our ranks. Let's drink of this new wine that enlivens through affirming the ever-evolving understanding of human nature, its development and manifestations. Let's applaud the wonder of sexuality, embrace it as grace and actively resist attempts to demonise, judge and divide. Let's become the wine skins of hope in a future unshackled from religiosity and enthused with a truth that's set us free'.[13]

Whatever happens, it is in our hands: The baptised, invoking the Holy Spirit, must claim their responsibility as the people of God and lead.

Endnotes

1. Waleed Aly, *The Age*, 3 January 2020
2. www.watac.net.au
3. www.catalystforrenewal.org.au/about/
4. www.e-arc.org/history.html
5. www.womensordinationcampaign.org/aim-and-mission
6. Australian Catholic Bishops Conference, *Woman and Man: one in Christ Jesus. Report on the participation of women in the Catholic Church in Australia* (Sydney: HarperCollinsReligious, 1999)
7. Gary Macy, *The Hidden History of Women's Ordination: Female Clergy in the Medieval West* (Oxford: Oxford University Press, 2008)
8. www.womensordinationcampaign.org-pink-smoke-over-the-vatican-vigil-in-rome-march-2013
9. *Irish Times*, 17/4/2015
10. Tony Flannery, '3rd International Conference of Church Reform Network; Chicago, October 2016', www.associationofcatholicpriests.ie/2016/10/3rd-international-conference-of-church-reform-network-chicago-2016/
11. Catholics for Renewal, *Getting Back on Mission: Reforming Our Church Together* (Mulgrave: Garratt Publishing, 2019)
12. George B. Wilson, *Clericalism: The Death of Priesthood* (Collegeville, Minnesota: Liturgical Press, 2008)
13. Francis Sullivan, 'New Wine, New Wine Skins', *Pearls and Irritations*, 26 February 2020

Chapter 4

The Church As We Know It Is Broken

Reflections from the *Voices of Hope and Challenge* Conference at Yarra Theological Union, 2019

Eleanor Flynn

This chapter was begun before the COVID-19 virus took hold of the world, so some of the ideas and suggestions may no longer be as pertinent as they were when I first considered them. Because of this major disruption to all of our lives, my proposition – supported by the numerous others I quote – is that the church as we know it is broken, requiring a major rebuild from the ground up which may now actually occur sooner than we had hoped. I am writing the final parts of this chapter in Holy Week and thinking of Easter without attending any service, something I have never done, not even when travelling in the Middle East. As someone very interested in death and dying and how the experience affects people, I am aware of the liminal, the uncontrolled time between structured events, the time between the old and the new. The world and the church are now truly in a liminal period, just as were those who waited in Jerusalem on the first Holy Saturday, waiting not knowing what would happen next.

I will discuss a series of 'conversations' that have made me realise that we must accept that the Catholic Church so many of us grew up in is broken, possibly beyond repair. And those of us still interested in her welfare need to be and do quite radical things in order to make those in power realise how malignant their behaviours are in stopping the voices of women and other marginalised groups even from being heard, let alone from having any input in the running of the church.

The first two conversations were just that – separate discussions (one a chance meeting) with two eminent Australian women theologians who both said quite flatly that the Catholic Church, as we know it, is broken and will need to be rebuilt if it is to have any meaning for those who come after us.

The other conversations I comment on were presentations at the *Voices of Hope and Challenge Conference* held at the Yarra Theological College campus of the University of Divinity in November 2019.[1] Although neither of my two initial conversationalists was present, the theme of a broken church needing root and branch renewal was dominant. And while the issue of a proper place for women in the church was not mentioned in the two initial brief conversations, it is something I know both my theologian-mentors embrace wholeheartedly.

The attendees at the conference were, like the writer, predominantly older, Anglo-Celtic and female – not unlike the audience/congregants at most Catholic Church activities

I attend. The presenters discussed past, present and future issues related to being a twenty-first-century Australian Catholic, albeit one from a primarily European background. I am limiting this discussion to the presentations that excited or depressed me, and those that showed a possible path towards a new church, or even a new way of being church. As a feminist from an Irish background, my biases will no doubt appear.

Bishop Vincent Long, OFM, began the conference proceedings by acknowledging that the church as we know it is broken, stating that the horrors of the Royal Commission's findings have demonstrated 'the rottenness in the state of the church'. Quoting Isaiah 43:19 – 'something new, making paths through the wilderness' – he talked about our need to 'rebuild from the ground up'. He discussed the problems of clericalism, and argued that continuing in the all-male, triumphalist model of church without engaging women as full members will lead to a church that is fit for no one.

I heard him mention Rosa Parks, the African American woman whose refusal to sit in the back of the bus was an integral part of the long continuing fight for justice for African Americans. However the transcript of his paper on the YTU website does not include the reference. I expect, like many of us, he either added extra notes to his talk as he was on the plane from Sydney to Melbourne, or possibly he didn't want the boldness of the suggestion to appear in the formal transcript, given the negativity of many of his brother bishops to anything approaching a real role for women in the church.

His answers to the many questions were models of honesty constrained by pragmatism – he could only say so much in public about the church hierarchy and their willingness (or not) to engage with the laity, or whether they will act to ensure that the Plenary Council (now rescheduled for 2021 once the virus has run its course) will lead to a transformed church. It seemed to me that he was challenging the organisers and attendees of the conference to stop talking and writing about the issues in ways that permit our thoughts and ideas to go around in a self-congratulatory circle, and instead to go out and challenge those we regard as the perpetrators of the ongoing clericalism of the Australian hierarchy.

The idea that we are in for the long haul of change in the church, a sustained task that requires us to stand up for our beliefs and ideas, is very challenging. As a privileged 'baby boomer' who has always had everything I wanted – free university, good jobs (in my case with equal pay) and the ability to afford a house and frequent overseas travel – I would need to change my attitude from one of 'they should fix it' to one of 'I have to be radicalised'. I would need to work with my sisters and brothers to define the problems carefully and then do something about them, and keep doing things until the situation improves, or I die.

In discussion afterwards, we decided that Bishop Long was calling us, particularly women, to resist the gender-negative messages many in the hierarchy impose on us; we should be strong and determined to push ahead with the ideas we have for change in the church. The Rosa Parks story is encouraging, but also a caution: change will prove difficult, with surges of progress followed by backsliding from those in power, who may be sitting back, waiting for someone else to effect the change, or hoping that no change will occur.

The Saturday morning session started with (recently deceased, June 2020) Dr Noel Connolly SSC, a member of the Plenary Council Facilitation Group. I had heard him speak earlier in the year on the Plenary Council, and was not very enthusiastic; however, I felt that I needed to hear what he had to say this time because of his role. His PowerPoint slides, available on the YTU website, apparently show that he discussed Pope Francis' calls for synodality and the need to listen to all, to encourage participation by all, and he mentioned the perils of clericalism. My memory is that he was explaining the processes of the Plenary Council and the pushes and pulls of the various groups, using a very blokey-jokey delivery that suggested he thought he was among friends who accepted his view of the issues. Interestingly, he was called out by a younger member of the audience, who objected to some of his comments. His style was more professional thereafter.

My concern about his role in the Plenary Council is that, as an older male member of a missionary religious order, he has not really engaged with the general Australian Catholic population to discover what many of them think about the church and why their children and friends no longer engage with the church at all. I was disturbed at his statement, repeated from the earlier presentation at a *Spirituality in the Pub* session, that inverting the clerical pyramid, as Pope Francis has suggested as a way to involve everyone in the conversation about where the church should be going, would leave him, as a priest, still in the middle. I found this statement odd when I first heard it, but as it was delivered in a blokey style I didn't think much more about it. The second time I heard it, it really bothered me because it implied that he didn't think that he, or any other priests, needed to change their behaviour or thinking even while considering ways in which the church must be different in the future. Given that his voice is predominant in the Plenary preparations, this is a major issue for women and the laity in general. He may suggest that I am disturbed by his style, not the content, and that I have misunderstood him. However, as those of us who work on improving communication in the health system know very well, the style of the conversation is as important, if not more so, than the content of the messages. A health care worker's manner can be crucial in ensuring that patients understand their problems and their proposed treatment.

The other Plenary Council issue of concern to the conference audience was how only six themes somehow magically sprang from the hundreds of submissions. The submissions are not available for all to see. Where was the transparency? All that effort and time spent attending meetings and submitting ideas to the Plenary website – then blackout. Was it because so many of the submissions advocated a role for women, something that the church at the higher levels seems to find so terrifying it cannot be discussed publicly?

Dr Andrew Hamilton SJ, editorial consultant of the online publication *Eureka Street*, spoke about clericalism through the prism of a Melbourne parish in the late 1940s, the 1980s, and now. He contrasted the changes in the community over that time with the less apparent changes in the clergy over the same period. He remarked particularly on the contrast between increasing opportunities for women in the community and in the church. He also mentioned the increasing informality of dress, discourse and ceremony, sometimes, but not often enough, taken up by the clergy. His take on the toxic behaviour that we call 'clericalism' is that it is a 'psychopathic manipulation of church structures and relationships for self-gratification'. And he asked, as others did over the weekend, why Catholics are still accepting this manipulative behaviour from those with power in the church.

He, like most of the speakers, made suggestions for the rebuilding of the church, and I was interested that he was one of the few to mention the need to take heed of the many migrant groups of Catholics, to ensure that anything that is developed does not leave them feeling the church is still as unfamiliar as when they first arrived in Australia. He also specifically mentioned the need to connect with the wisdom of the elderly, whose commitment keeps church activities running and whose voice may not be heard by those wanting youth to triumph.

Pondering Andrew Hamilton's discussion, I kept returning to this question: why do we, the laity and especially women, allow ourselves to be talked at, talked down to, not given the facts and in general treated as second class citizens in the church? As George Wilson discusses in his very pertinent work *Clericalism: The Death of the Priesthood*,[2] there are varieties of 'clerical' behaviour in other areas apart from the church. The one I know best is the medical sphere where, for decades, men ran the hospitals, university and specialist training programs, and entry into them. As women became more prominent in the medical workforce, they pushed for major changes to the processes of selection and training, as well as for equal pay for all. There is still a way to go to achieve full equality in most areas of medicine and even when an area is reformed there can still be backsliding. However, there is now an appreciation that women are integral to the proper running of a medical faculty, hospital or clinic, and that they must be included as equal members of governing bodies for these places. Nothing resembling this has happened in the church. In fact in recent years things have become worse in some places and we, the laity, must bear some blame for not calling the perpetrators out on their behaviour.

The speakers who really got me excited were those who spoke on the Sunday morning, Paul Bongiorno and John Warhurst, and a trio of educated feminists who really knew their subjects.

Associate Professor Mary Coloe PVBM, a highly regarded New Testament scholar, spoke about the place of women in the New Testament, and the parts of the text that were redacted by the later male editors. She provided ample evidence of the roles that women took in the early church, as deacons, priests and bishops, including the rules and prayers used for appointing women as deacons. What I found fascinating, as a doctor, was her argument that it was the incorrect biological interpretation of the Greek philosophers that was the basis for the view that women were inferior to men, rather than anything biblical. The Greeks assumed that men were the source of life and women just the receptacles, so 'obviously' women were inferior. Because this view was accepted by Augustine, it became the dominant trope in the church's teaching and practice from then on, leading to the view that women could not be active members of the clergy.

This totally mistaken idea of women's part in creation of new life is not just an issue for the church. As Dr Coloe showed, the medical men assumed well into the eighteenth century that this was true. Even now I have colleagues whose research in relation to women's health issues is demonstrating that much of what was thought true is now being discovered to be misogynistic rubbish, written by men who did not listen to women or examine them carefully. Another example of the toxic effects of another kind of 'clericalism'!

Professor Coloe finished by quoting John Paul II, writing to the Women's Gathering in 1995 in Beijing, declaring that it was a matter of 'justice and necessity' for women to achieve real equality. She emphasised five areas of change required for equality: reinstatement of women deacons and priests; use of inclusive language in the liturgy; representation of women at all levels of the church governance structure; equal access to funding for theology studies for men and women, and finally, equal access to acceptance for vocations and specific training for these vocations.

Her very personal statement about not being able, as a noted New Testament scholar, to break open the word in church but having to listen to 'dismal nonsense week after week' because men make up the rules, really focused my attention. The following week as I was about to read from Paul's letter to the Romans, I really wanted to explain why it is thought he wrote what he did. I refrained, but I was annoyed with myself for not speaking up.

The next speaker of the morning was Dr Rosemarie Joyce CSB, talking about how and why canon law should be changed to allow women and lay men to have a deliberative voice at the Plenary Council. As she said, both civil law and canon law can be changed to meet the needs of different times or circumstances. Canon law is 'merely ecclesiastical law' (canon 11) and is totally man-made, and therein lies a lot of the problem. To show the mutability of canon law, she gave pertinent examples of recent changes, such as the abolition of limbo and the improvements in nullifying marriages. She went on to argue the need for repeal of the laws that stop women and lay men from having any governance role in the church. As she and so many others have said since Vatican II, it is baptism that makes us all equal in the church. Ordination does not invest the priest with the right to be a leader, but rather a servant of the People of God. Her concluding challenge to the bishops – that they can and should change canon law – was to remind them of the general premise of canon law, that 'The salvation of souls must always be the supreme law of the church' (canon 1752).

The conversation that really had many of us if not jumping for joy at least nodding along very happily, was the presentation by Dr Patricia Fox RSM describing the way the Adelaide archdiocese encouraged and involved women at many levels of parish and diocesan governance. She spoke of her experiences working with two bishops who understood the need to engage all in the church, including women, in setting up pastoral councils in parishes, and in setting up a diocesan council with connections between the diocese and the parishes. Her account enthused everyone present to do the same in their own areas, while wishing they had bishops who accepted the teaching of Vatican II: that women and men are equal in the sight of God. She pointed out that an important part of Adelaide's success was that the work was informed by continuing theological discussion and reflection among all the participants – to be a 'substantive, people-centred diocesan renewal program that was seeking to implement Vatican II'.

In answer to questions, Dr Fox stated that the Royal Commission found there was less sexual abuse in the Adelaide Archdiocese than elsewhere in Australia. Also, she commented that involving women in all aspects of parish and diocesan life meant that when abuse was discovered, it was dealt with much more positively for the victims –

something that made many of us remember how poorly the victims in other states have been treated. So little succour! So little support!

I was aware that South Australia had a much better and more advanced child safeguarding system for the church because, when my Melbourne parish started to develop and implement our program, the pastoral associate, who was from South Australia, knew all about it, and had ideas about how to involve the whole parish and get everyone on side and signed up. The evidence about Adelaide's reduced sexual abuse and better handling is surely something we need to broadcast, so that church authorities realise there are better ways we can approach this matter than by tick-box education sessions being done in Melbourne.

I was very keen to hear Professor John Warhurst AO, as I have been reading his elegant pieces on the dysfunctional Australian Catholic Church for some time. His discussion about his experiences in the current church was both sobering and distressing. As a well-qualified and thoughtful member of several church bodies he is able to discuss issues of reform rationally and calmly. He is totally aware of the way the church works and of the clericalism that underpins so much of the failure of transparency and terror of change in the hierarchy. From his academic background in political thought, he suggests we need a model of church that is neither legalistic nor rule-bound, rather one that people who live Christian values in their daily work of teaching and those who provide for the old, the ill and the disadvantaged, will see as a body that works for the benefit of all, especially people who are currently marginalised by both society and church.

He described his recent defenestration from an important church-related committee. He sat, he told us, with others in the committee, and just said yes to the prelate who told them the news. All of us in the room were with him in that moment. Many of us have been in similar situations. We know we should speak up and say, this is not correct, this is not right, but reverence for the clergy is still so ingrained that we find it very hard to do so. Even so simple an action as not calling men who are very often younger than us 'father' goes against our reflexes. We, the non-clerical members of the church, are therefore compliant in the clericalism of the church because we do not call out inappropriate behaviour or speech, whether about a major issue like abuse of children or vulnerable adults, or something more minor like disbanding parish activities run by women.

My final reflection from the conference was prompted by the presentation given by well-known Canberra journalist Paul Bongiorno. He acknowledged his trepidation in filling in for Francis Sullivan (of whom more later), however his talk was riveting, full of information about the behaviour and statements of popes, cardinals and bishops over forty years. He accepts his bishop's description of him, and his fellow members of Canberra Concerned Catholics, as 'white, middle class grandparents'. But his experiences mean he is well acquainted with of the consequences of the long papacy of John Paul II, and the almost complete suppression of the reforms of Vatican II. The result: a dragging of the church back to a nineteenth-century absolutist model of papal governance and toxic clericalism.

Paul Bongiorno's discussion included aspects of the role of Cardinal George Pell in this restoration agenda, plus Pell's membership of the Congregation of Bishops, where he wielded great power working with the traditionalist US Cardinal Raymond Burke to get conservative protégés appointed to sees all over the world. Many current Australian bishops who owe their appointment to Pell's influence resist the idea of synodality, and are reported to consider the Plenary Council to be a waste of time and money because the laity will only ask for things like women's ordination that are not going to happen on their watch!

I found Bongiorno's explanations of why our children, brought up in the church, so often cannot cope with any form of religion, important and relevant. They 'see a Church that does not practise what it preaches and is more into fighting for its own privileges.' As well, they see the church rejecting the ideas and involvement of women, LGBTI persons and Catholics who have remarried outside the church – a large proportion of the Catholic population.

He did hold out some hope for the Plenary Council and potential for change while Francis remains pope and Mark Coleridge remains leader of the Australian bishops. I think he is hoping against hope. Francis has declined to consider married priests for the Amazon, even after the bishops asked him, and has again said that women could never be priests.

My final conversation was actually a session listening to Francis Sullivan at the Adelaide Festival in early March, where he provided a personal reflection on leadership before a choir sang ten Psalms on the same theme. Sullivan spoke of his time as the head of the Truth and Justice Commission, set up by the Australian Catholic Bishops as their response to the Royal Commission into Institutional Responses to Child Sexual Abuse. In one early meeting he sat and listened to a group of the abused tell their stories. This was followed by their challenge to him not to forget these stories in his interactions with the bishops.

Then he told us what he did to unwind from the pressure of the Truth and Justice Commission at the end of the Royal Commission, where his final task was documenting the recommendations of the Royal Commission in relation to the Catholic Church. This document, which the bishops refused to publicise for months, contains Sullivan's rational analysis of the issues, telling the bishops in very clear language what had to be done to meet the Commission's recommendations.

He walked the Camino for forty days and nights, carrying the Royal Commission's chapter on the Catholic Church in his backpack. When he arrived at the Cathedral in Santiago di Compostela he waited till everyone was busy climbing the stairs to embrace the statue of St James and then he went down to the crypt where the saint's bones are supposedly entombed. He took the volume and threw it through the upright bars around the tomb. It landed perfectly, open in the middle of the book, on the tomb. He left immediately, having done what he set out to do.

This moving story helped me understand what good lay leadership in the Australian Catholic Church can be: someone who sits and listens to the terrible things that have happened in the church; who documents the abuses; who provides a plan to move the hierarchy and the people of the church forward to overcome these abuses; who remains polite but very firm about what needs to be done for the church to be able even to start the necessary rebuilding. And finally, someone who, in spite of the dreadful narratives he has had to listen to for many months, is still able to take part in a Catholic ritual, and someone who takes time to look after his own mental and physical health.

Considering these conversations, as I have been writing this reflection, has made me even angrier at the majority of the Australian Catholic Church hierarchy for their wilful misuse of power in the cover-up of so much of the sexual abuse by the clergy, their insistence on the specialness of the ordained, including the non-existent ontological change at ordination, the refusal to allow women to have any real place in the church, and indeed their dismantling of structures to support women in the church.

I realise that to effect any change in the church, I need to become an active worker for justice, by whatever means I can, in collaboration with my sisters and brothers and with any of the clergy who want to join us for the ride. That it will be a long haul and not always straightforward, I do realise. However, if we believe that baptism makes us all people of God, then we need to accept that, and to work as people imbued by the Spirit to make a church worthy of all.

Endnotes

1. Transcripts of the Conference presentations are available at https://ytu.edu.au/voices-of-hope-and-challenge-conference-2019/ (accessed March 11, 2020)
2. George B Wilson SJ. *Clericalism: The Death of Priesthood.* Liturgical Press, 2008

Chapter 5

Suffer The Little Children

Judy Benson

For the extensive period during which the Royal Commission into Institutional Responses to Child Sexual Abuse sat to undertake its role,[1] conduct public hearings,[2] complete numerous private sessions with complainants,[3] and report its findings[4] – and indeed since – the general public has been overwhelmed by the sheer scope numerically, the repetition, the extent, and the nature of the accounts of sexual abuse perpetrated against children by clergy, religious, and others. On many occasions, whether the Royal Commission was sitting in a metropolitan or a regional centre, there was coverage of the day's hearing on the evening news channels, with footage of key aspects of what had emerged during the day, including excerpts from the testimony of witnesses, the questions of counsel assisting, and the oral exchanges passing between witnesses, counsel and various Royal Commissioners.

The Catholic Church, with its systemic failures over a long time, has had a high profile in the reportage of the Royal Commission. It has, along with other churches and organisations, borne the lion's share of shame and disgrace. Naturally this has left many in the Church, and indeed outside it, bewildered, grieving and perplexed that such things could have happened at all, and worse, that they should have been so surreptitiously covered up.

One message is painfully clear: for the Church to have any credibility at all in the future working with the victims and vulnerable of society – including children (and are not they the ones with which Christ said the Church's preference should lie?) – it must first and promptly get its own house in order. Of necessity, this must entail a commitment greater in scope than a mere *mea culpa*; real action must then follow. This will encompass an acknowledgment of wrongdoing in the past, but more importantly, putting in place and accepting and adhering to practices, procedures and protocols that reflect more accurately the expectations of the community, including embracing the consequences of redress.

Dealing with the consequences and outcomes arising from the abuse, sexual and otherwise, of children, is the tragic daily fare and 'core business' of the Family Division of the Children's Court of Victoria. In this instance, however, the abuse is perpetrated against children not by outsiders or powerful organisations but by their own parents, and by their immediate and extended families, mostly inside their own home. These matters hardly ever, if at all, achieve any publicity or profile, certainly much less than that which was accorded to the activities of the Royal Commission. Why is this so? Why the apparent secrecy?

Children Youth and Families Act 2005 (the Act)[5]

The protection of children[6] in Victoria is principally governed today by an Act of the State Parliament which over the years has undergone many revisions and amendments. The Children's Court of Victoria was originally established in 1906; prior to this time, children were dealt with in the adult courts of the day. Again, prior to 1906, the *Neglected Children's Acts* of 1864, 1887 and 1890 all had the effect, if not the intention, of criminalising children who had in effect done nothing more heinous than demonstrate that they were in need of protection. In the 1989 Act, the immediate predecessor to the current Act, the legislature determined on court proceedings for children who were in need of protection separate from those for children who had committed criminal offences in the way they were dealt with at court. The current 2005 Act deals with criminal offences committed by children in the Criminal Division of the Children's Court, and the protection of children from abuse and neglect is dealt with in the Family Division of the Court. The Court sits in a number of metropolitan and country locations throughout the state. Despite the formal division as stated, the Court and its practitioners have frequently noted the disproportionate number of young offenders who are, or were, also in need of protection.

Section 534 of the Act restricts the publication of proceedings of the Children's Court and prohibits the publication (or the causing to be published) of proceedings in the Court that may contain any particulars of that Court proceeding, the Court's location, the names of the child or any parties or witnesses involved in it, except with the permission of the President, a permission rarely granted. The penalties for breach of the prohibition are severe, including significant fines for corporations including media outlets, or in the case of a person, imprisonment for two years. Accordingly, any reference to cases in the Children's Court – either on the Court's own website or elsewhere – must be de-identified when referred to.

Given that the basic presumption in our court system is that courts and tribunals generally are – and should be – open to the public, and that anyone can go at any time and sit in and report on the proceedings being conducted in them,[7] the prescriptions applicable in the Children's Court are an apparent anomaly. In all other circumstances, the view has been taken that '[p]ublicity is the very soul of justice',[8] a dictum which is approved by the High Court of Australia[9] and reinforces the idea that justice can only be done when it 'shall be conducted publicly and in open view'. So the approach taken by the Children's Court needs some explaining.

Prior to the 1989 version of the Act, proceedings in Children's Courts were in fact closed to the public. They are still closed in some other jurisdictions, for example, in the United Kingdom and New Zealand. The current Act makes plain in section 523 that the proceedings of the Court *must* be heard in open court unless where, for specific and compelling reasons and in appropriate circumstances, the presiding judicial officer orders the entire court or a part of the proceeding to be closed to the public.

The *quid pro quo* for section 534 is that while the Children's Court in Victoria is now open to the public, and, of course, the media, the trade-off for the openness is the prohibition on reporting, that is, disseminating identifying information about children and their families and their litigation. This was considered by Parliament to strike an appropriate balance, thereby ensuring that no one would be permitted to identify, or heap opprobrium on or embarrass, the children or any individual involved in their case, including their parents and/or witnesses. The essential rationale is that the prescription is for the benefit of the children because children and young people in particular are very susceptible to stigmatisation.

The inevitable consequence of this, though, is that it is not generally possible to report on cases in the Children's Court with any degree of particularity, except for the rare instances where the media is given permission by the President of the Court to publish particulars of children who, for example, have either been abandoned (in an attempt to locate a parent) or children who have gone missing (who are considered to be in special danger). This makes it an unattractive proposition for the media to report on those cases, because 'the story' and interest is to be found in part in the very particulars that cannot be identified. Very little serious reporting, therefore, is done by investigative journalists. They have to rely on research into trends and tendencies, and consequently very little is known by the general public about what goes on in Children's Courts and what lies behind those cases.

Unlike the Royal Commission, which operated in public and disclosed many individual cases by name, institution and offending party, the Act prohibits a similar approach for good public policy reasons, and in the best interests of children. That is not to say that the abuse of children is not happening, for it surely is: at an alarmingly increasing rate in disturbing ways, without any apparent end in sight and by the persons in their lives closest to them.

What is child abuse and its scope?

The central focus of the Family Division of the Children's Court is the need to protect children from types of significant harm that either have been caused, or are likely to be caused to them, either by their being subjected to, or exposed to, abuse, ill treatment, violence or neglect from which their parents have not protected them or are unlikely to protect them. There are six categories[10] of abuse, some of which are overlapping as follows:

(a) *Physical abuse*
Examples of this might include a baby taken to hospital and being found to have multiple broken bones and unexplained fractures and a range of other unexplained injuries; an infant being found to have retinal and brain damage (shaken baby syndrome) when its parents present to hospital saying the baby is unresponsive; children being rendered paraplegic or cerebral palsied from being shaken repeatedly and/or dropped when they cried excessively; children who present at child care with severe bruising around their faces and on other exposed parts of their body.

(b) *Sexual abuse*

(c) *Neglect*
Examples of this might include children living in chronically filthy homes where old and moulding food scraps and animal faeces are left on every surface of the home and floor for them to crawl among and touch; hoarding in houses so that there is a

danger to children of fire or suffocation; children left unsupervised roaming around the neighbourhood in nothing but a nappy or in clothes inadequate for the weather; children who are not fed enough or at all; children who present to school late with chronic and untreated head lice, unkempt and without lunch.

(d) *The death or incapacity of a parent*
An example would be a child left unattended when a parent has overdosed on drugs and become unconscious.

(e) *The abandonment of a child or the parent cannot be found*
For example where a parent may have been involuntarily admitted to a psychiatric institution and the child has no other carer available.

(f) *Emotional or psychological abuse of a child*
This might become apparent through exhibited changes in the way a child acts, the child becoming withdrawn and uncommunicative, or lashing out with violent behaviours, or exhibiting a range of anti-social, atypical and difficult behaviours.

This latter category of emotional abuse is often invoked as one of the grounds for bringing a child before the Court, and frequently it is paired with the ground of physical abuse. But it has a number of different, individual and defined aspects, as follows:

1. Parental unavailability, unresponsiveness or neglect. For example, a parent may have a mental

illness, post-natal depression, or have substance abuse issues and be unavailable to give the child the attention and care it craves, needs and deserves.

2. Negative attribution, rejection or harsh punishment. For example, scapegoating a child. This is not an uncommon aspect when meted out to a child of a former partner by a parent's new partner; or it may be characterised as a type of punishment if the child is deemed to have been 'responsible' for the child protection authorities coming into the family's life.

3. Developmentally inappropriate or inconsistent expectations. For example, exposing a child to confusing or traumatic events and interactions during episodes of repeated or extreme domestic violence.[11]

4. Failure to recognise a child's individuality, for example using a child as a tool or pawn in disputes and arguments with other or former domestic partners.

5. Failure to promote the child's adaptation, for example failure to get a child to school each day.

How is child abuse brought to light?

As children are generally presumed to be adequately cared for by their family and parents to a good enough standard, it is only when a report is received to the contrary – that they are suffering (or are likely to suffer) one of the harms outlined above – that the Department of Health and Human Services (DHHS) may have grounds to intervene in the family's life. Reports or notifications about the welfare and safety of children come from a variety of sources, often from concerned or affected members of the general public. More particularly reports come from an array of mandatory reporters,[12] professionals – such as doctors, nurses, teachers, police and psychologists – who in the course of practising or carrying out their profession and duties form a belief that a child may be in need of protection from physical or sexual abuse.[13] In this instance, these professionals *must* make a report to DHHS. There is protection under the Act to ensure the anonymity of these mandatory reporters.[14] The public policy rationale for this is so that they can thereby fulfil their statutory duty without fear of retribution.

As the Church in general, and many of its individual adherents in particular, occupy the full range of categories that make up the field of mandatory reporters, they of course have a statutory duty to report any abuse that they see or suspect is occurring. However, before any abuse actually occurs, they also have a unique opportunity to occupy and initiate pastoral and outreach roles with the identified families and children to see 'how they are travelling' and what needs and actions might be discovered and implemented at grass roots level before a crisis actually occurs. Children who are disadvantaged can be easily identified at child-care and in a variety of community settings.

Following the receipt of a report or notification, the DHHS investigates the allegations made and determines whether or not the threshold of alleged risk to the child reaches the level of substantial harm as set out in the definition of abuse in the Act. It may, without further legal action, refer the family to a variety of community-based services for support and voluntary engagement, so that parents can address the concerns and safety issues identified for the children. The DHHS itself provides and funds a range of rehabilitation, accommodation and specialist support services, such as parenting support, in-home assistance and drug and alcohol counselling agencies, as do an array of other community and non-government agencies and services, including church agencies. Alternatively, DHHS may determine, after investigation – especially if the concerns are chronic or serious – to take a protection application to the Children's Court to seek orders removing the child from parental care, or seeking orders supervising the parents' care of the child for a period of time. In extreme cases, either initially or after a period of time during which the parents have demonstrated that they have been unable to address the protective concerns, it may seek an order that the children be permanently placed with other persons or extended family, either on a permanent care order, or placed for adoption.

For the period 2000-1 (note, only one year) there were 36,966 reports/notifications to the DHHS in relation to abused and neglected children. In 2013-14[15] there were 82,056 reports.[16] Of these latter reports 19,206 were investigated, 11,395 were substantiated (assessed as credible and reliable), and of these 4200 proceeded to court under a protection application (a 'primary' application).

An analysis of the statistics from the 2013-4 reports revealed a number of general characteristics:

(a) Very young children and infants were over-represented in the sample;

(b) Recurring themes among parents included family violence, drug and alcohol abuse, and psychiatric and/or intellectual and/or physical disability;

(c) 45% of the reports were in relation to a sole parent family (but by comparison, only 20% of the general population comprises a sole parent family);

(d) 77% were reports in relation to low-income families.

The picture from the statistics then invites us to draw a connection between social and economic disadvantage and isolation, and personal difficulties experienced by the parents, with significant harm arising for children in the care of those parents. When the perceived harm to children has not been able to be satisfactorily addressed by the parents by voluntary means of engagement within the community, as already indicated the DHHS may take a protection application to the Children's Court.

While the statistics present a sobering and confronting reflection of the reality, a more optimistic view might suggest that this presents a real opportunity for the Church to be seen as initiating and exercising compassion in action where it is most needed: at the point of crisis. While there are of course Catholic agencies active in the field of child and infant welfare, and parental drug and alcohol rehabilitation, could more be done with pastoral and community-based outreach to prevent the worst excesses of abuse and neglect from reaching a point where litigation and statutory involvement is the only outcome left? The answer is obvious; but what is needed is the will to reallocate priorities and resources to make any presence at this human coalface effective and ongoing.

However, both the statistics and the lived experience of practitioners in the jurisdiction also suggest some additional broad propositions:

a. The Child Protection system has been characterised as being in 'crisis' for at least the past two decades. Despite the increase in community and non-government agencies (in addition to those directly funded by DHHS itself) who offer voluntary services to families in order to avoid the need to proceed to statutory intervention, the number of reports overall continues to increase exponentially. Referrals to court under statutory intervention have also increased exponentially.[17] One postulated reason is that there are large numbers of dysfunctional families and parents about whom repeated numbers of reports are made. In criminal circles they would be referred to as 'repeat offenders'. But the so-called 'offence' that the families and parents 'commit' in the child protection system is often nothing more than being disadvantaged and overwhelmed: poor, often a single parent, isolated and without extended family support; sometimes homeless, sometimes a victim of domestic violence; mentally ill, intellectually or physically disabled, overcoming or in the grip of alcohol or substance abuse; cognitive impairment; sometimes combinations of some or all of these. The children, and the parenting of them, become collateral damage of this despairing scenario. Cuts in the funding available to services are a perennial threat, and long waiting times for referrals to and help from those services are a pervasive reality. The question then needs to be asked: what is the priority here if, as the Charter says,[18] protection of families and children is so important, and families are the fundamental unit of society *entitled* to be protected by society and the State. [my emphasis]

b. The intervention by child protection bodies, while considered necessary to address the identified abuses, can have potentially adverse impacts on children, especially on the very young ones (disproportionally represented in the statistics). It can disrupt their secure attachment. The effects of this are acknowledged among psychologists to be adverse, especially in the early years. Secure attachments are known to be the essential foundations for the solid and secure development of healthy social, emotional and intellectual growth. The impact of removal of children from an attachment figure is profound, affecting development of the core of their personality and emergent self. The 'removed' child may feel rejected or abandoned by its parent. There is a very real tension between what child protection does (and has to do) in appropriate cases and the unintended consequences and outcomes for the children.

c. Because parental substance abuse (and difficulty in staying off drugs) has long been identified as one of the factors inhibiting parents' capacity to have their children successfully reunited with them, the Family Drug Treatment Court was launched in May 2014. It began as a pilot program designed to engage parents whose substance use, abuse and dependence played a key role in the removal of children from their care. The Court uses intensive case management co-ordination and therapeutic intervention to wrap around the parent in order to address not only the substance abuse issues but also any associated factors that might have led to the abuse. These can include undiagnosed mental health problems, lack of housing, financial management difficulties, and parenting deficits. The objective is to ensure that a parent can sustain the reunification with the child, and avoid the revolving door of repeated relapses. It is a much-lauded initiative, modelled on collaborative practice, and involves dedicated multi-disciplinary teams working with the Court and the parent to achieve goals and report back on a regular basis.

But! The eligibility screening to identify suitable candidates for the program requires them to make a considerable commitment to the process, typically over a year, with repeated testing of urine screens and attendance at Court, often on a weekly basis. The program only operates at one metropolitan and one regional Court in the whole state. As at the end of the first year of its operation, only one child had been reunited with a parent. Another four parents were still in the program, affecting another eight children. As at 2018-19, the Court was dealing with 65 referrals affecting 56 parents and 85 children, but only 52% of parents succeeded in achieving reunification with their children, by demonstrating a very real prospect of remaining clean of illicit substances.

This initiative was, and is, a good start. However, in this writer's view more funds and personnel are sorely needed to enable a rollout of this initiative across the whole state and in all courts if there is to be a more systematic success in defeating what is universally agreed to be the insidious societal problem of substance abuse. It is suggested that this is another forum in which the Church, in a practical and committed way, could walk with the parents who are undertaking this journey, to support and encourage them to be successful and to be reunited with their children. The process does not encourage the presence of lawyers, so the support the family member receives comes from those who are assisting at a practical level. The Church can and should be present as a support, with no agenda other than to walk with the parent and show what a practical Christian life is all about - being there when needed.

What happens for children and parents once legal intervention is undertaken?

Once the DHHS has filed a protection application at Court alleging one or more of the grounds of abuse identified above, the Court assumes case-management control of the steps then to be taken to achieve an outcome in the best interests of the children. The framework of the Act sets out the principles the Court must apply when considering what is in the best interests of children (called the 'best interests' principles),[19] including the important principle that a child must not be removed from its parent(s) unless there is an unacceptable risk of harm.[20] The Act also sets out the principles the DHHS must apply and consider before coming to any decision in relation to a child.[21] There are additional principles that apply to Aboriginal children.[22]

In 2018-19, 5866 protection applications were brought by the DHHS in Victoria, an increase of 10.7% over the previous year. The majority of these applications were brought on the grounds of both physical and emotional abuse of children and in the latter instance on the basis of their exposure to domestic or family violence. The number of protection orders made by the Court in 2018-19 in Victoria was 7456, an increase over the previous year (7034).

The special position of indigenous children is recognised in the Act and requires amplification. For the period of the last available statistics[23] there were 15,188 Aboriginal children in the Victorian population (1.25%), with non-Aboriginal children numbering 1,214,399. But Aboriginal children accounted for just over 10% of finalised investigations of reports made to DHHS (1064 cases as opposed to 10,404 for children generally). In the field of child protection it appears that, consistent with reports of Aboriginal youths being over-represented in the criminal justice area, children of Aboriginal parents are more represented statistically in the child protection arena.

Specialist lists of the Court for Aboriginal children have been established in the Children's Courts at Broadmeadows and Shepparton. Called *Maram Ngala Ganbu* ('We Are One'), they adapt the practices and procedures of the Court so that they are more culturally sensitive, aware and responsive to the needs and sensibilities of Aboriginal people who come before the Court. This initiative has been well received; however, in this writer's view, more needs to be done to make this the standard practice and procedure in all Court settings where Aboriginal people come before the Court in child protection proceedings. This is yet another avenue where the Church could - and should - be more active in showing solidarity with the plight of Aboriginal people and their disproportionate representation in the child protection system, by walking with them through the minefield of whitefella law to achieve some dignity and outcomes commensurate with their rights and dignity.

The Court must accord procedural fairness to all parties who come before it, the DHHS and parents and children. It has extensive powers of case management in the conduct of proceedings in the Court,[24] and it may inform itself on any matter in such manner as it sees fit, subject always to the proper application of the principles of justice and fairness.[25] Children over the age of ten years are entitled to separate representation based on their direct instructions, and those under ten may in some circumstances have an independent children's lawyer appointed by the Court to advise the Court on what is in that child's best interests. The Court then manages each case through to completion in a number of preliminary (interlocutory) steps, often involving referral of the matter to a conciliation where there is an effort made to resolve the matter informally by consent of all parties.

The statistics reveal that while many cases brought to Court proceed to at least one interim contested hearing, usually in relation to whether and where a child should be placed out of parental care, only 5% of protection applications filed at Court proceed to a final contested hearing, that is, where the application proceeds to an adversarial trial with the calling of witnesses and the testing of evidence.

In recent years, one very noticeable difficulty for all parties challenging the actions of the DHHS has been the increase in the number of unrepresented litigants coming before the Court trying to argue their own case. This may be because legal aid assistance is unavailable to them under that organisation's eligibility guidelines. Alternatively, the party may have originally been granted aid but had it withdrawn at some point for failure to appear at court and advance their case, or for other reasons. In part it is due to the particular temperament, presentation and psychology of the litigant, who is often not amenable either to legal advice or assistance or who can neither accept nor agree with what advice or assistance is given. The strain this places on the Court and its procedures – not to mention the other parties involved and the children – cannot be overstated. While the Court has the overarching duty to be fair, neutral and impartial, that duty cannot of necessity include the giving of legal advice to any party, even an unrepresented one; and therefore it is often the case that a parent with obvious and real personal disadvantage is further disadvantaged by having to represent him or herself at Court in a matter involving their child, an emotionally charged situation at any and every point along the procedural continuum.

Outcomes in the Court [26]

The most recent records collated by the Court in its statistics list both primary and secondary applications. A primary application has already been referred to (above) as including a protection application. A secondary application might include breaches of existing court orders, variations, revocations or extensions of existing orders, applications for further additional or different orders, and applications for safe custody warrants (an emergency power invoked when children have absconded and need to be found, apprehended and brought to court for their safety). It is noted in passing that in 2018-19, 8017 safe custody warrants were sought and obtained, an increase over the previous year (6505) of just under 25%. The Court also notes that over the past five years the number of primary and secondary applications has increased by 25% from 14,879 in 2014-15 to 18,722 in 2018-19. In the last year reviewed (2018-19) 31,650 cases were finalised of which 51.9% were in the Family Division of the Court (as opposed to the Criminal Division) and in addition another 3028 Intervention Order cases were finalised.

Waving or drowning?

Jesus is said to have uttered the famous words[27] 'suffer the little children to come unto me... for of such is the kingdom of heaven'. What an enormous challenge this poses for today's Church in light of what is revealed in this chapter. Unless heaven is to be populated by multitudes of broken, traumatised and unhappy little souls with memories of an earthly life that left much to be desired, the urgency to turn things around cannot be overestimated.

The need is great, and the scope of the task seemingly overwhelming, but as Nelson Mandela reminded us, every impossible-looking journey starts with just one step. The Church can hardly disagree with what the Charter says[28] about the family and children being the fundamental unit of society, and children having the right, without discrimination, to the protection they need. As the Church looks to heal and redeem itself from its own shameful past, is it too much to ask that it walk with all the broken towards a new model of collaborative, inclusive and compassionate unity?

That would indeed be something to proclaim as living out by example the values of the gospel.

Endnotes

1   January 2013 - December 2017.
2   Of which there were 57.
3   Of which there were 8013.
4   In addition to its formal recommendations, there were 2575 referrals made to authorities including police.
5   The author is indebted to the Research Materials on the Children's Court website authored by former Magistrate, later Reserve Magistrate, Peter Power.
6   The protection of families and children is also one of the headings of power set out in section 17 of the Victorian Charter of Human Rights and Responsibilities Act 2006. The Charter relevantly provides:
    (1) Families are the fundamental group unit of society and are entitled to be protected by

society and the State.

(2) Every child has the right, without discrimination, to such protection as is in his or her best interests and is needed by him or her by reason of being a child.

7   With some limited exceptions.
8   *Scott v Scott* [1913] AC 417 at 477-8.
9   In *Russell v Russell* (1976) 134 CLR 495 at 520.
10 Section 162 of the Act.
11 The Court estimates that in recent years about half of all applications for protection brought before the Court involve domestic violence.
12 See section 182 of the Act.
13 See section 184(1) of the Act.
14 See sections 189 and 190 of the Act.
15 The last year for which the Court holds DHHS statistics.
16 It is estimated that the figures are well over 100,000 now.
17 See below under Outcomes in the Court.
18 See note 6 above.
19 Section 10 of the Act.
20 Section 10(3)(g) of the Act.
21 Section 11 of the Act.
22 Section 12-14 of the Act.
23 2009-10.
24 See for example Sections 215 and 215B of the Act.
25 See *Weinstein v Medical Practitioner's Board of Victoria* [2008] VCSA 193 at paragraphs 28-29.
26 The writer gratefully acknowledges figures derived from the Annual Report of the Children's Court of Victoria 2018-9.
27 Matthew 19:14.
28 See note 6 above.

Chapter 6

Julian: A Mystic For Today

Janette Elliott

Introduction

Julian of Norwich is a mystic for today. By 'today' I am referring to its most profound biblical sense as we encounter it in the Book of Deuteronomy when Moses handed down the *Torah* on the Mountain of Horeb. 'Although heaven and the heaven of heavens belong to the Lord your God, the earth and all that is in it, yet the Lord set his heart in love of your ancestors alone and chose you, their descendents after them out of all the peoples as it is today' (Deuteronomy 10:14-15). By 'today', I am also referring to its most immediate and pregnant sense, because of the silent and stealthy intrusion of COVID-19 into our lives as a global pandemic. For Julian who lived through the first wave of the Black Death in Norwich as a young girl of six in 1348, and a second wave when the Black Death hit England in the 1360s, she would certainly have understood our anxieties, concerns and earnest prayer for a cure today. Julian would also exhort us as Moses did, to

'Choose life... loving the Lord your God... holding fast to him; for that means life to you...' (Deuteronomy 30:19-20).

Julian offers us an extraordinary resource for reminding us, that the Lord has indeed set his heart in love for us today, and for all our 'todays'. Her work *Revelations of Divine Love* bears this out.[1] This chapter flows from the conviction of the value of the Mystic's insight into our relationship with God as profoundly intimate from our origins to our future in eternity. It also flows from the conviction of the Mystic's reminder that the human story belongs to God as Creator, Sustainer and Lover.[2] Julian's understanding of what we today refer to as 'Deep Incarnation'[3] is empowering, given it confirms that we were created whole in God, that we are partners with God in caring for all creation, and that our deepest desires for holiness or in fact wholeness, are inclusive of our thirst and struggle for justice. Julian's lived experience in an anxious age of disease and death; of war, famine and heavy taxation; and of the desire for reform in the church brings her closer to our lives today than we might imagine. In our current COVID-19 reality, when we are more people from the pews, rather than 'people in the pews', it is worth making these experiential connections to Julian before moving to her insights that reveal our lives as preciously enfolded in Divine love and longing.

As the people from the pews, we are immersed in and value life's worth even in the midst of its often messy, grimy, heart-breaking realities. We cannot escape so easily, but nor would we want to for the flecks of beauty that emerge through life's challenges and even brokenness. We trust in the constancy of a loving God whose magnificent creation, even in our fragile world, witnesses daily to God's presence holding us in being, in love, in desire and in hope. When we gather together as the people in the pews, our feet are planted in the beauty and paradox of our lives with its mix of wheat and weeds, of light, dark and shade, in hope and trust. We are grounded in the earthiness of our lives, and we gather to re-member that we are first grounded in the fullness of life itself who is God, and Mother of all life. Julian wrote, 'In our creation we had beginning, but the love in which he created us was in him from without beginning' (LT 86). As one we, the people in the pews, stand together before the image of our Saviour as Julian did for she stands with us in solidarity. We might ask who Julian was, and why would Julian – as a Mystic – care about us, our deepest desires and our concerns?

Julian, her Context and her Writings

Julian of Norwich (ca. 1342-1416) lived as an anchoress in medieval England at the heart of the bustling city of Norwich. Her anchorhold was attached to St Julian's parish church of Conisford, Norwich, and close to the River Wensum that fed into the major trade and commerce operations of her day. As much as from the liturgical prayers and the intercessions of the folk attending her church, as from the sounds, smells and occasional sights from her window onto the world, Julian imbibed the 'signs of the times'.[4] In this way, she is not unlike us 'the people in the pews' who listen to the signs of the times, and seek by our prayer and our action to birth a new church into being.

Historically, we know extremely little of Julian. Even her name is believed to have been taken from the church named after St Julian where she lived as anchoress. It is only through her writings, and bequests left to her to support her life of prayer that we can identify her as a woman. Indeed, she is credited with being the first woman to write in English. Living in an anxious age more like our own now than ever, given the fear around the coronavirus pandemic in our world, marked by war, famine, taxation, unrest, resurgent waves of aggressive nationalism, and the need for reform in the church, Julian's historical context gives her voice credibility and weight. In this purview, there is something quite tender about the fact that Julian wrote in the vernacular available to her, presumably meaning she could not read or write in Latin. In her writings, she made God's unconditional love accessible to her readers though not without risk being a woman.

Julian's writings flow from her experience of a Vision she received at the age of thirty and a half. In a *Short Text* Julian set down this Vision of 'Sixteen Revelations of Divine Love'. There is much evidence to suggest that women's writings arose out of visionary experience, in its own way a sign of the times, given the situation of women in the medieval era. The contrast of Julian's anxious age with the riches of the medieval mystic tradition and the phenomenon of anchoritic life, beguines and other forms of religious life attest the fecundity of the spirit amidst so much suffering and hardship. Julian is unique in this context, seeking not further visions to advance her soul to God through ascetic practice that blinded her to the needs of her neighbour, but to go deeper into the heart of the Crucified Lord to understand what this Vision meant for her and all her 'evencristens' or fellow Christians.

Thus, Julian wrote her longer version of the *Revelations* sharing her maturity and wisdom with us, which remains a powerful resource for enkindling our deepest desires for wholeness and holiness, for healing, justice and peace. If Julian contemplated the five wounds of Christ – a popular medieval devotion befitting her context following the Black Death – Julian also contemplated our own wounds and woundedness, desperately longing for them not to blind us to the Lord who set his heart on us with love. Julian is thus no aloof mystic, but one who desires to bring us along with her, inviting us in to her 'heartscape' pulsating with her enduring longing to long, the desire to desire that we may 'Choose life' loving the Lord our God... 'holding fast' to God, for this is life and leads to well-being (Deuteronomy 10:1).

Julian and the Desire to Desire

The greatest gift of the Christian mystic to us is that, right in the midst of the creative tensions at play in their lives, through whatever circumstances that set up that tension, their focus remains on nourishing their deepest desires for at-one-ment with God.[5] Julian understood the profound importance of nourishing desire, and the desire to desire. As a youth, Julian prayed for three graces at the heart of which was her desire for the 'wound' of earnest longing toward God. While it is important to understand the language and content of her prayer in the context of her times, Julian directs us to an essential insight into our innate capacity for God. In Julian's understanding of the relationship of the soul to God, this capacity for God is within us from the moment we were conceived in the mind of God, even before we received life from our human parents.

Julian writes that we were knit and oned to God in our very making (LT 53). We share in the very substance of God, and through the Word made flesh, that is Christ, even in our body and sensual lives we are oned to God in an unbroken chain of Divine desire and love. Within us is a 'Godly (or goodly) will', writes Julian, that never assents to evil, but desires only good (LT 37; 53). Yet, as Julian recognises, wounds and woundedness can blind us to how 'preciously loved' we are in God's sight. So the importance of praying for the desire to desire, the longing to long for God is our deepest need. Our capacity for God is innate, and therefore natural to us. Like watering a seedling and giving it the right amount of sun, we are to nourish our desire that it may grow, mature and seek after its Divine Source. Let's consider how we, the people in the pews, might recognise our innate capacity for God. Let us also consider what this might look like in our current ecclesial context.

Our Capacity for God

Nestled deep inside each person who enters a church taking their place as a person in 'the pews' is vulnerability and desire, searching questions and a thirst for justice. All this sits beside the formation we have received through the Church. Whatever the context of our lives – religious, historical or political – we know this to be true. It is fair to say also that our context has been and continues to be subject to extraordinary change at every level of society, and the Church is not exempt. We, the 'people in the pews', more often than not, find ourselves wrestling with the creative tension of the interplay of our broader context, what we have been taught by the Church, our deepest desires and questions, and our thirst for a better world and, in our times, a better Church. We, who are the remaining 'people in the pews,' dare to engage with this creative tension as uncomfortable as it is and as inspiring as it is, because we still aspire to live as followers of Christ in our fragile world and fractured Church.

We the people in the pews care intensely for our fragile world and fractured Church, and for each other who share this growing, seemingly 'marginal' space.

In our particularly challenging, rapidly changing and often upsetting current context following the Royal Commission into Institutional Responses to Child Sexual Abuse, we find ourselves distracted, or rather fully focused on the problem in a way that allows us to be driven by it. We may call this listening to the 'Signs of the Times', a phrase attributed to John XXIII. This may be so, but in the full reality of the creative tension we experience, are we sufficiently in touch with our vulnerability, desires, searching questions and thirst for justice nestled deep within our hearts and spirits? We, the people in the pews, have received formation in faith that has not systematically encouraged emotional literacy, much less an understanding about desire, Eros and our affective life. In fact, the opposite has been taught, promoted, fostered and often enforced. The point here is not the identification of a central problem within our broken Church – brokenness is at the centre of being Church – but it is the identification of what it means to be human. We are vulnerable and we have within us deep longings, which do not mean that something is wrong with us, nor that they are bad. Our searching questions often arise out of these longings and are related to our thirst or desire for justice.

Our desire is itself prayer; our thirst for justice too is prayer. This does not mean action is not required; far from it. However, the recognition, awareness and attention to our deep inner longings bears the promise of a new future. God does not stop creating. 'See, I make all things new' prophesied Isaiah (Isaiah 43:19). God, writes Constance Fitzgerald, 'comes to meet us from the future'.[6] Were we to sit with our deep inner longings for a few quiet moments upon entering a church, or now in our quiet places, we might well encounter this God waiting for us in the midst of those desires. No doubt a few of us would need a few more quiet moments to switch off the voice telling us our desires are silly! The truth is that God awaits us in the midst of our desires, for Christ who was 'knit' to our flesh, which relates to all our sensory perceptions and psychological sensibilities, sits in the midst of our heart in rest and in peace.

(a) Each time we attend to the deep inner longings and even stirrings of our heart, we in some way answer the question put to Adam 'Where are you?' (Genesis 3:9). Much energy has been directed to the question of 'Who told you you were naked?' (Genesis 3:11). Yet the question 'Adam where are you?' is a more significant one both existentially and psychologically. Attention to our desires will help us. Thus, the work of the mystic is our work too by very nature of our humanity and capacity for God. The theologian Nicola Masciandaro makes the connection between the content of longing and place as we read: 'The content of mystical longing as the impossible desiring questioning of impossible place... the most intimate wrestling partner through which and with whom we struggle to get a grip on ourselves, cast off sleep, determine the truth about things, find where here is'.[7]

(b) The connection between longing and place for finding where 'here' is carries especial significance at present, as we grieve accessibility to gathering spaces both sacred and secular. For while we may still connect in a virtual electronic way to those we would gather with, the accessibility of that physical place that facilitates the space in which to attend to our inner desires is denied us during the current COVID-19 crisis. So while we are, in the words of St Paul to the Community in Rome 'waiting for our bodies to be set free' (Romans 8:22-23), we are challenged to find that place, our own 'anchorhold' in which we can attend to our inmost desires.[8] This work is more critical than ever for the people in the pews given the fact that we are less 'bound' to systemically cold and structurally loveless forms of ecclesiastical living that dry up all affectivity and true compassion. Yet, we all have memories that attest a happier time in our churches when the healthy dynamism of Vatican II filled our hearts with hope in a more emotionally healthy Church. The despair around sick governance structures was not on our collective radar as it is now. The following anecdote from my childhood speaks to this.

A Child's Hope for 'The Church in the Modern World'

In preparing this chapter, while considering myself as one of the people in the pews, a strong memory from childhood returned about choosing a book from the bookcase in the hallway behind our front door. The book was called *The Church in the Modern World*. My mother's conversion from the Church of England to Catholicism coincided with the early years following Vatican II. Guided by a fine priest who was both pastoral in his approach, and conscientious about his own ongoing formation, mum was the happy recipient of some excellent resources. This actually served to prepare her for a new role as organist in our parish. My memory of finding this book was one of excitement; first, because I could read it at a young age, and also because the message it gave was that the Church cared about people. This was beautifully symbolised in the Blue Cross affixed to the roof of my parish church dedicated to Our Lady of the Way which lit up at night. I could see it from home, and it was a strong reminder of the message of that 'book' which was in fact a simplified version of the Vatican II Document *The Pastoral Constitution on the Church in the Modern World*. Whilst reading it now, I baulk a little at the approach that jars in the sobering aftermath of the Royal Commission into Institutional Child Sexual Abuse, not to mention its non-inclusive language to which we are more sensitive, the spirit in which it was written displaying that the best of the Catholic Faith in terms of understanding of the human person 'the mystery of man' and our social nature still have a place. In fact they align beautifully with the deep insights of Julian of Norwich into the relationship of the soul with God, as also the relationship of desire with justice.

The enduring phrase 'the signs of the times' which has entered into the Liturgy is a poignant metaphor for continuity with the best of the Church arising from Vatican II and our post Royal Commission era now. It highlights the collective responsibility of the whole Church – not just the hierarchy, or just the ordained, or even just the laity – but all of us together listening. Were we to write a new Pastoral Constitution for today, what would it look like? For written in the post war era, it too marked the significant change across the world, and couldn't we add to that now! The current coronavirus crisis would certainly place its stamp on it.

Desire and Justice

Julian of Norwich and other medieval spiritual writers challenge contemporary ideas of desire, which only reduce the concept to a merely natural movement. The result of such reductionist thinking is that there is no requirement to nourish or foster desire which makes sense when contemporary understandings of desire do not extend beyond the merely physical desires related to hunger, thirst and sex. It makes sense that this narrow understanding serves a spirituality as Grace Jantzen describes 'which sees it as private, apolitical, set apart in a tranquil realm of its own from the injustices of the world'.[9] A medieval understanding of desire highlights its intimate connection with the thirst for justice as we read, 'the struggle for justice is at the centre of desire for the divine'.[10] Julian's understanding that her visions were granted as much for her evencristens as for herself ring true as she writes: 'God never removes his hands from my works, nor ever shall without end' (LT 11), and 'God regards sin and sorrow as pain to his lovers, to whom for love he assigns no blame' (LT 39). These statements are summed up in her conviction 'the sweet eye of pity and love never turned away from us' (LT 48). The early *Lesson of the Hazelnut* brings these teachings into a unified whole, when Julian is told that as small as a hazelnut is, God loves it, God keeps it and this is true of the smallest of things that God has made. Applying this teaching even further, Julian wants us to know that whether we find ourselves experiencing weal or woe (LT 15), that is good times or bad, well-being or suffering, God keeps secure and preciously loves us.

In a more sobering fashion, Julian's struggle for justice at the centre of her desire for the Divine is indicated within the context of her deeply personal wrestle with the problem of sin. In this context, she writes that 'the Holy Church will be shaken in sorrow and anguish and tribulation in this world as men shake a cloth in the wind' (LT 28), and God will 'completely break down in you your empty affections and your vicious pride' (LT 28). The auspicious title of the 'Warring Bishop' given to Bishop Despenser of Norwich who most likely interred Julian in her anchorhold, and also put down the Peasant's Revolt, as well as leading a Crusade, reveals something of the 'vicious pride' Julian spoke of. Yet, in Julian's understanding of the theology of Creation, of the Incarnation and Redemption, we are shown that God judges according to what is unchangeable, and humanity judges according to what is changeable (LT 45). God does not blame us for our falls nor are we ever separated from God's love as Julian wrote:

> *God is closer to us than our own soul, for he is the foundation on which our soul stands ... For our soul sits in God in true rest, and our soul stands in God in sure strength, and our soul is naturally rooted in God in endless love. (LT 56)*

Thus the nourishing of desire that Julian prays for is a prayer to hold fast to God, whose cherishing love enfolds us and draws us to remain in God's endless and unchanging 'gift'. Julian's desire that all be well is born of the experience, and church teaching that sin and evil get in the way of our longing, cause pain, and blind us to this gift. Julian writes we have of both nature and grace to long (LT 46), and we need Christ to give us this grace drawing our 'Godly will' to seek after God that we may hold fast to God and so find Life.

Divine Desire and the Love-Longing of Christ

Julian is unique in her presentation of Divine Desire. In terms of her writings, it flows out of the central motif of Christ's Passion and is expressed as 'spiritual thirst' (LT 17). All of the Sixteen Revelations which Julian received are communicated by the crucified Lord of glory. Many of the earlier Revelations are marked by graphic descriptions befitting the Middle Ages of Christ's passion and suffering, yet this is the most accessible lens for Julian to open up on to the profound lessons of love that come together in the second half of her Long Text. The spiritual thirst of Christ is a case in point and connects with the 'All Shall be Well' teachings, answering her deepest questions about the harm caused by sin (LT 27; 29; 31). In the Revelation highlighting Christ's thirst on the Cross, Julian graphically describes the drying out of Christ's body through exposure to the cold winds buffeting him from his place of crucifixion, the place of greatest intended shame (LT 17). As if to emphasise the drying out, the lack of moisture with the pain suffered as a result, Julian brings to our awareness the accompanying spiritual thirst of Christ. Thus, the words 'I thirst' have a double meaning for Julian, one physical as we would expect, and one spiritual.

There is a poignancy in Julian's presentation of this double thirst that over-rides any cheap shot about medieval devotions. For, when Julian unpacks the deeper meaning of Christ's spiritual thirst, it is in the context of her deepest place of wrestling with the pain of sin on one hand, and the assurance of God's absolute love on the other – and both against the teaching of the Church in her day. With all the intensity of the pleading psalmist, Julian searches for answers, and learns that Christ's spiritual thirst is ultimately the love-longing of God, the pathos of a waiting God to draw us into God's fullest embrace of love and mercy, compassion and joy (LT 31). There is here no place for shame, only cherishing love (LT 38-39). There is no place for despair, only the true knowing of love (LT 74).

Depending on our age and our years of experience as 'people in the pews' as regards the teaching we have received in our parish contexts, education and formative spiritual experiences, we will have varying degrees of understanding about what might be meant when Julian wrote that 'All Shall be Well'. For some, it will be clear that there is a relationship between this well-known phrase and the eternal life. For some, this phrase reflects the 'Pollyanna' grasp of Julian where suffering and pain seem all too glibly bypassed in favour of some ideal (and unreal) approach to life. Of course, there is the more popular understanding of this phrase as just one of so many words of comfort that Julian offers. However, it is little known but less understood that this four word phrase expressing hope and trust was wrestled out of the 'creative tension' experienced by Julian noted above. It sits alongside the invitation to a deep trust that God keeps us secure whether we are in well-being or in woe.

How can all be well in our immediate context? How will all be well in this current COVID-19 crisis? Will we see a time when all shall be well after so much suffering in the health sector, for our economic and social well-being, not to mention spiritual well-being which is essentially a social and emotional reality as personal one? Julian was given an answer to her questions, which speaks to our own, and it draws together the theological themes that permeate her writings giving depth to her words of comfort that many have clung to for hope. It is this answer – this Example (or parable) I turn to next.

True Knowing of Love in 'Weal and Woe'

Drawing on the spiritual wisdom of her age and making it her own as a kind of discernment tool, Julian wrote of 'four dreads' (LT 74). In medieval English literature, these four dreads sit within the broader context of our loves and dreads, and provide us with insight into what is not well. The worst of these is the third described as 'doubtful dreads' or, despair; and the best of these are reverent dread when our soul is in peace and at rest. Julian in her wisdom assigns a remedy for each of these except for reverent dread, and the remedy for our despair is the 'true knowing of love'. In answer to Julian's own searching, wrestling questions about sin and whether or not God assigns any blame for our failures and falls, she is given an example or a parable as noted above (LT 50). We receive an understanding of what her earlier lessons on well-being and woe, and the true knowing versus unknowing of love look like in this Example. The Example reads as follows:

> *I saw two persons in bodily likeness, that is to say a lord and a servant... The lord sits in state, in rest and in peace. The servant stands before his lord, respectfully, ready to do his lord's will. The lord looks on his servant very lovingly and sweetly and mildly. He sends him to a certain place to do his will. Not only does the servant go, but he dashes off and runs at great speed, loving to do his lord's will. And soon he falls into a dell and is greatly injured; and then he groans and moans and tosses about and writhes, but he cannot rise to help himself in any way... And all this time his loving lord looks on him most tenderly... with great compassion and pity (LT 51).*

It is fair to say that Julian's presentation of the Example and her lengthy exposition of its meaning are as rich as it is complex. For readers today we need to take account of the fact that it reflects the feudal system of medieval England with the apparently vassal lord and servant fief. It helps if we note how Julian works with the characters in a double sense with the lord as both the Father God and Christ Glorified, and the servant as both Adam and Christ as 'suffering servant' or second Adam. These double characters contain strong resonances with Julian's Trinitarian hermeneutic that effectively brings us with her into the Trinitarian circle of communion (LT 4). The Rublev Icon of the Trinity reflects this open invitational space into Communion. For Julian, access to Christ is access to God the Father, Son and Holy Spirit, and it is more because she presents God as Mother in the fullness of the Trinity. 'As truly as God is our Father, as truly God is our Mother' (LT 59).

Julian develops a rich understanding of Christ as our Mother through the metaphor of 'Deep Wisdom' (LT 58). A mother's care is akin to wisdom in its unconditional love, ready service and counsel in Julian's mind. A mother's care is also imbued with mercy and Julian refers to Christ as our Mother in mercy, as also in nature and grace (LT 58). Julian's profound reflections on the roles of Christ within the fullness of Trinitarian love reveal that her Example is not a story about feudal living, but of healing, of restoration and of rising up to our full dignity as the beloved of God. As regards Julian's presentation of Christ as Mother, this is Julian revealing Christ as the most compassionate icon of constancy and tenderness available to her, and it is disarming since it witnesses to the love-longing of Christ to draw us to himself.

At the climax of Julian's revelation about God's mercy and compassion is the Deep Wisdom of the Trinity, which is Christ our Mother. Julian is not a mystic seeking spousal intimacy in a spiritual way, but a mystic revealing Christ who ever draws, thirsts and longs for us to come into his embrace within the communion of the Blissful Trinity (LT 75). This is part of that 'deep Incarnation' where Christ meets us where we are, including in our falls and failures. As one who himself fell undergoing the shame of the Cross, he comes to us in our lowest of needs. An Ancient homily for Easter Saturday describes the deeper implications of Christ's coming among us and his 'coming to us' in this way:

> *I am your God, who for your sake have become your son. Out of love for you and for your descendants I now by my own authority command all who are held in bondage to come forth, all who are in darkness to be enlightened, all who are sleeping to arise. I order you, O sleeper, to awake. I did not create you to be held a prisoner in hell. Rise from*

the dead, for I am the life of the dead. Rise up, work of my hands, you were created in my image. Rise, let us leave this place, for you are in me and I am in you; together we form only one person and we cannot be separated.[11]

With this in mind, and recalling in particular the servant of the Example who fell, we first note that he fell by accident and by surprise. We also take stock of the fact that Christ who goes down into hell to rescue the 'first Adam' displays not judgment, but profound concern for the dignity of Adam and indeed all of us. We are recalled to our first image and to the fact that we are already whole in God, because we were 'knit and oned' to Christ from our beginning. The same sentiment is in Julian's understanding of the relationship of the human person with God. These three points, that we fall by accident and often by surprise; that we are not judged by God, and that we are already whole through our eternal 'oneing' with Christ – all serve to reassure us that God does indeed keep us secure in well-being and in woe.

The Unknowing of Love

For all the victims of child sexual abuse in the Church, who have lived through decades of self-recrimination, an over-burdened consciousness, and endured painful memories, would indeed have blamed themselves for their 'falls' caused not by them but by those who professed God's love. As Julian writes of the Lord looking on his servant, he only sees the good will and desire of the servant to carry out the errand with a heart full of love. Julian's insight into the deepest suffering of the servant, of the one fallen, is profound and recalls again the words of the Deuteronomist in the opening paragraph of this chapter. The greatest suffering the servant experiences is:

> ... lack of consolation, for he could not turn his face to look on his loving lord, who was very close to him, in whom is all consolation; but like a man who was for the time extremely feeble and foolish, he paid heed to his feelings and his continued distress... (LT 51).

The servant becomes absorbed in his pain, and is deeply embarrassed if not ashamed of falling. In the fall, he becomes bruised and stunned all at once. He 'takes full great sore' and then he groans and moans and tosses about and writhes, but he cannot rise or help himself in any way' (LT 51). While all this is going on for the servant, the lord sees how deeply his beloved servant is suffering and desires only to reward him since he recognises that it was only the inner goodness, longing, love and joy that led to this fall. The lord seeks to replace his shame with joy, his travail with peace. Julian writes that the lord regards his servant as 'unloathsome' as when he set out with joy and love to do his will (LT 61).

Julian's record of the seven pains suffered by the servant highlights not just his pain and suffering, but his complete isolation as he experiences it. Although no blame is assigned to him by the lord for his fall which again I stress was *accidental*, his isolation on top of his pain make him vulnerable to the 'unknowing of love'. These seven pains (LT 51) include the following:

1. The sore bruising through taking the fall
2. Heaviness of the body

3. Feebleness as a result of these
4. Blinded in reason and shattered in his mind
5. The servant may not rise
6. The servant lies alone with no help
7. The place where the servant lies is long, hard and grievous.

Among these seven pains, two are identified by Julian as linked to the 'doubtful dread' which leads to despair. The first is bodily heaviness as a result of the fall with the surprise and shock of it all. The second is blindness, which Julian describes in the Example as 'blindness in reason' with the effect of causing our mind to be shattered, or stunned, or – in current drug-related use – stoned. There is a further consequence of the cumulative effect of these pains and that is the servant 'almost forgets his own love' for the lord who loves him. He becomes disillusioned and unwise. As the situation is described by Julian, it appears that there is nothing left for the servant but to attend to his feelings and enduring in woe as is described by Julian in this way:

> But often when our falling and our wretchedness are shown to us, we are so much afraid and so greatly ashamed of ourselves that we scarcely know where we can put ourselves (LT 61).

It is clear that while the lord regards his servant as favourably as when he first set out, it is *within the servant* that the experience of woe, of dread and of personal loathing resides. As Julian reflects 'only pain blames and punishes' (LT 51). In his vulnerable, wretched state, the servant becomes utterly disconnected from himself. He certainly can't see or love himself as the lord sees and loves him. Particularly in his 'almost forgetting his love for the lord' (LT 51), he experiences a kind of 'unknowing of love.'

Rising in Dignity and the Remembering of Love

Even without falling in a literal sense, a pandemic such as coronavirus can in effect drop us to our knees. Yet we all understand what falling does to us. A simple trip or stumble can cause embarrassment. A failing that causes pain to others can have the felt effect of falling, and, as with the servant, it can come by surprise. In unpacking the pains of the servant, Julian draws on her vocabulary of what is not well which comes under the umbrella term of 'woe' to use the Middle English terminology. We not only recognise the depth in which we can fall, but also how stuck we can get in our own 'attending to feelings of woe and enduring in our pain'. The doubling of characters in the Example places the Christ the suffering servant before us, reminding us that Christ too fell.

Julian is creative in this space, drawing on the metaphor of falling to the Incarnation. Christ 'fell into the maiden's womb' (LT 51), and she masterfully links Christ's own motherhood to the fact that he was first 'mothered' in Mary's womb. Christ took our flesh, and was knit to our sensuality, that is our bodily and sensual life. Thus, Christ became Mother of all life taking flesh from flesh, and restoring us to peace. We may well think this is all very well, and even quite beautiful, but what can make us unstuck when our falls and failures place us in difficulties? What can draw us out of despair, and even guilt and shame? After all, most of us have been formed too well in this area given the more disobedience- and sin-focused theologies, rather than Julian's approach where the constancy of God's loving gaze is unbroken through Christ's 'deep incarnation' into the messiness of our lives.

We might recall that among the seven pains of the servant, he 'almost forgets his love' but does *not totally forget* his love. The servant in his feeble, heavy, stunned and isolated state cannot fully remember who he is, much less how the lord sees him (LT 51). At this point, his knowing of love becomes 'unknowing' and yet his capacity for God that is innate does not allow for utter forgetfulness of love. The Godly will, which Julian notes in this context, is kept safe in the lord's sight even while he fell. The yearning for wholeness will come flowing from our innate capacity and desire for God. Like the *ek-stasis* or reaching out toward healing, toward hope, toward an embrace that speaks to body and soul of the true dignity of humanity, our more hidden 'shy self' discovers that inner spark that can re-member that it is loved, and ever loved.

We would be wise not to discount the re-membrances of love that pass our way. Like butterflies. they are not so far from us if we are attentive to the stirrings of our heart, spirit and sensibilities. Consider the seasons of nature and life, the seasons of our heart and spirit – that area often reflected in our liturgies connecting us to Christ and to mystery. The early fragrance of spring energises and enlivens our spirit. The delight of children in play stirs up joy within. A 'real' hug from someone dear who knows us and whom we have not seen for a long time brings home that we are loved. The contentment that flows when family or friends come together in unity of heart with real affection. Whatever in nature and in life delights and moves us; whatever in our hearts, affections and spirits rings true in our depths; whatever re-minds us of the gift of our very existence and re-minds us that we are preciously loved is the celebration of who we are in God. Our hidden, shy and even uncertain self *knows* itself as loved, and through the beauty, joy and peace of this knowledge can gift others with that 'knowing of love'.

The mystical element of the Example is an invitation to allow Christ who is the Lord whose loving gaze never leaves us, and Christ, who humbled himself even to the point of death to re-kindle this spark within us. Julian realises this in herself when she makes her choice for Christ whether she finds herself in well-being or in woe. For she understands that Christ who lives within her draws to his loving embrace that part of her that is subject to suffering, guilt and pain. So the great teaching of 'wellness' in Julian's writings is that we are never separated from our being in love, because when our sensuality came into being, God's work of mercy and grace began (LT 55). Julian reminds us that listening to our hidden self is key; allowing that inner spark to reveal the deepest desires of our hearts is essentially God in us. The stirring of our hearts to prayer is itself the work of the indwelling Christ who sits in our soul in rest and peace (LT 41-43). Julian went so far as describing this in terms of a home as follows:

> *The place that Jesus takes in our soul he will nevermore vacate, for in us is his home of homes and his everlasting dwelling (LT 68).*

The remembering of this 'homely' love supports our rise to our true dignity, trusting all the while that even while dwelling within us, Christ's love-longing is drawing us to peace.

Choose Life

Julian undertook a profound journey of faith towards a real understanding about the 'true knowing of love' that took place throughout her life and in the fifteen to twenty years she spent reflecting on her 'Vision'. With Julian, we learn that whether we are in well-being or woe, knowing or unknowing of love, love or dread, we are already whole in God. For 'We shall truly see that we were never hurt in his love, nor were we ever of less value in his sight' (LT 61). We can take great comfort from her words describing the intimacy we have as God's beloved creatures:

> ... as the body is clad in the cloth, and the flesh in the skin, and the bones in the flesh, and the heart in the trunk, so are we, soul and body, clad and enclosed in the goodness of God (LT 6).

This statement reflects Julian's grasp of the relationship of the soul with God, and is a testimony to the 'marvellous melody of the endlesse love of God' (LT 47). The Divine memory is accessible within us. God is the very Ground of our being. God is enclosed in us in rest and peace, because Christ 'fell' into our flesh and loved us from within as we read:

> He wants us to trust that he is constantly with us, and that in three ways. He is with us in heaven, true man in his own person, drawing us up; and that was revealed in the spiritual thirst. And he is with us on earth, leading us... And he is with us in our soul, endlessly dwelling... (LT 52).

Loving us from within, Christ loved us in our entirety – body, soul and sensuality. Nourishing our desire is about attending to our innate capacity for God, to Christ within us, allowing our desire to mature into a thirst for justice while not neglecting our more hidden shy self.

The mature Julian engages with the Christ of the Revelations wrestling as it were for a blessing that 'all shall indeed be well' as was promised to her numerous times throughout her Vision. We are invited to wrestle with our desires, with our questions, with our thirst for justice, nourishing a true knowing of love which it is too easy to become blind to. True knowing of love does not mean that there is no sin, suffering, sorrow, pain or shame. True knowing of love means that a deeper reality is carrying us through woe as also 'weal'. Assuring us further about this, Julian wrote God did not say:

> *You will not be troubled, you will not be belaboured, you will not be disquieted; but God said: You will not be overcome. God wants us to pay attention to these words, and always be strong in faithful trust, in well-being and in woe, for he loves us and delights in us, and so he wishes us to love him and delight in him and trust greatly in him, and 'all will be well.'*

Julian concluded that her *Revelations* represent a 'book not yet performed' (LT 86). This is a direct invitation to take up Julian's 'book of life' alongside our sisters and brothers, *attending* to what stirs our hearts to 'choose life' clinging to God's goodness that enfolds us all in endless wisdom and endless love.

Endnotes

1. All references to Julian's Long Text in this chapter are taken from the Colledge and Walsh edition of Julian's *Showings*. See: Julian of Norwich, *Julian of Norwich Showings* [in English]. Translated by Edmund Colledge and James Walsh. The Classics of Western Spirituality: A Library of the Great Spiritual Masters edited by Richard J. Payne. (New Jersey: Paulist Press, 1978)
2. Julian often gives expression to the Trinity in terms of triads such as this emphasising the relational nature of the Trinity.
3. Edward, Denis. *Deep Incarnation: God's Redemptive Suffering with Creatures*. (Maryknoll, N.Y: Orbis Books, 2019).
4. The phrase 'signs of the times' is attributed to John XXIII and used in *Gaudium et Spes* and *Pacem in Terris*.
5. The term at-one-ment is one expression of Julian's use of the term 'oneing' or 'oned' meaning united.
6. Constance Fitzgerald, "From Impasse to Prophetic Hope: Crisis of Memory," *CTSA Proceedings 64* (2009).
7. Nicola Masciandaro, "Eros as Cosmic Sorrow: Locating the Limits of Difference in Julian of Norwich's Revelations of Love and the Cloud of Unknowing," *Mystics Quarterly* 35, No. 1-2 (2009).
8. Some spiritual writers would use the term 'enclosure of the heart' here rather than anchorhold.
9. Grace Jantzen, "Julian of Norwich: Desire and the Divine". Lecture given at Norwich Cathedral, July 1996.
10. Jantzen, "Julian of Norwich: Desire and the Divine".

11 Robert Gantoy and Romain Swaeles, *Days of the Lord: The Liturgical Year*, trans. Greg and Donald Molloy LaNave, Volume 3. Easter Triduum/ Easter Season (Collegeville, Minnesota: The Liturgical Press, 1993), 6.

PART II

Theology Responds

Chapter 7

Clericalism, Women And The Family Of Jesus In The New Testament

Constant J. Mews

Pope Francis is particularly fond of synodality as a concept he hopes can give a new energy to his sense of local collective endeavour that must underpin the Church. At the same time, he is troubled by the Church's pernicious and enduring culture of clericalism.[1] His vision of regenerating the Church at a local level is informed by a profound sense that true catholicity is developed by all the people of God coming together, not just the clergy.[2] Synodality derives from the Greek term *synodos*, meaning a common road, akin to the ancient Sanhedrin (from *synhedrion* or sitting together) that assembled the elders of Israel. Francis' conception of the term is very different from the more centralised vision of the Church held by John Paul II and Benedict XVI. Its theological roots are explained in a key document, issued by the International Theological Commission in 2018.³ It rightly observes that although the term synodality was not used in the documents of the II Vatican Council, a sense of the Church as a local collective gathering of the faithful underpins its thinking. It thus builds on the notion of conciliarism, namely that supreme teaching authority is vested in the Ecumenical Councils of the Church, but seeks to capture the vitality of local communities, involving all the people of God, not just the bishops.

This chapter offers the thoughts of a medievalist interested in how the New Testament has been interpreted over the centuries, with regard to both 'synodality' and clericalism, that is, the tendency to entrench power within a specific elite. While clericalism is often considered a legacy of Constantine, the abuse of leadership has been a matter of concern since the very beginnings of Christianity, which was a movement that transcended traditional barriers of ethnicity, gender and legal status. It was not easy to bring together different groups, each with their own stories. The texts assembled in the New Testament deserve to be examined, not just as literary constructions, but as responses to the ambitions of Roman political authority. Many reform movements would look back to their stories to promote a vision of the kingdom they saw being preached by Jesus of Nazareth. Developing consensus or synodality within and between these communities was never easy, but retelling familiar stories helped them in that process, as it may still do today.

Critiques of clericalism within the Gospels

Every community needs ministers, symbols and structures that can help it survive. It also needs stories that transmit not just a historical record but a moral compass that reminds the community how leadership should function. The Gospels attributed to Mark and Matthew offer what were originally oral traditions, akin to the songlines of Indigenous Australian communities, which communicate its version of sacred Law pertaining to that community and its land.[4] They relate the travels of a spirit ancestor from the Dreaming, an idealised image of the path to which society must reconnect. Jesus, culturally a Galilean, saw the twelve apostles as working towards a new Israel, even though his family claimed descent from the royal line of David. While key members of the Twelve, like Simon Peter (crucified c. 67), were not Roman citizens, there were others who did enjoy that privilege. Because James the Great, brother of John, was beheaded by Herod Agrippa in 43/44 (Acts 12:2), he must have been a Roman citizen, like the rest of his family and like Paul.

The linking together of the feasts of Peter and Paul on 29 June was a way of asserting that two saints, with very different legal status and cultural backgrounds, were of equal importance in the Roman church. Paul is referring to James the younger when he speaks of 'James, the Lord's brother' (Galatians 1:19) and as one of three acknowledged pillars, alongside Cephas and John (Galatians 2:9). By looking closely at how the evangelists refer to both the mother of the sons of Zebedee and the family of James, brother of the Lord, we can observe something of the great diversity of early communities who all looked to Jesus, as well as the challenge they faced in finding consensus about his teaching. The roots of both synodality and clericalism go back to the time of Jesus. In any attempt by the Church to renew its rules and practices, it must be aware of its complex history and the stories that it inherits.

The years 67-70 witnessed a determined move by Rome finally to crush all attempts to restore the Herodian kingdom of Judea with its capital in Jerusalem, or the Roman province of that name, also involving Galilee and Samaria. In sacking the Temple in 70, Vespasian extinguished the ritual structure of second Temple Judaism, with its dynastic and privileged priestly class. The Sanhedrin, in which there were, among its rabbis, diverse views about Roman authority, was forced to move to Galilee. The early apostles had to work out how far Jesus, whom they believed to be *Christos*, anointed by God, required them to observe the Torah. Out of their various churches emerged the image of a catholic or universal *ekklesia*, of which all those local communities were part.

The failure of the apostles to grasp Jesus' teaching about the kingdom of God and true servant leadership is formulated in different ways in the Gospels. Mark 10:35-45 reports that James and John, the sons of Zebedee, once recklessly asked Jesus: 'Grant us to sit, one at your right hand and one at your left, in your glory.' Mark had already emphasised that these two brothers, namely James (subsequently known as 'the Great', to distinguish him from James the younger and John, 'the beloved disciple'). They formed with Peter (the closest disciples of Jesus) the trio presented as witnessing Jesus' true identity as heir to both Moses and Elijah at the transfiguration (Mark 9:1-8; Matthew 17:1-8; Luke 9:28-36). Jesus refused to comply with their request, except to say that they would encounter the same baptism as himself. When the other apostles grumbled at what seemed to be the elite status of this inner group, Mark reports a pithy response of Jesus as a lesson to any who claimed authority in this world: 'You know that among the Gentiles those whom they recognise as their rulers lord it over them, and their great ones are tyrants over them. But it is not so among you; but whoever wishes to become great among you must be your servant, and whoever wishes to be first among you must be slave of all. For the Son of Man came not to be served but to serve, and to give his life a ransom for many (Mark 10:42-45). The sons of Zebedee were nicknamed by Jesus *Boianerges*, 'the sons of thunder' (Mark 6:13) and had been the first to join him after Simon (Cephas/Peter) and Andrew. According to Mark, they were like Simon Peter in having to learn from their mistakes.

Matthew 20:20-28 repeats Mark's account, but with a small, but significant change. Instead of saying that it was the sons of Zebedee who were asking for a position of honour, he assigns the question to their mother, presenting her as excessively ambitious. Matthew's subtle modification of Mark's story is reinforced by a shift he makes when revising Mark's account of the Galilean women who accompanied him to Jerusalem, and subsequently witnessed his crucifixion. Mark 15:40 singles out three as particularly important: Mary of Magdala, Mary mother of James the younger and Joseph, and Salome. He subsequently reports (16:1) that all three women sought out Jesus' body, as if they were more faithful than the three leading apostles. The variations in the way the evangelists identify the women alongside Mary of Magdala is significant. Matthew 27:56 repeats Mark's list of those watching the crucifixion, but replaces Mark's reference to Salome by 'the mother of the sons of Zebedee'.

In the process, Matthew explains Salome's importance among the apostles. Luke 24:10 replaces Salome by Joanna, a figure to whom we shall return. Matthew 28:1, however, says that only Mary of Magdala and 'the other Mary' sought out the body, as if Zebedee's wife did not follow through with her devotion to the Lord. The woman Matthew describes here as seemingly unimportant, namely 'the other Mary', alludes to his description of her as Mary, mother of James (and Mark 15:40 as mother of James and Joseph). These are the names of the first two brothers of Jesus, according to Mark 6:3 and Matthew 13:55. It is normally assumed by modern exegetes that John has invented the presence of Jesus' mother at the execution and his dialogue about her closeness to John, alongside a woman he calls his sister, 'Mary the wife of Cleophas (also spelled as Clopas)'. Another possibility is that Mary of Cleophas had previously been betrothed to Joseph, when she conceived Jesus, who had many half brothers and sisters. This reading of John 19:25 implies that the evangelist invents the image of Jesus' mother as having a sister in order to identify the mother of Jesus' half-brothers as quite distinct from his true mother, to whom he assigns a symbolic significance.

All four evangelists emphasise that Jesus saw his true family as separate from his biological kin. Both Matthew 13:55 and Mark 6:3 refer to four brothers (*adelphoi*, not *anepsioi* or cousins), namely James, Joseph, Simon and Jude, and some unidentified sisters. They both report Jesus as saying that his parents, brothers and sisters are not his kin; Matthew expands on Mark's terse reference to Jesus' family by adding a classic Jewish phrase, that his true family are those who do the will of their Father in heaven (rather than of God).[5] Even John 6:23 develops this theme, but in more cosmic dimensions, when he contrasts the popular view that Jesus was the son of Joseph with a mystical discourse about Jesus as the bread of life. Matthew's hostility is towards the priests of the Temple. In 21:31-32, he reports Jesus as saying that tax collectors and prostitutes would enter the kingdom before them (Luke 7:29-30 refers only to tax collectors). These were all ways of saying that, for Jesus, all were equal in God's kingdom, whatever their gender or legal status in the Roman Empire.

As gentiles became interested in Jesus, a serious question arose as to whether they had to follow the Law of Moses, in particular its precepts on circumcision. Paul insisted that he had been trained by Gamaliel in all the traditions of the Law, but argued that there was an unwritten law or wisdom originally present in people's hearts, brought back to life in Christ. Yet there were also political and cultural issues shaping Paul's rhetorical distancing from the written Law. In 41, Herod Agrippa I (d. 44) reclaimed the title king of Judea, after Pontius Pilate had been ousted as governor of the province. Herod saw James the Great as a threat to his political authority, and had him beheaded (Acts 12:1). Cephas was arrested, but escaped from Jerusalem to Antioch with the help of Mary, the mother of 'John Mark' (probably Mark the evangelist), and her servant, Rhoda (Acts 12:2-17). More Romanised than his father, Herod Agrippa II (44-67) ruled over regions outside Judea, allowing it to revert to Roman control. This incurred hostility from Judean zealots, keen to restore the independence of their nation. Josephus, sympathetic to Roman rule, tells the story of how Judean resistance would lead to Roman military intervention, and finally the looting of the Temple in 70. Four years later, almost a thousand Judean zealots preferred to sacrifice their own lives at Masada rather than submit to Rome.

Paul reports in Galatians 1:19 that when he first went to Jerusalem (c. 36), about three years after his conversion experience, he saw only Cephas and James, brother of the Lord. He then recalls that fourteen years later (c. 49), he went there again to settle a serious disagreement about whether gentiles needed to be circumcised. He recalled that James, Cephas and John, 'these acknowledged pillars' (2:9) agreed that, just as Peter, then based in Antioch, was an apostle to the circumcised, so Paul was entrusted with preaching to gentiles. John may already have moved to Ephesus, but returned to Jerusalem for this important meeting.[6] The relationship between John the Apostle and the author (or authors) of John's Gospel is highly problematic. John 19:25-27 claims that the beloved disciple made a place for Mary in his home, a verse that promoted subsequent tradition that she went with him to Ephesus. In any case, the Mary wife of Cleophas mentioned in John 19:25 must be the same person as the one whom Mark, Matthew and Luke call Mary, mother of James – namely the brother of the Lord. Because medieval commentators never questioned the literal truth of John's assertion, they interpreted Paul's epithet as meaning that he was Jesus' cousin. Whereas Mark 15:40 calls him 'James the younger', Paul accords him respect in Galatians 2:9 as one of three pillars, presumably referring to his authority in Jerusalem, parallel to that of Peter in Antioch and of John in Ephesus.

Both the Pauline letters and the Acts of the Apostles speak only about multiple churches, not a single *ekklesia*. Among the evangelists, only Matthew uses the word – once in 16:19 when he has Jesus say that he is building his church on Simon as 'the rock' (Cephas or *Petros*), with a mandate that whatever he willed on earth would be considered as bound in heaven. On the other occasion (Matthew 18:17) he uses *ekklesia* as meaning community in a general sense, as the final arbiter in any dispute, after the failure of two or three witnesses to resolve a problem. The voice of Matthew is that of judge, formulating a legal principle about the way conflicts are to be resolved. He recognises that the community is ultimately superior to individuals who might be in conflict with one another. For this reason, Matthew would be quoted much more than Mark as the primary source of canon law in the medieval period. In his rhetoric about scribes and Pharisees, Matthew was responding to other rabbis who in their own interpretation of the Torah were developing what would become known as Judaism, a religious tradition by then based much more on the experience of exile than around the no-longer-existing kingdom of Judea.

The final version of the Gospel attributed to John took a long time to evolve. Scholars have observed many different voices in its text; possibly, these are stages of reflection, formulated over time. Heavily Hellenistic in literary and intellectual style, it both adopts and responds to gnostic ways of understanding Jesus as manifesting a higher wisdom.[7] The absence of any explicit quotation from, or allusion to, the synoptic Gospels implies that it developed, presumably in Ephesus, quite independently from the other accounts. According to later tradition, John, 'the beloved disciple', lived until the time of Trajan (98-117), which could only have been possible if he lived to over ninety, after attaching himself to Jesus aged around twenty. Another possibility is that a disciple, also called John, developed his master's insights.[8]

John's Gospel could have initially been planned at the same time as other Gospels were being drafted, namely the late 60s or 70s, when so many of the apostles were facing arrest and execution. Many of its historical details about both Galilee and Jerusalem are very precise, although the discourses attributed to Jesus are clearly subsequent elaborations on his key themes. John's Gospel responds to the preaching of Paul with a greater sense of Jesus as a person, while being more theologically sophisticated than the synoptic evangelists. Like Paul, John did not wish to exacerbate tension with Roman authority, as is evident from his presentation of Jesus' dialogue with Pilate (18:28-19:16). While its frequent references to Judeans (*Judaioi*) are often read as about Jews in general, they can also be understood as referring to Judean zealots, such as those who promoted insurrection, and the final Roman assault on Jerusalem between 67-70. Galileans were not as uniformly hostile toward Judeans as Samaritans. Many of them, like Jesus, saw in what had happened to the Temple a betrayal of the original message of Moses and the prophets.

Mark introduces Jesus as announced by John the Baptist, without any attention to the circumstances of his birth.[9] John imitates Mark in introducing John the Baptist as a forerunner to Jesus, but only briefly as a beacon to the light of the world. John avoids any reference to how the Baptist's beheading was secured by the step-daughter of Herod Antipas, identified as Salome by Josephus, as told by Mark and Matthew. Matthew brings in John the Baptist only after presenting the genealogy that shows how Jesus was connected by Joseph to the line of David, and indirectly to some remarkable non-Judean women, like Tamar, Rahab, and Uriah's wife, with whom David had coupled. The genealogy functions like an Indigenous songline, recited by heart by a community which recognised the allusion to Jesus as heir not just to David, but also to Bathsheba. Matthew was telling his readers that Jesus' lineage fulfilled the prophecy of Isaiah 7:14 that a young woman (*almah*, translated in the Septuagint as *parthenos* or virgin), would conceive a saviour for Israel. This had meaning for those who valued the family from which Jesus came.

Prior to the nineteenth century, Matthew's Gospel was considered to be the earliest because it was believed to have been translated from the Hebrew. Mark was thought to have abbreviated Matthew, and so Mark's Gospel never attracted a commentary until the task was taken up by an Irish monk in the seventh century. Jerome mentions that there still survived at Caesarea in the late fourth century a Gospel written in Aramaic, in Hebrew letters, that was used by Nazarites (Jewish Christians). He noted that it recorded Jesus as saying that the mother of Jesus and his brothers said to him: 'John the Baptist baptises into the forgiveness of sins; let us go and be baptised by him.'[10] While Mark was certainly not an abbreviation of Matthew (as its references to Salome attest), there could well have been an earlier Aramaic version of the Jesus tradition that Matthew drew on to expand the narrative offered by Mark. Each of the Gospels brings together a range of voices about Jesus. Mark was familiar with the Hebrew phrase used by Jesus, as when (5:41) he tells a young girl, apparently dead, to rise from her bed: *Talitha, cumi*, a detail that Matthew does not give.[11]

Matthew and Luke both present Jesus as combining traditions of Judea through the family of Joseph, and of Galilee through Mary, but in different ways. Matthew explains the connection to Nazareth in terms of Jesus' fulfilling an unidentified prophecy that the saviour would be a *Nazaraios*, a Nazarite (Matthew 2:23, often translated as Nazarene), someone who has taken a vow to be holy unto God, according to Numbers 6:1-21, rather like John the Baptist. Yet while Matthew revises Mark's perspective by transmitting a perspective shaped more fully by Jewish Law, he is also aware of the universal mission of Jesus, and the place of Peter among the Twelve. He ends his narrative with Jesus appearing in Galilee, as if this was where he was writing.

John's account also concludes in Galilee, but presents only Mary of Magdala, Peter, and the beloved disciple, as each coming to realise the true identity of the risen Jesus (John 20:1-10). This implies that John honoured Mary of Magdala, but avoided any reference to Salome, his mother. John's Gospel makes no reference to the sons of Zebedee or to their mother, except in an additional chapter (21:2), which says that the two brothers were part of a small group of apostles around Simon Peter, prophesying his death by crucifixion (67), while implying that the beloved disciple is still alive. The passage reads like a story told to honour Peter, even after offering a narrative very different to that of Mark.

Luke, on the other hand, introduces his account in a way that is more focused on the Temple. He presents John the Baptist as miraculously conceived by Zechariah, a Judean priest who served in its sanctuary, and Elizabeth, a kinswoman of Mary and descended from Aaron, thus also of a priestly class. Luke addresses Theophilus as someone fully familiar with these Temple traditions. He concludes his account with Jesus appearing in Jerusalem, thereby connecting with the narrative in Acts that tells how the followers of Jesus were collectively inspired in that city at Pentecost. This feast commemorated Moses' bringing of the Law to all the people of Israel, Judeans and proselytes alike, many of whom were scattered across the Mediterranean world, even as far as Rome. Acts (introduced as following on from Luke's Gospel) concludes with Paul preaching in Rome, but without any allusion to his arrest or execution, as if it had been written before 67. While the Gospels of Mark, Matthew and Luke are conventionally assigned to after 70 because they contain prophecies about the destruction of the Temple, it is quite possible that these passages were interpolated into an earlier text.

The account in Acts of the so-called Council of Jerusalem, the basis of subsequent ecclesiastical teaching about the authority of synods and councils, presents an irenic picture of the meeting between two divergent positions. It reports that James acknowledged that gentiles should respect the Law, and acknowledged that they did not have to observe all its precepts, notably that of circumcision (Acts 15:13-21). Yet consensus was not so easily achieved. Paul reports (Galatians 2:11-14) that, even after the meeting, certain friends of James were still insisting that gentiles should be circumcised, and persuaded Cephas to go back to his perspective, thereby incurring his anger. This was still a pressing issue when Paul wrote to the Galatians, and then more fully to the Romans, between 54 and 57. He recalls that James urged him not to forget 'to help the poor, as indeed I was anxious to do' (Galatians 2:10).

Paul and James both saw themselves as Jews, bound by commitment to the Torah. They differed in their relative focus on faith and righteous action, and they also differed in other, more practical ways. Paul was a cosmopolitan Jew, fluent in Greek, and enjoyed the privileges of a Roman citizen (including that of execution by beheading – as happened to James the Great), while James was more committed to the traditions of Judea and the line of David, with Aramaic as his natural mother tongue, as it was for Jesus.

The author of the letter to the Hebrews presents Christ as High Priest and drew heavily on Temple imagery to show that Christ was the true mediator between people and God, not the ritually appointed High Priest (traditionally from an aristocratic family close to the Judean king). Bringing this letter together with those of Paul and other early Christian writers, and allowing one text to speak to another, was a way of balancing alternative perspectives – not easy to achieve at a time of heightened hostility between the Roman Empire and a pro-Judean Herod. These tensions created an immense crisis for the Sanhedrin, in which there were voices, like that of the Pharisee Gamaliel, reported as arguing that this movement was more likely to last than others (Acts 5:34-39).

While the evangelists each claim to offer a particular eye-witness testimony about Jesus, they all agree that he established the Twelve (Matthew 10:3; Mark 3:17; Luke 6:15; Acts 1:13).[12] Even John mentions the Twelve (John 6:71-72; 20:24), without identifying each by name. The Twelve symbolise a new Israel (traditionally comprising twelve tribes), in an ideal community that transcended the petty divisions of Judea, Samaria, and Galilee. Unfortunately, this distinction is lost in the contemporary practice of thinking about Israel as a purely Jewish State, whereas Israel originally embraced many tribal groups, including Galileans, who acknowledged the Law of Moses, but not the political authority of Judea.

All three synoptic Gospels identify the apostles in a similar way, namely in three groups. The first group was the most senior, involving two sets of brothers: Simon and Andrew, and the two sons of Zebedee, who worked in their father's fishing business on the Sea of Galilee, serving its affluent urban communities. The comment of Mark 1:20 that Zebedee engaged employees in his fishing business suggests that he and Salome were prosperous Roman citizens (as also indicated by the fact of James the Great's being beheaded rather than crucified, Acts 1:1-2). The second group contained Philip and Bartholomew, Thomas (the twin, according to John) and Matthew, the tax collector. John's comment (20:24-28), about ('doubting') Thomas the twin needing to see before he believed, may allude to subtle friction between these factions. The third group involved James of Alphaeus, Thaddeus (Greek for Jude), Simon the Zealot (or Canaanite, namely from Cana, in Galilee) and Judas Iscariot, probably from Kerioth, and thus the only apostle from Judea.

While the identity of James of Alphaeus (mentioned in Matthew 10:3; Mark 3:17; Luke 6:15; Acts 1:13) is disputed, the first three names in the third group are exactly those of Jesus' brothers, according to both Mark 3:18 and Matthew 13:55: James, Simon and Jude. At the opening of his brief epistle, Jude describes himself as the brother of James. This Simon is identified by Matthew as from Cana, or as 'the Zealot' by Luke, to distinguish him from the other Simon, nicknamed Cephas. Matthew is always listed in this middle group, between its leaders and the third group, led by James of Alpheus (perhaps another version of Cleophas), involving Jesus' three brothers and Judas Iscariot, the weakest link in the group.

John is the one evangelist to assign a particular role to Jesus' mother, introduced not through Joseph and the line of David, but through her presence at Cana in Galilee, perhaps alongside his brothers (2:1-12). He also has her majestically present at the crucifixion, alongside Mary of Magdala, and a woman John 19:25 describes as 'Mary of Clopas (Cleophas)', whom he describes as the sister of Jesus' mother. This key statement has always been interpreted literally, as a way of explaining that the so-called brothers of the Lord were in fact his cousins. In the fourth century, Jerome reasserted

Mary's miraculous perpetual virginity, a claim first made in the apocryphal *Protoevangelion* from the late second century, spuriously attributed to James of Jerusalem, brother of the Lord. Aware that the genealogies of Matthew and Luke only spoke about Joseph, it presented Mary's parents as Joachim, a priest, and Anne, both of the line of David.

Jerome's assumption, based on John 19:25, that the Virgin's mother had a sister, married to Cleophas, was expanded further in the later ninth century by Haimo of Auxerre, who imagined that Anne took three husbands: Joachim, by whom she begot the Virgin; Cleophas, father of Mary, mother of James; and Salome, understood as the father of a third Mary, who married Zebedee.[13] This made their two sons, James and John, cousins of Jesus, like James of Jerusalem. A more plausible scenario is that Mary conceived Jesus while betrothed to Joseph, but that after his death, she married Cleophas (his brother according to Hegesippus, to whom we shall return), and went on to have at least four more sons, and daughters besides. The evangelists never spoke much about these relationships; they chose to emphasise (unlike James of Jerusalem), that Jesus was establishing a kingdom quite removed from his Jewish family.

Mark was not interested in the family of Jesus, and makes only minimal allusion to the house of David. He introduces Jesus as heir to both Moses and John the Baptist, but as a leader opposed to those false religious leaders whose concern was more for legal exactitude than the spirit of the Torah. Matthew, by contrast, respects the importance of lineage in opening with a genealogy that connects Jesus, through Joseph, to the royal house of David and back to Abraham. Given the power and ambition of the family of Herod the Great, the Romanised king of Judea, Matthew's genealogy could be read as implying that, according to Jewish Law, Jesus was the rightful heir to the line of David. From Herod's perspective, Jesus the Nazarene could be seen as challenging Roman authority in claiming to be king of the *Judaioi*, (meaning the inhabitants of the kingdom of Judea, rather than all those circumcised in the Law of Moses, as the word subsequently came to mean in the usage of later Christian writers).

Luke is less overtly critical of Herod than either Mark or Matthew. He omits reference to Matthew's story of the massacre of the Innocents (Matthew 2:16-18), and mentions only briefly the imprisonment (not the execution) of John the Baptist. Luke follows his account of tension between the disciples of Jesus and of John the Baptist with unusually detailed information about the Galilean women who accompanied the Twelve to Jerusalem: 'Mary of Magdala, Joanna, the wife of Herod's steward Chuza, Susanna and several others who provided for them out of their own resources' (8:3). Luke's respectful way of acknowledging Joanna implies that Jesus had high support from within elements of the Herodian court. She is very likely to be the Joanna whom Luke 24:10 says was present at the crucifixion, a remarkable action given the politically divisive nature of the arrest and crucifixion of Jesus. Joanna could have been a source of stories about Jesus for Luke, just as Salome could have told Mark, whose mother was a friend of Peter.

By chance, a funeral slab was discovered near Jerusalem, belonging to a certain Joanna, daughter of Jonathan and granddaughter of Theophilus, High Priest in Jerusalem between the years 37-41. Whether this Theophilus was related to Luke's addressee cannot be proved.[14] Nonetheless, Luke's avoidance of direct criticism of the Herodian dynasty suggests Theophilus belonged to a similar elite circle, or group, perhaps resident in a Romanised city like Caesarea in Samaria. The fact that Manaen, one of the early Christian teachers at Antioch, is described as foster-brother of Herod Antipas (Acts 13:1), implies that its early Christian community enjoyed political support at a high level.

In Jerusalem, however, Judean zealots were a significant force. The Acts of the Apostles presents Jesus' followers in idealised terms, as a community in which members looked after one another, came together at the Jewish feast of Pentecost, and pooled their resources. Yet there were significant tensions evident in the community, described in Acts 6:1-6 as initiated by Hellenists who complained that they were being overlooked in distribution of food. In consequence, the whole community decided to appoint seven deacons, all men (although in Romans 16:1-2, Paul recommends the ministry of Phoebe, a deaconess at Cenchreae). Outside Jerusalem, there were also difficulties. Acts 18:18-24 describes how Simon 'Magus' in Samaria tried to use his own money to argue that he could preach the Gospel (Acts 8:18-24). The account effectively defined the crime of what came to be called simony, the medieval term for clerical corruption, that is, the buying of ecclesiastical office for personal gain.

During these early decades, it took time for the followers of Jesus to work out common rituals and formulate methods for conveying his teaching. The Eucharist quickly became a central ritual, based around coming together to talk and share recollections. Doctrines like God as a trinity had not yet been crystallised. Luke says that they were first called Christians in Antioch (Acts 11:26) and by Herod (26:28), although neither Paul nor the evangelists use the word, which otherwise is used only once in the New Testament (I Peter 4:16). According to Acts 24:5, Paul was accused of being a ringleader of the Nazarites, as the sect was known. Paul is remembered in Acts 18:18 as having cut his hair in fulfilment of a vow at Cenchreae, near Corinth, when he was with Priscilla and Aquila. This reversal of the traditional practice – of a Nazarite not cutting his hair – may reflect an adaptation to Hellenistic culture, which associated the long hair and beards of priests and Nazarites in Mosaic law as the very definition of a barbarian (which means bearded).

There are few allusions to clerical structures in the Pauline corpus. One of the earliest may be 1 Timothy 3:1-13 (written towards the end of his life, c. 65), in which Paul rules that wanting to be an *episkopos* (bishop) was not wrong in itself, but such a person had to be of exemplary reputation, and not married more than once, like any deacon. Paul may have been following the example of Simon Peter, whose mother-in-law was the focus of a significant miracle by Jesus (Matthew 8:14-15, Mark 1:29-31, Luke 4.38-39). Paul commends Phoebe to the community in Rome as ready to serve it in that capacity, as if he considered it normal for women to have such a role. He did not speak of such deacons as ministers, or as priests. And there was as yet no general imposition of tonsure as the sign of a male clerical elite.

All the evangelists in their narratives depict women as being always more faithful than the Twelve, whether during the ministry of Jesus or at his death and in the claims to his resurrection. Salome gets only passing mention in Mark, and then only allusively as the mother of the sons of Zebedee in Matthew. Yet her inclusions, along with Joanna, wife of Herod's steward, is one of the features of the followers of Jesus that differentiates them from others, like the Essenes and the disciples of John the Baptist, who defined their identity by rejecting marriage and sexual relationships. Jesus could not be bracketed as either pro- or anti-Roman in his politics.

For all the differences between the communities established by the apostles, they were bound by common bonds of practical support. At the end of his letter to the Romans 15:22 to 16:16, Paul says that he wanted to send money to help the poor among the saints of Jerusalem, and speaks of many friends there, including 'those outstanding apostles Andronicus and Junias, my compatriots and fellow prisoners, who were before me in Christ' (Romans 16:7). Peter is not mentioned as being in Rome either in that letter or in the closing section of Acts. It could be that Peter and Paul directed quite different communities within Rome, one Jewish, the other gentile. And it also may be that only after their executions a common clerical structure started to emerge, drawing on traditions of the priesthood familiar to Israelite tradition, and amenable to Roman society, in which pagan priests held positions of respect.

Only by the second century did imagery develop of the *episkopos* as having a priestly role like the pagan pontifex of Rome (from which the word pontiff derives). In Mosaic law, the priest had to wear special linen vestments and have a respectable wife (Leviticus 6:1-34). The title of priest connoted respectability in pagan Rome. The Roman clergy were acquiring respectability. Paul's injunctions were still being quoted in fourth-century Rome as the authority that permitted bishops and priests to marry. Yet there were also ascetic Christians, who argued that clergy should stand apart from Roman social convention. Notable among them was Jerome, who argued that monks who aspired to a virginal state were of superior moral character. Jerome's zeal for virginity was such that he refused to acknowledge that Jesus could have had any brothers, and insisted that his mother always remained a virgin.

Hegesippus, Cleophas, and the extended family of Jesus

A shift towards Roman dominance among different churches was already beginning to happen after 135, when the Emperor Hadrian sought to remove all traces of the past from Jerusalem, renaming it Aelia Capitolina, and expelling its native population. The story of the followers of Jesus in Jerusalem, in particular of James 'the Just', brother of the Lord, was told in detail in the second century by Hegesippus, whose five books of *Memoirs* (*Hypomnemata*) were much used by Eusebius of Caesarea (in his *Ecclesiastical History*, in particular *HE* II.23.1-25) to take the story of the Jesus movement beyond the account in the Acts of the Apostles.

Hegesippus is an historian who deserves to be much better known to modern readers because he articulates the voice of a community largely minimised in the canonical Gospels. He was an educated, Hellenised Jew, who tells us (*HE* IV.11.7 and 24.3) that he went to Rome during the time of bishop Pius in Rome (c. 142-55), and completed his *Memoirs* under Eleutherius (174-89). Because Eusebius only seems to quote from its fifth book, it may be that the previous four books were the four Gospels, referred to as *Memoirs* by Justin Martyr (c. 100-165).[15] Justin was another early Christian who moved to Rome in around 135, becoming part of a disputatious circle in which Marcion was arguing from the authority of Paul that Jesus had effectively abrogated Jewish tradition.

This was the context in which the corpus we know as the New Testament was assembled, although not all versions included the letters of James, Jude and the second letter of Peter (*HE* II.23.25 and III.25.3).

In his narrative, Hegesippus gives much more emphasis than the Acts of the Apostles to James, whom he calls the first *episkopos* of Jerusalem (*HE* II.1.2, IV.5.3). He reports that James's successor, Simon, son of Mary and Cleophas (the same as Clopas), was chosen because of his kin connection to Jesus, and that he was crucified as a very old man in the time of Trajan (98-117), on suspicion of belonging to the royal house of David. Hegesippus also mentions that the grandsons of Jude (one of the other brothers of Jesus) were still alive in the time of Trajan, and had been interrogated by Domitian (who had entered Jerusalem in 70 alongside the Emperor Vespasian) for the same reason. He emphasises that although the grandsons could trace their royal lineage to David, the kingdom preached by Jesus was not of this world (*HE* III.19, 20.1-6 and 32.1-6; IV.22.4), and so did not constitute a threat to the established order.

Hegesippus describes James, brother of the Lord (*HE* II.1.2 and II.23.1-18) in glowing terms, as devoted to God from infancy, never shaving or bathing (like a Nazarite), and as 'the only one able to enter the sanctuary', because he wore the linen vestments prescribed by the High Priest on the day of atonement (*HE* II.23.6; Lev. 16:31). To do all this, James must have been supported by sympathetic elements within the court of Herod Agrippa II. Hegesippus' emphasis on the dignity of James, whom he singles out as 'the Just', heightens the drama of James's fate and how, despite the support of his followers in Jerusalem, he was opposed by other scribes and pharisees, who accused him of blasphemy. They had him thrown off the parapet of the Temple (still standing despite being sacked in 70), after which he was stoned by a Judean crowd, and finally clubbed to death by someone with a rod used for beating cloth (*EH* II.23.7-18). Hegesippus reports that James was buried near the Temple and that his death took place during the disorder that followed the ousting of the procurator Festus in 62, in turn provoking Vespasian to crush the Judean revolt.

Hegesippus also reports a detail never mentioned by the evangelists: that Cleophas was a brother of Joseph (*EH* III: 11). While John 19:25 maintained that Mary of Cleophas was a sister of Jesus' mother, it seems implausible that two sisters, both called Mary, married two brothers. It seems more likely that after Joseph's (perhaps premature) death, Mary married his brother Cleophas, with whom she raised four more sons (James, Joseph, Simon and Jude) and unnamed daughters. In this reading, we should read John's statement in 19:25 about Jesus' mother and her sister as a literary device. John wanted to distinguish Jesus' mother from the Mary of Clephas honoured by the Jerusalem community.

According to Deuteronomy 25:5-10, in Levirate law, if a woman's husband died without legal issue, the woman could marry his brother, if he accepted her, and so could legally continue the male line. Mary might not have been troubled by this legal issue in marrying Cleophas. The evangelists did not mention that Joseph and Cleophas were brothers, because it could have detracted from their sense of the universalism of his message. But in local tradition, as attested by Hegesippus, James, the brother of the Lord, wanted to emphasise that he and his brothers were also descended from the line of David, alongside Jesus. The evangelists were troubled by the use of kinship to assert quasi-clerical authority within the

Christian community. Jesus defied convention by choosing not to marry. Instead he created an alternative family, structured around twelve male apostles, but also involving key female disciples to whom he was not related by kin. They included Mary of Magdala and Salome, mother of James and John. The Jerusalem community had its own way of recalling Jesus, rather like a songline which connected Jesus and his brothers to a legendary past that they saw as restored in Jesus. It emphasised a different story from that of the four evangelists preserved in the canonical New Testament.

The account in Luke 24:18 about Cleophas encountering the risen Christ as he walked from Jerusalem to Emmaus in Judea, was a skilled way of showing that Jesus' broader family did eventually come to understand his identity – but in their own way. John 19:25 creates Mary of Cleophas as a sister of Jesus' mother to articulate his sense of the transcendence of Jesus' true family over that of his half-brothers, who dominated the church of Jerusalem. It fits with John being a son of Salome and Zebedee in Galilee, but conflicts with the imagery of the other James, who asserted authority in Judea by claiming physical kinship with Jesus and the royal line of David. For John, Jesus was a quite different kind of king.

Conclusion

Each of the evangelists offers a distinct angle on Jesus, and the new vision of community that he offers. They all attest, however, that the apostles had great difficulty in grasping the implications of Jesus' teaching about the kingdom of God for their understanding of traditional models of religious authority. They also all present certain female followers of Jesus as ultimately more loyal than those apostles in both witnessing his crucifixion and wanting to care for his body after death.

The evangelists differ in identifying precisely which women came to the tomb. While Mark is the only evangelist to mention Salome, it is clear from comparing his account to that of Matthew that he is speaking about the wife of Zebedee and mother of James and John. By contrast, Matthew only speaks of Mary of Magdala and Mary mother of James as visiting the tomb. I argue that this second Mary could be the mother of James the younger by Cleophas as well as the mother of Jesus, James's half-brother. According to Hegesippus (who was well informed about the family of Jesus), Cleophas was a brother of Joseph Cleophas and could have married Mary if Joseph died unexpectedly. While James the younger became leader of the community in Jerusalem, he gave much more attention to the Law of Moses than did John, to whom the fourth Gospel would be attributed. Hegesippus alerts us to the perspective of Jewish followers of Jesus, whom Matthew was seeking to address.

The New Testament is remarkable in the way it transmits such a range of views on Jesus. James the younger has a different view on Jesus from that of Salome, the Galilean mother of James 'the Great' and his brother, John. The modern Church needs to be equally respectful of a diversity of views on Jesus, who crossed so many social boundaries.

Reference List

The NRSV is used for scriptural translations, unless otherwise stated.

The text of the Greek New Testament can easily be accessed with transcription and translation of one of its most important manuscripts, at http://codexsinaiticus.org/en/.

Hegesippus can be read in extracts quoted by Eusebius of Caesarea in his *Ecclesiastical History*, cited according to the book, chapter and verse of the Greek text, edited and translated by Gustave Bardy, Sources chrétiennes, vol. 1 (Paris: Cerf, 1952) and available in English translation, *The History of the Church*, trans. G. A. Williamson (London: Penguin, 1965).

The Loeb version of the Greek text of Eusebius, with the 1932 translation of Eusebius by Kirsopp Lake, vol. 1, is available at https://archive.org/details/ecclesiasticalhio1euseuoft/page/n5/mode/2up. For English translations of the writings of other early Church Fathers, see for Justin Martyr, First Apology, http://www.newadvent.org/fathers/0126.htm and for Jerome, Dialogue against the Pelagians http://www.newadvent.org/fathers/30111.htm

Endnotes

1. This chapter has been written without the detailed footnotes conventional for academic readers. Many of the issues it considers relating to identification of individuals mentioned in the New Testament have long been contested. More detailed discussion of these perspectives is reserved to a later date. I am grateful to Fr Michael Elligate for his regular Gospel homilies at St Carthage's Church, Parkville, and its community, including Berise Heasly, author of *Call No One Father: Countering Clericalism in the Catholic Tradition* (Melbourne: Coventry Press, 2019), for discussion of themes in this paper. I also express my gratitude to various former graduate students at Monash University, including Rina Lahav and Sam Baudinette (now at the University of Chicago) who have helped me edit, translate and contextualise the writings of Maurice of Kirkham and Herbert of Bosham, two twelfth-century scholars, who both questioned unfounded mythologies about Salome, mother of James and John. These writings will appear in *Maurice of Kirkham and Herbert of Bosham on Salome, British Writers if the Middle Ages and the Early Modern Period* (Toronto: University of Toronto Press, forthcoming).

2. http://m2.vatican.va/content/francesco/en/speeches/2017/september/documents/papa-francesco_20170907_viaggioapostolico-colombia-celam.html

3. 'Synodality in the Life and Mission of the Church', available at http://www.vatican.va/roman_

curia/congregations/cfaith/cti_documents/rc_
cti_20180302_sinodalita.en.html

4   On these songlines and their relation to Law, I am indebted to John Bradley, *Singing Saltwater Country: Journey to the Songlines of Carpentaria* (Crows Nest: Allen & Unwin, 2010) as well as to the reflections of Max Charlesworth on Indigenous spirit ancestors, as I discuss more fully in 'Songlines, Sacred Texts and Cultural Code: Between Australia and Early Medieval Ireland', in Peter Wong, Sherah Bloor, Patrick Hutchings and Purushottama Bilimoria (eds), *Considering Religions: Memorial Volume for Max Charlesworth*, Sophia Studies in Cross-Cultural Philosophy of Traditions and Cultures 30 (Dordrecht: Springer, 2019), 201-217.

5   I am indebted to Emily Fero-Kovassy for alerting me to the specifically Jewish character of 'the will of the Father', frequently used in Jewish discussion of the Torah, in her MA thesis, submitted to Monash University (2020), '"Doing the Will of the Father in Heaven" in the Gospel of Matthew: The Confluence of Law Observance and Moral Behaviour'.

6   Eusebius of Caesarea, *Ecclesiastical History* (*HE*) III.1.1 and 20.9. For bibliographical details, see Further Readings. Eusebius reports that John went to Ephesus, from where he was sent for a short period into exile in Patmos during the time of Domitian (81-96), but subsequently lived to the time of Trajan (98-117), and (III.23.1) governing various churches in Asia. The tradition that Mary went to Ephesus is not based on Eusebius but relied only on the report in John 19:25-27 that he took Mary into the

house of John. If Jesus was born c. 6 BCE and was active in his ministry 27-30 and John, 'the beloved disciple', was about 20 when Jesus died, the report of Eusebius (based on Papias) implies that he lived to around ninety years or more. Mary's cult developed strongly in Ephesus. Needless to say, all estimates about the ages of the apostles are highly speculative.

7   The literature on John's Gospel is immense. Brendan Byrne focuses on its theological message, with attention to its literary structure, in *Life Abounding: A Reading of John's Gospel* (Strathfield: St Paul's Publications, 2014). Robert Crotty argues that it emerges out of a gnostic context in *Jesus, His Mother, Her Sister Mary and Mary Magdalene: The Gnostic Background to the Gospel of John* (Kew East: David Lovell Publishing, 2016). While Crotty focuses on what he sees as gnostic features in John's Gospel, he does not consider as much its implicit dialogue with Judean tradition (often rejected by gnostics), and refers only briefly (p. 237) to John's reference in 19:25 to Mary's sister, which he thinks may be a scribal intervention rather than a rhetorical strategy on the author's part.

8   Eusebius, *HE* III.23.3-4, refers to Irenaeus (c. 130-202) as claiming that John lived to the time of Trajan. Eusebius also cites Papias (fl. 100-160) in *HE* III.39.5 as reporting that there was another elder, called John, distinct from the apostle. Possibly Irenaeus confused the two.

9   Peter E. Lewis argues that the surviving text of Mark's Gospel might have lost both its original introduction

and ending in *The Ending of Mark's Gospel* (Burleigh: Zeus Publications, 2020, 2nd ed.). The dramatic quality of Mark's opening, coupled with his lack of interest in the line of David, argues against this possibility.

10 Jerome, *Dialogues against the Pelagians*, 3.2; http://www.newadvent.org/fathers/30113.htm

11 *Talitha, kumi* is Hebrew, also used in Judeo-Aramaic, meaning 'Little girl, wake up (or arise)' in Hebrew. As explained to me by both Rina Lahav and Nathan Wolsi, *kumi* is correct when addressing a girl, *kum* a boy. Although the standard Greek critical edition of Mark 5:41 reads *kum* (reproduced in translations like NRSV and the Jerusalem Bible), the editors of the version in Codex Sinaiticus http://codexsinaiticus.org/en/ read the text here as *kumi*, the grammatically correct form.

12 For discussion of the Gospels as reflecting different perceptions, see Richard Bauckham, *Jesus and the Eyewitnesses: The Gospels as Eye-witness Testimony* (Grand Rapids, MI: Eerdmans, 2017, 2nd ed.).

13 For further detail, see the publication announced in n. 1 above.

14 Dan Barag and David Flusser, 'The Ossuary of Yehohanah Granddaughter of the High Priest Theophilus', *Israel Exploration Journal* 36 (1986), 39-44. Was this Theophilus related to the Theophilus to whom Luke (1:4) addresses his Gospel? While Matthew was anti-Herodian and proud of Jewish tradition, Luke minimises references to the family of Herod, omitting the story of the massacre of the innocents (and mentioning only the imprisonment, not the

death of John the Baptist (Luke 3:19-20)). His version of the nativity of Jesus situates John the Baptist as the son of Zechariah, a priest of the Temple, and Elizabeth, a kinswoman of Mary, re-asserting family connections, but in a way that connected Jesus to both John the Baptist and the line of David. Bauckham, 166-168 (n. 12 above) has suggested that Joanna could be the Junias mentioned by Paul as an outstanding Jewish apostle in Romans 16:7.

15   Justin Martyr, *Apology* 66.1-3, available at http://www.newadvent.org/fathers/0126.htm

Chapter 8

Rediscovering Jesus: Reimagining Church

Ian Hamilton

The reason for Historical Jesus scholarship[1]

The aim of Historical Jesus scholarship is to retrieve key characteristics of the earthly life of Jesus of Nazareth. It seeks to discover and rediscover his human actions and infer his beliefs and motivations. It is essentially an historical inquiry using historical methods. It works from source documents, archaeology and hermeneutical[2] principles. It endeavours to read the data with fresh eyes, leaving aside, for the moment, the detailed workings of Christological[3] theology and the complex layers of cultural appropriation[4] of Jesus that have occurred over the centuries.

In Matthew's gospel, Jesus' final words are 'My God, my God, why have you forsaken me?' (Matthew 27:46 NRSV)[5]. By contrast, John has Jesus utter 'It is finished' (John 19:30 (NRSV); 'It is accomplished' (JB). This stark contrast of

Messianic[6] theology should immediately alert us that the gospel texts are not univalent about Jesus' life and mission. The work of Historical Jesus scholars has newly explored the basis upon which we build Christian faith, and their insights have great potential also to inform our ecclesiological thinking (the way we imagine the Church).

In other words, how will we perceive the nature of the Christian Churches if we approach the gospels with Historical Jesus questions such as: 'What formed Jesus as a person?'; 'Can we know his perception of his purpose and mission?'; 'Is it possible to know the Jesus of history in an unveiled way: with fewer cultural and theological accretions?'

Jesus the Jew

One of the most significant outcomes of Historical Jesus scholarship has been to retrieve Jesus Christ from centuries of Eurocentric portrayal and return him to first century Judaism. One of the seminal works in this regard was *Jesus the Jew* by Geza Vermes. He describes his book as '... no more than an endeavour to clear away misunderstandings which for so long have been responsible for an unreal image of Jesus' (Vermes, p. 224). To do this he takes up several important themes about the contexts within which we find the Historical Jesus. First, he discusses rebellion as a characteristic of Galilean history (following the lead of Dubnov's 1967 book *History of Jews I*), and whether Jesus may have been a Zealot (an idea he rejects, in contrast to Brandon's argument in his 1967 publication *Jesus as Zealot*). These are bedrock discussions for the Historical Jesus scholar, as they seek to enhance our understanding of the world within which Jesus was formed and to which he reacted.

Secondly, he complements our understanding of the exorcisms and healings undertaken by Jesus by placing them not in a medical context, as we would, but in a religious one. He puts it succinctly: 'In the world of Jesus, the devil was believed to be the basis of sickness as well as sin' (Vermes, p. 61). We may interpret Vermes' exposition as implying that Jesus' healing was a political act, as well as a compassionate one, in the sense that it either usurped the role of the priest as authorised healer or it assumed the role of prophet as anointed healer.

Thirdly, Vermes uses two key descriptions of Jesus: charismatic and prophetic. He justifies these adjectives in detail. The terms are also used by other writers and discussed below. Interestingly, he notes that Christian theologians have, perhaps, become too concerned with the issue of whether Jesus is the *final* prophet (incidentally, a point of contention with Islam), rather than what his prophetic mission implies for us about authentic discipleship. Vermes also examines other key titles given to Jesus but, as I note elsewhere, this is a complex area of Biblical scholarship and I have chosen to omit it from this overview. Notwithstanding, Vermes offers a powerful set of conclusions. Prominent among them is this quotation:

> *The prophets spoke on behalf of the honest poor, and defended the widows and the fatherless, those oppressed and exploited by the wicked, rich and powerful. Jesus went further. In addition to proclaiming these 'blessed', he took his stand among the pariahs of his world, those despised by the respectable. Sinners were his table-companions and the ostracised tax-collectors and prostitutes his friends. (Vermes, p. 224).*

Some aspects of Marcus Borg's work

As noted above, Historical Jesus scholarship essentially concerns itself with questions such as: 'What can we know of the historical figure of Yeshua[7] *before* his death?' For scholars such as Borg this leads away from at least some of the commonly held truisms about Jesus. The Christian tradition has become largely dominated by stress on his salvific mission (Christ died for our sins), which is so closely linked to atonement or appeasement theology (Christ's death reconciled us to God). Are these really the core missions of Jesus, as gleaned from a fresh look at what we can know of his life?

This chapter limits itself to the work of a few distinguished scholars. They are rarely iconoclastic, although they do apply sharp thinking to questions of historicity[8] and interpretation. Borg notes that dominant images of Jesus (as Saviour, for instance) are not to be discounted or belittled. He notes that they are true in the sense that they 'appropriately describe what Jesus had become in the life of the post-Easter Church' (Borg, p. 10).

These scholars alert us to the limits of literalism. They present the idea that applying a post-Enlightenment empirical mind to late first-century texts is problematic. Given this, it can be argued that to expect literal historicity of every gospel text (especially John's gospel) is to read with faulty eyesight. Borg, though cautious about literalism, asserts some clearly historical statements about Jesus. He names him as a charismatic[9] who was a 'healer, sage, prophet and revitalization movement founder' (Borg, p. 15).

One of these names is especially significant: Jesus as a prophetic voice, rather than proto-priest. It is certainly clear that Jesus did not belong to the Sadducean priestly caste and that he vigorously disapproved of some of the ways at least some of the Temple priests 'dishonoured'[10] God by extorting the faithful who came to change secular money for temple money (Mark 11:15-19). While Borg's fellow scholar E. P. Sanders warns against over-interpretation of this episode, it does communicate an act of at least symbolic disgust (see Matthew 22:21). It also suggests that Jesus was alert to the abuse of power that can follow from meshing priestly duties with high social status and concomitant power and prestige. The Temple priests stand accused of allowing imperial pollution of Judaism's most sacred space.

Anyone familiar with the Christian tradition will recognise the prophetic nature of Jesus' teaching. Indeed, according to Luke, the tone is set by his first acts of preaching (for example, Luke 4:16ff). In that text he unequivocally identifies himself with the Jewish prophetic voice (Isaiah 61:1-2 and Zephaniah 2:3):

> The spirit of the Lord has been given to me,
> For he has anointed me.
> He has sent me to bring the good news to the poor....

Historical Jesus scholarship alerts us to the fact that our familiarity with this scene (which Luke places within the synagogue at Nazareth) may have blunted our appreciation of its significance. Here we have an apparently unauthorised *tektōn*[11] presuming to proclaim the essential nature of God's expectation of righteous ideals and behaviours. As one chosen for a sacred mission, Jesus has a spiritual duty to follow the prophetic imperative. Borg identifies three common elements of the prophetic mission: *indictment*, *threat* and *call to change*. These are briefly discussed below.

The first disturbing role of the prophetic voice is to name the ways in which the sacred covenant between God and humanity (Genesis 17:1ff) is being violated. The *indictment* is that the ruling elites, those who, by definition, exercise power and wealth, are accused by the prophets of wilful exploitation of the marginalised and powerless, in direct contravention of God's kingdom. Insulated from the lives of ordinary Jewish people, those responsible for compassionate leadership were, in fact, calloused and hardened. That is to say, the prophets 'charged that Israel's relationship to God had become distorted' (Borg, p. 152). Specifically: 'Though Israel's religion was organised around the God of Israel, and though priests and prophets and religious practice flourished, those in charge of Israel's religious and political life no longer knew God' (Borg, p. 152).

The indictment of hypocritical and wanton carelessness is sharpened by accompanying *threat*. This aspect of prophetic proclamation may explain why there is often a misconception that the role of a prophet was (is) to predict the future. Broadly, the threats were intended to shock and alarm the wayward: if nothing changes, you will experience great defeat and suffering. One instance of such a threat by Amos and Hosea was that Assyria would destroy the northern kingdom (for example, Amos 1:5f).

To restore right order and avoid destruction, the prophets proclaimed *a call to change*. It was necessary that the collective life of the Jewish people experience repentance – a dramatic, but most importantly, sincere, change of direction from sinfulness to virtue, from the mere formalism of belief to hearts aflame with the love of God (as succinctly expressed by Jesus in Matthew 22:37ff). Indeed, the word *metanoia* calls for more: a willingness to go beyond the strictures of our present mind; to think again and understand anew. One might see this as an existential ultimatum: the voice of the prophet asserts that Israel's reason for being is to live in true covenant with God. Any departure from that is a hideous betrayal of their call to holiness.

All this offers no departure from a 'mainstream' understanding of the preaching of Jesus until we ponder the silences and absences. Jesus identifies himself with one type of voice and implicitly distances himself from another. He evidently understands himself to be in a privileged and sacred relationship with the Divine One, whom he dares to speak of as 'Abba'. What is also clear is that he seems highly suspicious of self-important elites who claim to be those 'authorised' to allow people access to God. He joins his voice to previous prophets who felt called to name loudly the ways in which religious authority-figures, and the institutions with which they identified, were failing in their calling. He does not appear to endorse the existing religious leadership, or their understanding of covenant. In short, we lose something key to the Jesus story if we do not emphasise his prophetic self-identification, and make the connection between that emphasis and our present realities.

The way the Christian Church conducts itself will never be truly holy unless we test ourselves against that prophetic voice. Even a cursory glance at Church history makes it clear that when we favour hierarchical, institutional and priestly world-views over the authentically prophetic, we, like the people of Israel, lose our way. Is it too harsh to say that the hierarchical, institutional and clerical world-views have been, and are, inimical to the demands of the truly spirit-filled mission of the church, as exemplified by the spirit-filled mission of Jesus?

In his presentation of Jesus as a spirit-filled prophet, Borg contrasts him to those who convert holiness into a political weapon. Most famously, but perhaps somewhat unfairly (as both Borg and Sanders point out) the Pharisees have been portrayed as figures of sublime hypocrisy precisely because they gave preference to the outer show of ritual purity over heart-felt faith (*pistis*).[12] The Levite and the Priest in the story we call 'The Good Samaritan' (Luke 10:39ff) are faithful to the rules of purity but unfaithful to the call to compassion, which is one of the great themes of Jesus' teaching (and indeed the teachings of other religious leaders).

Borg describes Jesus as an 'epiphany' whose holy motivation was to always act out of love (*agapē*). This contrasts to the religious elites who were fearful of defiling themselves. They allowed such fear to impede their compassionate and loving responses. We are all too aware that fearful compliance with outward appearances has caused great harm to the Church's mission, both in the distant and recent past. Any ecclesiology that favours protection of institutional reputation and prestige above natural justice for the poor, oppressed and abused is an ecclesiology that betrays Christ's teaching. Historical Jesus studies point to a recurring theme of his teaching: worldly hierarchies of holiness[13] are condemned.

Some aspects of John Dominic Crossan's work

The insights communicated to us by other scholars are also worthy of our attention. John Dominic Crossan writes in fine detail about the contexts within which he believes we need to appreciate the life of Jesus.

After explaining his scholarly methodology[14] he explores aspects of first century Palestinian life. He is keen to place Jesus within his Mediterranean context, including Mediterranean ecology and its influence on prosperity, peasant village life and wider social structures. One of his more arresting assertions is that Jesus needs to be seen as a provincial peasant and, therefore, of relatively low social status. His extensive discussion of the causes of, and expressions of, social stratification chiefly focus on the nature of an honour and shame society and on patronage, slavery and clientage. Each of these produce asymmetrical power relationships, and scripture vividly portrays Jesus as a man largely marginalised from worldly power. This message of Jesus as outsider recurs both in the body of scholarship considered here and the wider academic corpus.

Crossan adds to this portrait of first-century Jewish society by noting the work of Ramsay McMullan. Crossan reports that McMullan draws the conclusion that not only was society rigidly stratified, the literate upper classes saw no reason to hide their sense of superiority over the lower-class worker (such as a *tektōn*). Woven into this is their sense that their elevated position in life entitled them to claim honour, and to be ever ready to shame those they deemed unworthy. Consider the story of the woman caught in adultery (John 8:1ff) and Jesus' defiant riposte to the 'righteous'.

Further detailed writing follows about the nature and role of peasantry. Suffice to note that being a peasant is not intrinsically a position of power or influence, although peasant revolts are not unknown in history. Crossan portrays the time before, during and after the life of Jesus as times of social unrest. This is hardly surprising given that the chosen people experienced exile and oppression (most pertinently, the military dictatorship of Rome). We have no evidence that Jesus perceived himself as rebellious leader, which would have been in contradiction to his profound commitment to just non-violence (cf. The Beatitudes, Matthew 5:1-12; Luke 6:20ff). He did, however, fit the more pervasive characteristics of peasants: he lived in a rural environment and it is reasonable to infer that he had little material wealth (certainly not large landholdings or luxurious riches) and little opportunity for social advancement.

Another unexpected description that Crossan applies to Jesus is that he displayed many of the characteristics of a cynic. The term is being used precisely to name a Greek-influenced view of life. The cynic[15] adopted disdain for society's superficial values, judgments and assumptions. This extended to assumptions about who was to be revered as honourable and who was to be scorned as shameful. Indeed, it was often an inversion of these assessments, as many gospel stories testify, for example, Eating with Sinners (Mark 2:15-17; Matthew 9:10-13; Luke 5:29-32) and Who is the Greatest? (Mark 9: 33-37; Matthew 10:40; Luke 10:16). The inversion applied similarly to the prevailing rules of patronage and clientage, which existed to ensure that the power and wealth of elites were unassailed, unquestioned and unchallenged.

Crossan furthers his thesis about how we should imagine the Historical Jesus by adding another term that is startling to most modern readers: he names him as a magician. Our modern understanding of the term has a pejorative dimension because we see magicians as clever but, ultimately, deceitful. He could also have used the term 'miracle worker' (or thaumaturgist) but wants to retrieve the idea of the magician as essentially religious: one who brings a personal experience of divine power into the lives of individuals.

This is the context within which Crossan believes we should understand many of the healing stories. He offers the provocative insight that the most accurate way to see the healing acts of Jesus is that they belong outside the 'rabbinisation'[16] process necessary to have contemporary and later magicians included in the rabbinical corpus (Crossan, p. 157). This is a helpful frame for us to see the sharp criticism levelled at Jesus when he does his 'magic' (as defined above) (consider 'Which is easier?', Mark 2:1-12; Matthew 9:1-8; Luke 5:17-26). Leaving aside any discomfort caused by the term 'magician', here we have another strand to our image of Jesus as one who acts independently of the approval of established religious authorities.

One of the most familiar Gospel phrases is the 'Kingdom of God'. It is usually seen as the state of covenant between God and God's people where 'Your will be done on earth as it is in heaven' (Matthew 6:10; Luke 11: 2). Crossan opens up the meaning further. Much ink has been spent on the question of whether Jesus is announcing a state of divine love (*agapē*), which is our *future* promise (heavenly reward), or our *immediate* reality.[17] He distinguishes the world view of John the Baptist (apocalyptic)[18] from that of Jesus (who did not embrace 'apocalyptic asceticism', Crossan, p. 260). Perhaps more appealingly, he uses exegesis of several relevant passages to come to the conclusion that the fundamental nature of God's reign of love is that we cannot understand it unless we become like children (see Mark 10:13-16). Moving swiftly from any sentimental reading of this text, he notes that children have little status in Jesus' society. They are not taken seriously. We see that Jesus subverts any expectation that the coming of the Kingdom will ensure that already self-important people will become even more important. Indeed, 'a kingdom of children is a kingdom of nobodies' (Crossan, p. 261).

The intent of this point is amplified by Crossan's linguistic analysis of the first Beatitude ('Blessed are the poor', Luke 6:20b).[19] The word *ptōchos*, which is translated as poor, is a stronger reference to the marginalised – to the outsider. The *ptōchos* are shamefully destitute. They are reduced to begging and have no claim to honour (or, indeed, righteousness). Crossan's scholarship takes us into a deep consideration of texts sometimes dulled by familiarity.

The last element of Crossan's text to which I wish to turn my attention is his evaluation of the importance of Jesus' itinerancy. He refers to Gerd Theissen's work because it asserts that Jesus' itinerant existence (at least from the point in his life which begins in the Jordan River) is not a minor vagary or whim. Crossan agrees with Theissen that it is a deliberate and authentic aspect of Jesus' understanding of the mission he undertakes.[20] It is, Crossan maintains, a vivid reassurance that Jesus has an egalitarian proclamation:[21] one does not have to be a figure of (apparent) honour to be worthy. It is not outward piety or rigorous attention to ritual purity that opens the Kingdom. Later theologians call this invitation a theology of grace. The point is that Jesus does not settle in one place, does not establish any kind of institution, and does not align himself with any existing agencies of religious authority.[22] Crossan links his itinerant life to his mission by opining 'that the Historical Jesus had both an ideal vision and a social program' (Crossan, p. 349).

How does Jesus emerge from this very thorough scholarly examination? Crossan draws together his extensive and detailed work in this way: 'Miracle and parable, healing and eating were calculated to force individuals into *unmediated* [my emphasis]physical and spiritual contact with God and unmediated physical and spiritual contact with one another. He announced, in other words, the brokerless kingdom of God.'²³

Some aspects of the work of Theissen and Merz

Theissen and Merz list Crossan, amidst many others, as a frequently cited thinker, and they take up several of his motifs. They are exemplary Historical Jesus scholars in that they seek to interrogate available sources, and place Jesus within the milieu of his times. They add a note of warning that this sometimes leads to some commentators locating Jesus *against* his Jewish contexts, rather than, more positively, *within* those contexts. Although they certainly see him as marginalised, they note that much of his world-view would have been profoundly compatible with mainstream Jewish thought. It would be wrong, for instance, to think that he stood against the heart of Jewish identity as a monotheistic, covenanted people, with the Temple as the unique centre of worship. This does not obviate the fact that Jesus had no authority within the context of Temple priesthood, although he is recorded as speaking at the synagogue.²⁴ We also know that apparently core pieties (avoiding the unclean, and strictly observing Sabbath restrictions, for example) were rejected by Jesus when they usurped sincere belief with outward show, hypocrisy or self-righteousness.

In a similar way to other scholars, these authors pay attention to the social, cultural and political (imperial) contexts of Jesus' times. They place Jesus within the scope of other renewal movements, and encapsulate their findings in this way: 'All these (renewal) movements ultimately go back to the challenge posed to Judaism by Hellenistic culture' (Theissen and Merz, p. 147). This idea is followed by a highly detailed analysis of those Greek influences and the role of the Sadducees, Pharisees and Essenes.[25] In addition, discussion is offered about the distinction between Galilee and Judea. Using a range of evidence, including archaeology, they present the idea that Galilee was seen not only as a fringe province but less purely Jewish, separated as it was from Judea by Samaria. Theissen and Merz present this not so much as a shortcoming but as Galilee's being more 'open to the world' (Theissen and Merz, p. 163). This is certainly compatible with Jesus' acts of inclusion, such as the conversation with the Samaritan woman (as portrayed in John 4: 1-30).

Other elements of Crossan's thinking are echoed in this work: 'As land was the primary source of employment, social stratification was closely connected with the ownership of land' (Theissen and Merz, p. 171). Indeed, a major theme of Borg's thinking is also found here. In Chapter Eight there is a detailed discussion of Jesus as charismatic, which includes the following helpful quotation from Max Weber: The charismatic's power (and consequent authority) '... are not accessible to the ordinary person but are regarded as of divine origin or as exemplary...' (Theissen and Merz, p. 186). It is important to hold in balance the two key ideas here: we may infer that Jesus is an outsider in terms of worldly prestige but possesses an extraordinary charismatic wisdom that allows him to preach and heal with authority.

In addition to these insights, their work includes intellectual contributions about the description of Jesus as magician. Here they disagree with Crossan's use of the word but not with the connection he makes between Jesus' acts and the radical nature of his mission. While they note that: 'Jesus' understanding of himself was prophetic, not magical' (Theissen and Merz, p. 306), they attribute great significance to his gift of healing: 'Nowhere else do we find a charismatic miracle worker whose deeds are meant to be the end of an old world and the beginning of a new one'[26] (Theissen and Merz, p. 309). They add to earlier work by exploring Jesus as poet, as rabbi, as the founder of a Eucharistic cult and as martyr.[27]

Atypically of this genre, they write two detailed chapters entitled 'The Risen Jesus: Easter and its Interpretations' and 'The Historical Jesus and the Beginnings of Christology'. As noted, most Historical Jesus scholars restrict themselves to the events up to, and including, his death. Perhaps then the last word we take from Theissen and Merz should be:

> *The death of Jesus is the consequence of tensions between a charismatic coming from the country and an urban elite; between a Jewish renewal movement and alien Roman rule; between someone who claimed cosmic change which was also to transform the temple and the representatives of the status quo. (Theissen and Merz, p. 467)*

Jesus and Women

A relatively recent voice in Biblical criticism can be heard in the work of female scholars. For the most part they frame their theological thinking within the broader academic phenomenon of feminist theory. This leads to a reading of the gospels as written for men, about men and by men. Not surprisingly, they express discomfort with what they perceive as the dominant androcentric world-view within the scriptures. In doing so, these exegetes have alerted us to the role of women in a fresh and arresting way. Joanne Dewey[28] offers a helpful summary of the purpose of feminist work: it is to expose those ways in which women have been rendered invisible or subordinate and, more positively, to promote the 'liberating egalitarian vision of the gospel' (Dewey, p. 470) that their analysis unveils. It is interesting to note how this complements much of what we have noted of the work of Borg, Crossan and Theissen and Merz.

Not only is the reign of God[29] immediate[30] and powerful but it is inclusive. Dewey notes that one example of this is the way in which Jesus wipes out discrimination, not only of the ill or deformed (thereby unclean) but against women (also often seen as offensive to purity). Women are often the ones most open to, and perceptive about, the spiritual freedoms within Jesus' preaching and actions (consider Mark 5:21ff, Mark 7:24ff, Mark 15:40-41, Matthew 26:6ff, Luke 7:36ff, Luke 8:1-3, Luke 21:1-4 and Luke 23:55ff as examples). From close scrutiny of Mark 5:25-34, Mark 14:3-9, Mark 15:40 and Mark 16:8 Dewey draws the following conclusion: 'Mark clearly had available to him stories of women who played central roles in Jesus' story', and further: 'The prominence of women in the oral tradition is such that Mark does not ignore them' (Dewey, p. 508).

Theissen and Merz also contribute to this topic. Having described the ways in which the canonical[31] texts are androcentric, they note: 'Over against the patriarchal features stand the inclusive elements in the Jesus tradition. A strikingly large number of women appear in the narrative tradition, sometimes in roles that are not typical of their sex. The anointing of the Messiah by a woman in Mark 14:3-9 might be mentioned as an example' (Theissen and Merz, p. 220).

The impression one derives from feminist textual studies is that the evangelists, almost despite themselves, do convey that there were female disciples, and that at least some women were figures of insightful and sincere faith. Some of these may well have been confidantes and benefactors. We seem entitled to say that in this, as in other aspects of his behaviour, Jesus 'pushes the boundaries' of the *morēs* of his times. One principle of Historical Jesus scholarship that gives credence to such a conclusion is the 'Criterion of Embarrassment'. This principle states that extant Scriptural stories which are at odds with proper behaviour for a devout Jewish man are very likely to have happened. There would be no incentive for an evangelist to compose an embarrassing episode.

Lastly, it is worth noting that much attention has also been paid to the role of women in the early Church. While this is, strictly speaking, outside the orbit of Historical Jesus scholarship, it does seem important to ponder the characteristics of the earliest life of the Jesus movement once the earthly Jesus is no longer with them. Several women are named in Romans 16, most tellingly Junia, who is given the title of 'apostle' by Paul.[32]

Upon this Rock

The question of female apostleship leads neatly into the question of whether the Historical Jesus can be accurately seen as a religious founder (that is, founder of what became 'The Way' and eventually Christianity). In the Catholic tradition, much emphasis has been placed on the Petrine texts. These are normally cited as: 'And I tell you, you are Peter, and on this rock, I will build my church, and the gates of Hades will not prevail against it' (Matthew 16:18) and 'He said to him the third time, "Simon son of John, do you love me?" Peter felt hurt because he said to him the third time, "Do you love me?" And he said to him, "Lord, you know everything; you know that I love you." Jesus said to him, "Feed my sheep"' (John 21:17). Although neither text has, strictly speaking, multiple attestation, they have been used as proof-texts for the role of the priesthood and the hierarchical clerical structures that have been built from interpretation of these pericopes.[33]

As B. A. Johnson notes, early Christian writers were at variance about who exactly is 'the rock'. While Cyprian follows Tertullian in seeing Peter as the rock, later thinkers diverged from this interpretation. Augustine saw the rock as Jesus Christ, not Peter, while Chrysostom stressed the expression of faith ('You are the Christ' – Matthew 19:17) as the rock. Johnson further notes: 'Origen believed that all who professed the same belief as Peter also could be called "rock". Indeed, he even held that those gifts which were conferred to Peter were no less conferred to any other believer!'. J. C. Fenton neatly aids us to understand the further words: *mou tēn ekklēsian* – my church. Bearing in mind that our

English rendering comes from Aramaic via Greek[34] Fenton reminds us that *ecclesia* may be translated as 'the people', 'the assembly', 'the congregation' (Fenton, p. 269). Even a brief dip into exegetical scholarship, and without any survey of views about the historicity of the pericope, seems to indicate strongly that Matthew 16:18 is a very poor proof-text for supreme Petrine authority and the ecclesiology the Catholic tradition has built on it.

It is also quite common to view John 21:17 as a commissioning of Peter, and it is clearly so. But what is the context of the commission and the nature of the commission? First, this is not an historical encounter, in any normal sense of the word, as it is a post-Easter narrative about a post-Easter event, written for a post-Easter faith community. In it Peter has an experience of the Risen Christ. The resurrection narratives present a rather enigmatic portrait of a Christ who does not appear to dwell in time and space in exactly the same way as the historical Jesus did (consider Luke 24:36ff; John 20:19ff); whose disappearance from the tomb is seen as suspicious (consider Matthew 28:11ff); and who is not readily recognised (consider Luke 24:13ff; John 21:4). These texts alert the reader to the need to be attentive to context and literary inferences.

The second important factor to note is that this exchange may be read as much as an admonishment of Peter, as a praising of him. The Risen Christ seeks assurance three times (twice to love as *agapē* and once as the less demanding *philia*), which both recalls Peter's triple denial (Mark 14:66ff; Matthew 26:69ff; Luke 22:56ff; John 18:17ff) and seems to have the literary purpose of presenting Peter as a figure of vacillation, simplistic incomprehension and unreliability. A possibly divergent interpretation is given in catechetical style by the 'free Catholic online resource' Agape bible study site.[35]

Thirdly, what are we to make of 'feed my sheep'? We may take it as a familiar reference to pastoral care. It does imply attentiveness to the needs of the many and willingness to work for their welfare. It does not, intrinsically, denote authority over others. It is interesting, also, that the Marcan commissioning[36] has the Risen Christ showing himself to the Eleven and saying to *all* of them: 'Go into all the world and proclaim the good news to the whole creation' (Mark 16:15). Both the commissioning, and the commission, are open-hearted and expansive. It is not by a caste for an elect (although the next verse does require that those who receive the Good News believe and be baptised).

One should note that the early chapters of Acts do present Peter as a leading speaker (Acts 1:15, 2:14, 2:38, 3:7) but other apostles are also significant (John the beloved, Philip, Barnabas and, especially, James in 13:17). The latter part of that book is dominated by the initiatives taken by Paul, and it may be argued that it is he who is the dominant figure in early Church history and possibly should be credited as the founder of Christianity. And as already noted, many current scholars ponder the role of women in the earliest life of the church, particularly as they have a uniquely important role in the gospel narratives. All four gospels name Mary of Magdala as the one to whom the Risen Christ appears (Luke 24:10, Matthew 28:1, Mark 16:1 and John 20:1).

It may be concluded then that even a cursory examination of these Petrine texts casts at least some doubt on their value as justification for the emphasis on Petrine primacy, apostolic succession, and clericalism in general. Despite the work done at Vatican II, these three tenets continue as foundational beliefs for many Catholics. They are usually presented as Christ's intentions for his evangelical legacy, especially about who may be ordained and why it is they who qualify for ordination.

Some conclusions

Within the limits of a relatively brief chapter, the question 'What is Historical Jesus scholarship?' has been broached.[37] That is to say, I have sought to investigate what view of the church emerges when we focus on fundamental questions such as: 'What formed Jesus as a person?'; 'Can we know his perception of his purpose and mission?'; and 'Is it possible to know the Jesus of history in an unveiled way, with fewer cultural and theological accretions?'. In my view, this scholarship offers us a chance to 'see again'. Much of the work of the Christian Church is motivated by compassionate generosity; however, any glance at history reveals that the institution of the Church has quite often lost its way. We live in one of those times. How do we, the wider Church, nurture the life of the institutional church and propel it towards the unwavering authenticity found in the life of Jesus the Christ?

If we accept the assumption that the mission of the Christian churches should be congruent with the mission of Jesus of Nazareth, then honest re-reading of our sacred texts is imperative. Historical Jesus scholarship is crucial to this for two reasons: it avoids literalism, which is often simplistic and misleading,[38] and it seeks to separate later cultural and theological elements from the Jesus of Nazareth story. The seemingly naïve question 'What would Jesus do?' becomes, in fact, a profound bedrock of discernment if the answer is founded on sober scholarship complemented by prayerful humility.

Although I have not directly dealt with J. P. Meier's monumental work, *A Marginal Jew: Rethinking the Historical Jesus*, that volume's title is a powerful summation of what I believe Historical Jesus scholarship teaches us. Jesus is not a figure of high social or religious status. In many respects he is an outsider. More importantly, this status frames his self-understanding as one within the Jewish prophetic tradition. Even more importantly, he does not seek to become an insider. His charismatic life is profoundly formed by his love for other marginalised members of his society, whom he anoints as 'Blessed' (Matthew 5:3ff). His life of courageous grace is the template of discipleship. Provocatively, that discipleship may be interpreted, indeed perhaps it should be interpreted, not as the path of priestly, or other, authority, but of prophetic discomfort with the human tendency to institutionalise, and thereby tame, our call to authentic holiness.

Though it may not be historically accurate to name him as the founder of Christianity, it is certainly accurate to say he is its source and inspiration (in the poetic, etymological, sense of the One who breathes us all into life). The future of the Catholic Church in Australia is uncertain in many ways. The 'People in the Pews', while certainly not a single voice, do appear to be 'voting with their feet' by deciding that the institution (as led by its clerical hierarchy) is unworthy of their loyalty. Perhaps the frailty of the church lies not so much in a discomfort with the immediate past and with our future directions but in a neglect of our origins. If that same leadership were to ponder the lessons of Historical Jesus scholarship with open minds and open hearts, then the Holy Spirit of Hope would have a chance to spread its wings.

Reference List

Author unknown :http://www.agapebiblestudy.com/John_Gospel/Chapter%2021.htm (Accessed November 7, 2019)

Borg, Marcus, *Jesus, A New Vision* (San Francisco: Harper, 1991)

Crossan, John Dominic, *The Historical Jesus: The Life of a Mediterranean Jewish Peasant* (San Francisco: Harper, 1991)

Dewey. J., 'The Gospel of Mark' in *Searching the Scriptures Vol 2* (New York: Crossroads, 1994)

Dunn J.D.G., *Jesus Remembered* (Grand Rapids: Eerdmans, 2003)

Fenton, J.C., *Saint Matthew* (London: Pelican New Testament Commentaries, Penguin, 1963)

Johnson, B.A., *Is Peter The Rock? Early Interpretations of Matthew 16:18-19*
https://owlcation.com/humanities/Who-Was-The-Rock-Interpretations-of-Matthew-1618-and-19-in-the-Early-Church (Accessed October 30, 2019)

Levine A-J (1997) *A Feminist Companion to Matthew* (Sheffield Academic Press).

Marsh, John, *Saint John* (London: Pelican New Testament Commentaries, Penguin, 1968)

Perrin, Norman, *The Resurrection Narratives: A New Approach* (London: SCM Press, 1977)

Sanders, E.P., "Jesus and the Temple" in Dunn J.D.G. and MacKnight S. (Eds), *The Historical Jesus in Recent Research* (Philadelphia: Pennsylvania State University Press, 2005)

Theissen G. and Merz A., *The Historical Jesus: A Comprehensive*

Guide (Minneapolis: Fortress Press, 1996)

Vermes, Geza, *Jesus the Jew* (Philadelphia: Fortress Press, 1981)

Endnotes

1. Historical Jesus scholarship is normally described as having had five phases: Early Critical Impulse (Reimarus, Strauss); Liberal Quest (Baur, Hotzmann); Collapse of the Liberal Quest (Schweitzer, Wrede); The New Quest (Käsemann, Braun); The Third Quest (Sanders, Vermes, Theissen, Crossan), see Theissen and Merz, p. 12.
2. Hermeneutics concerns itself with the principles of interpretation (especially of Scripture).
3. Christology is the branch of theology which concerns itself with Jesus as the anointed One (Messiah = Christos) and his place within the Trinity. High Christology, as frequently found in John's gospel and the doctrinal developments of Nicaea and beyond, stresses Christ as the second person of the Trinity, whereas Historical Jesus scholarship stresses the human existence of a man who was born, lived and died within particular historical, social, cultural, political and religious contexts.
4. Devotion to the Infant of Prague is one vivid example of Christian beliefs which have little direct or obvious connection to Jesus' first century Palestinian Jewish life.
5. Biblical quotations are from the NRSV translation (Catholic edition).
6. The terms 'Messiah' (Hebrew *mashiah*) and 'Christ' (Greek *Christos*) both mean 'the anointed One'.

Expectations of who the Messiah would be and how the Messiah would change Judaism were not uniform within Second Temple Judaism. Whether Jesus perceived himself as the expected Messiah is an interesting Historical Jesus question (Vermes Chapter Six is one treatment of the issue).

7 'Yeshua' is a more accurate rendering of Jesus' name, but 'Jesus' will be used in the chapter.

8 Perhaps the most famous enquiry into questions about what Jesus may not have said or done (in the eyewitness sense of historical reportage) is by the Jesus Seminar.

9 Borg is using 'charismatic' to mean a person deeply in tune with the Holy Spirit and a gifted channel of holiness.

10 Sanders attributes this view to E. Trocomé.

11 A *tektōn* is a craftsman or worker (Liddell and Scott Lexicon). We may reasonably assume two things from this description of Jesus: he did not belong to an especially high-status occupation and he certainly did not belong to a social rank that would have been identified with religious authority.

12 The Greek word carries two meanings: what we normally mean by faith (assent to a set of beliefs) and trust (a more affective understanding of the divine-human relationship) (Liddell and Scott Lexicon).

13 We might posit that one of the dangers of clericalism is that it assumes that the priestly caste is holier than others.

14 He does this from pages xxvii to xxxiv in the preface to the book being discussed. In brief, he chooses to discuss texts which are in more than one primary

source (that is, multiple attestation). Those sources include the four authorised (canonical) gospels plus the Gospel of Thomas. He also draws on the source known as Q (a presumed lost source which accounts for material which is in Luke and Matthew but not in Mark – Mark's gospel being the foundational text of the other two synoptic gospels, Matthew and Luke). In addition, he uses the *Didache* and for historical comparison he draws on Josephus, Tacitus *et al*. Another very thorough exploration of methods used in Historical Jesus scholarship is found in the first one hundred and thirty-five pages of Dunn's *Jesus Remembered*.

15 Presumably the term was never intended to be complimentary, as it derives from the Greek word for dog.

16 The rabbis had some status within the Jewish community. It is unlikely that Jesus was perceived as a rabbi within his own lifetime, for the reasons which Crossan and others articulate.

17 Crossan calls the former an 'apocalyptic' vision of the kingdom. It is also sometimes called an unrealised eschatology. Theissen and Merz offer a nuanced response to this matter: 'The Jesus tradition contains both future and present statements about the Kingdom of God. Those who regard a "non-eschatological Jesus" as historical must dispute the future statements; those who only accept the "apocalyptic Jesus" must dispute the present statements. Nowadays both series of sayings are usually accepted as authentic' (Theissen and Merz, p. 252f).

18 Meaning that John the Baptist was preaching about a future final judgment time (the apocalypse).
19 This does have multiple attestation but Matthew adds 'in spirit' which Crossan considers a gloss.
20 We know little of how willingly he comes to a realisation that he has a part to play in the restoration of his Jewish brothers and sisters to an authentic understanding of the Kingdom. The synoptics stress that immediately after his Baptism he experiences deep anxiety and worldly temptations (Mark 1:12f; Matthew 4:1-11; Luke 4:1-13).
21 A contrary view is found in J. H. Elliot's article 'Jesus is not Egalitarian' in *Biblical Theology Bulletin*, 2002.
22 Or even with groups who perceived themselves as forces of renewal, such as the Pharisees.
23 It is interesting to note that in a rather different context, *Why Priests?*, 1971, Hans Küng wrote: 'In contradistinction to the Pagan or Jewish cult, a Christian does not need the mediation of a priest to enter the innermost sanctuary of his temple: that is, to reach God himself (*sic*). On the contrary he (*sic*) is admitted to the ultimate immediacy of God, which no church authority can spoil or forbid him' (p. 19).
24 Surprisingly perhaps, synagogue is a Greek word, rather than a Hebrew/Aramaic one. It means 'assemblies' and becomes applied to places of gathering.
25 Theissen and Merz put this material into table form on page 138.
26 This is a vivid way to understand the story of the wedding feast of Cana (John 2: 1-12).
27 Of Jesus as poet they offer this valuable insight: 'For God

can be spoken of appropriately only in images and similitudes' (Theissen and Merz, p. 343). Of the title Rabbi, they note that there is little connection between the use of it in reference to Jesus and the subsequent (post 70 CE) connection between the term and the scribes.

28 I have limited my focus here to the work of one writer because she focuses on aspects of Mark's gospel. Many feminist scholars write across a wide range of themes. Some of the more prominent thinkers include: Osiek, Wainwright, Schüssler-Fiorenza, Ruether, Levine, Genest and Kitzberger.

29 Dewey notes, as others have done, that the 'Kingdom of God' is not a very good translation of the Greek term *basileia* because that word refers more broadly to the act of ruling, regardless of gender.

30 The question of the immediate nature of the Kingdom (*baseleia*) is an area of debate (see end note 17).

31 The canonical texts are what we know as the normal New Testament. Non-canonical texts include the Gospel of Mary, the Gospel of Thomas, The Sophia of Jesus Christ, the Acts of Paul and Thecla.

32 The scholarly consensus is that Junia is, in fact, a woman not a man. One of the many studies of this matter is by Hope Stephenson, 'Junia: woman and apostle' in *Women in the Biblical World* (Lanham: University Press of America, 2009).

33 A pericope is an identifiable, arguably discrete, section of text. It may have complex editorial elements (as revealed by redaction criticism).

34 In *Jesus Remembered* (Eerdmans, 2003) James D. G. Dunn argues that we only have access to what

is remembered about the words and actions of Jesus. We do not have direct access to the events themselves. While this does not automatically imply that events and words are historically inaccurate, it does remind us that narrators (both oral and written) were recalling, from the shared memories of the 'keepers of the memory'. It also reminds us that the Gospels are to be read as post-Easter proclamations.

35 *Question*: In the first two exchanges Jesus uses the verb form *apage* (sic) signifying the kind of self-sacrificing love with which He calls Peter to love His Church, but Peter responds each time with the word *philo* meaning brotherly love or love of family. What might Peter's response indicate?

Answer: Some scholars contend that the use of the two verbs for 'love' means nothing significant but John never uses double words or double meaning words without some hidden significance. It is possible that the difference in meaning between these two verbs for 'love' signifies that Jesus is calling Peter to a higher form of love and Peter is not yet ready to commit himself to that kind of self-sacrificing love.

36 Most Scripture scholars think that Mark's gospel ended at what we know as Chapter 16 verse 8. Chapter 16:9-20 appears to have been added later.

37 This overview has not attempted to include every aspect of Historical Jesus scholarship. It has certainly not even remotely dealt with every scholar working in this field. It has endeavoured to present a helpful sample of the oeuvre. I have included only brief treatment of the sayings (including parables) and

miracles (including nature miracles). There has been no treatment of the much-discussed titles given to Jesus by the evangelists (Rabbini, Lord (Kyrios), King of the Jews, Son of Man, Son of God) nor examination of the extensive attention given to the Eucharistic passages, the Passion narratives or the Resurrection accounts. Each of these would require many 'column inches'. Even so, I believe this survey does allow us to draw some inferences, as I have done in the final section of the chapter.

38 Literalism is usually characterised by little or no knowledge of the contexts within which a text was composed, insensitivity to the complexities of composition (as revealed by tools such as redaction criticism) or any linguistic/translation issues that may apply.

Chapter 9

Clericalism And Reforming The Church In History

Constant J. Mews

Clericalism has always been a problem within the history of the Church. Yet there have also been many efforts over the centuries, both to reform the Church as a whole, and to generate alternative models of ecclesial community. Every major reform movement within the Church has been shaped by a particular socio-economic and political situation. This is a story that deserves to be told.

Within the time of Jesus, Roman colonisation in the Holy Land created particular circumstances that shaped the way Christianity developed. In the fourth and fifth centuries, the creation of an officially Christian Roman Empire prompted monasticism to develop as a structure for preserving a contemplative way of life. With rapid urban expansion and mercantile prosperity, Francis of Assisi reframed the vision of the Gospel to adapt to a new world. The religious orders he inspired were much more mobile than in the past. They were committed to seeking out those not benefitting from the new prosperity of the merchant class from which he came. In the sixteenth century, the invention of printing, coupled with the emergence of nation states, led to a much more educated laity challenging the clerical dominance of the Roman Church. In many ways, it was only with the Second Vatican Council that the Catholic Church realised that it had much to learn from its Protestant brothers and sisters, as well as from the Eastern Churches, if it was to move towards true catholicity.

A slim chapter like this can only suggest a few moments in the long history of the Church as illustrating how, in each generation, the ideas and images offered in the New Testament were rediscovered and reinterpreted to provide a stimulus for reform. Any effort to promote new directions for the Catholic Church in the twenty-first century, whether at the macro level of canon law, or at the micro level of new interpretations of community, can benefit from precedents provided by the past, *if* we can see how new situations demand fresh readings of the vision it calls the Gospel.

The early centuries

For the first two hundred years or so, there was no clear delineation of authority in a movement that was not so much a single institution as an association of regional churches, all of whom claimed to share a universal or catholic faith. Communities met in people's houses. While lists of bishops of Rome start to be compiled by the later second century, their historicity is uncertain. Among various Christian teachers becoming active in Rome after 135, Marcion (84-c. 160) and Valentinus (c. 100-c. 160) established their own churches, but would be remembered by more mainstream figures, like Irenaeus of Lyons (c. 130-202), as too gnostic and intellectual in their tendencies, because they rejected any sense of continuity between Jesus and Jewish tradition. The formation in Rome by the mid-second century of a canonical New Testament, comprising a range of perspectives on Jesus, implies the evolution of a mainstream tradition with collective authority over more partisan views of local communities. Many local churches had their own version of a Gospel (many of which would be rediscovered only in the twentieth century in places like Nag Hammadi in Egypt).

By the mid-third century, churches were developing a common institutional structure to preserve their traditions, and ensure their survival in the face of periodic persecution. Within these communities, mostly urban in character, authority was becoming vested in deacons, presbyters (elders) and bishops.[1] These developments inevitably generated factionalism. In 251, Novatian (d. 258), a senior presbyter and prolific author, claimed election as bishop of Rome. By resisting the election of Cornelius (251-3), Novatian created the first known schism in papal history. As a theologian, Novatian was firmly opposed to all heresy. He was also a rigorist, who refused to give communion to those who had submitted to Rome during the persecution of Decius in 250, even if they repented. He insisted that commitment to the Gospel required refusal to submit to secular law, a position that would continue to cause controversy across the centuries.[2]

Novatian was opposed by Cyprian, bishop of Carthage (c. 200-58), who argued that the great majority of the people and clergy supported the authority of Cornelius as bishop of Rome, and thus as leader of the Church. Cyprian used the image of Christ's undivided tunic to argue that those who had apostasised should be allowed to return to communion. He was a pastor, profoundly moved by a savage pandemic that ravaged the Roman world 249-62, which he describes with great vividness in his treatise, *On the Mortality*.[3] He encouraged his communities to look after the sick and remember the dead, transforming involvement in Christianity within the Roman world.[4]

A core part of Cyprian's argument against Novatian was that Cornelius had been chosen as bishop of Rome 'by the suffrage of the clergy and the people' (*cleri ac plebis suffragio*).[5] Cyprian was voicing a principle that had become established over the previous two centuries. He was looking back to the account, in Acts 6:1-6, of how the first deacons were chosen not by a bishop, but by the community in Jerusalem. Cyprian's appeal to the role of both clergy and people in choosing their pastor countered the practice within the Roman Empire of authority being vested in an autocratic emperor, who relied on the army to assert his authority. He was hearkening back to the formula of the Roman republic, in which laws were decided 'by the Roman senate and people' (SPQR: *Senatus populusque Romanus*), a formula still invoked by the Empire to maintain the fiction of republican government. Cyprian's formula (often with *populus* replacing *plebs*) would be repeated by those Popes concerned to re-assert canon law.

Needless to say, this reference to the people or laity being involved in the choice of bishops would become as much a fiction within the Church as in the Empire. Nonetheless, the theory that a bishop was to be chosen by clergy and people, before receiving the pallium (the symbol of pastoral office) from Rome, remained in place until the reform of canon law in 1917. In the hierarchical society of the medieval West, shaped by that of the Roman Empire, the role of the laity was largely to accept what had been decided by the senior clergy, the new senatorial class of the Roman world.

Clericalism and reform in the medieval Church

The military chaos of the early fourth century resulted in Constantine's lifting of the persecution of Christians and granting special privileges to Christian clergy, above all exemption from imperial taxes. After Constantine moved the capital of the Empire to Byzantium, the Christian churches in the Latin West took over many of the functions of government. Overnight, bishops became civic as much as religious leaders. In major urban centres, clerics took over the entrenched power of the Roman civil service. Within churches, the bishop came to be seen as participating in the priesthood of Christ, with presbyters sharing in the bishop's priestly function. The title of priest (*sacerdos*), familiar to pagans, had been dropped by Jews after the destruction of the Temple in 70 CE, but provided respectability to the Christian community. The title pontiff, originally used for any bishop, derives from *pontifex*, a senior priest responsible for the bridges in a city. The big difference between pagan temples and Christian churches was that whereas only a priest (or in Jerusalem the high priest) could enter a temple, a church was open to all.

Within Christian churches, however, the practice gradually developed of creating a screen behind which the bishop or priest would go, to participate in what was seen as participation in the sacrifice of Christ on the altar (reminiscent of the way only the High Priest could enter the holy of holies in the Temple at Jerusalem). The laity were kept at a distance so they could not potentially pollute the sanctuary. Ecclesial communities took over the structure and symbolism of the Temple and its clergy in the name of representing a New Jerusalem.

The only movement capable of challenging this clericalising tendency was monasticism, which grew out of an ascetic reaction against the way aristocratic families were using clerical positions to re-assert their authority. It started with ascetics fleeing cities and establishing communities in remote regions, especially in Egypt and the Holy Land. Its most articulate exponent in the late fourth century was Jerome (342-420), whose rejection of marriage was supported by powerful Roman widows. These women wanted a way of rejecting marriage as an institution that served to perpetuate dynastic interests in a society where women had few legal privileges. Jerome saw monks as able to resist the snares of clerical corruption.[6] Whereas urban churches focused on sacramental worship, monks emphasised close study of the Bible.

The leaders of monastic communities, both male and female, were chosen by all members of the community. Their election was thus more authentic than that of bishops, who came to be chosen by the canons of a cathedral church (often from prominent families), rather than the whole clergy and people of a diocese. The only way bishops could keep control on monastic communities was through ordaining abbots so that they could celebrate the sacraments. Female monastic communities were always fewer in number, and remained dependent on the local bishop, as women could not be ordained, at least in theory. In practice, monasticism evolved into an alternative kind of clerical structure, defined by a celibate way of life, and distinct from that of normal clergy, whose mission was defined by service to the community rather than rejection of the world. The fourth century thus laid the foundations for the reforms of the late eleventh and twelfth centuries, which imposed a quasi-monastic life-style on clergy in the hope that the move would improve standards among what was called 'secular' clergy.

Many bishops were cautious about ascetics acquiring authority in society by speaking out against clerical corruption. From around 400, Augustine (354-430) started to engage in a continuing polemic against Pelagius, whom he (inaccurately) accused of denying God's grace. Augustine started to develop his doctrine of original sin, namely that the consequences of Adam's sin were so grave for human psychology that even though sin was forgiven through baptism, its effects could only be countered by the continuing infusion of divine grace. Thus Augustine transformed Cyprian's commitment to a conception of the Church as embracing sinners by introducing an increasingly pessimistic sense of human selfishness. Augustine may not have been as enthusiastic for monasticism as Jerome, but nonetheless he encouraged a psychology that was cautious about any expression of sexual desire, and which discouraged any idea of moral perfection in this life.

Monks, clergy, and people in an age of reform

The idea that monasticism provides a valid way of committing oneself to the vision of Christ became, for many centuries, the dominant interpretation of a committed Christian life, certainly between the fifth and twelfth centuries. Gregory the Great (590-604), the first monk to become pope, successfully combined what he saw as the best of Augustine's insights about humanity's need for divine love and forgiveness with recognition of the ascetic principle, that we all have a responsibility to turn to God through our own effort, whatever the hardships we face. Gregory did not speak much about original sin or heresy. He emphasised, for example, the mutual love and respect between Mary of Magdala and Jesus as a model for religious devotion. As a monk, he was troubled by bishops engaging in what he calls simoniac heresy, namely the practice of using money to acquire senior office in the Church. In his *Dialogues*, Gregory presents Benedict of Nursia and Benedict's sister Scholastica as embodying a monastic ideal open to both women and men. He saw them as far more effective than those clerics who had not renounced the world.[7] He insisted on going back to the Gospels to reconsider how the Church should be run.

Pope Gregory's reforming vision had a powerful effect in places like Ireland, where there were none of the entrenched traditions associated with urban centres as in Italy and Gaul. One illustration is offered by Carthach (Carthage in Latin, known as Mochuda in Irish). He was remembered for his concern for lepers, who flocked to his community at Rahan (Co. Offaly) in central Ireland.[8] Late in life, Carthach was forced by various powerful abbots, resentful of his success, to take refuge at Lismore (Co. Waterford) in around 632. His biographer presents him as a charismatic figure who appealed to both men and women. It was just at this time that there was heated argument in Ireland between those who followed a traditional date for Easter and a calendrically more advanced system, promoted in Rome.[9] Carthach belonged to the latter faction, as did Cummian, a brilliant scholar, who appealed to the authority of Cyprian and the great Councils of the Church. This was a way of combining monastic renewal with a vision of the Irish Church as part of a much larger movement, understood as embracing both Eastern and Western Churches. Irish monks travelled as far as Egypt and the Holy Land, even in the early decades of Islamic expansion. Pope Gregory was perceived as promoting a new future for the Church.

This vision of moral reform is also articulated by a short text from mid seventh-century Ireland, *The Twelve Abuses of the Age*, attributed in its earliest manuscripts to Cyprian, whose prose style it imitates. It shares his vision of social responsibility by identifying twelve types who do not live up to their calling: a wise man who does not do good; an old man without religion; an adolescent without discipline; a rich person without almsgiving; a woman without modesty; a lord without virtue; a contentious Christian; a proud pauper; a bad king; a negligent bishop; an undisciplined laity, and a people without law[10] – 'For this way justice is suffocated.' By identifying these abuses, its author was arguing that no-one was exempt from acting responsibly under the law. Because the text was attributed to Cyprian (and in later manuscripts to Augustine), this short text helped shape the moral imagination of the Latin West.

By the mid-eleventh century, lip-service was being paid to Cyprian's ideal that the bishop of Rome should be chosen 'by clergy and people'. Between 1045 and 1048, five candidates from German or Italian noble families vied for the Petrine office. To resolve the situation, the German 'Holy Roman' Emperor, Henry III, secured the election of his relative, Bruno of Egisheim (bishop of Toul) as Pope Leo IX (1049-54).[11] Leo opened his papacy by calling a council at Reims where he proclaimed that all bishops who had obtained their office through financial transaction or simony (the sin of Simon Magus according to Acts 8:18-24) had to resign and receive their appointment from the pope. Leo had to invoke conciliar authority to authorise his reforms, which pitted the papacy against ambitious aristocratic families.

Pope Nicolas II (1059-61) took Leo's reforms a stage further by calling a council at the Lateran, which declared that not just bishops, but the pope himself, should be chosen, not by the Emperor, but 'by clergy and people'. To achieve this, he instituted a College of Cardinals, to represent different ranks of clergy who would elect the pope, prior to the people giving their assent. The pope's ruling, delivered in Council at the Lateran Palace, would be repeated in the twelfth century by Gratian, thus becoming a central document in canon law.

> *When the pontiff of this universal Roman church dies the cardinal bishops shall first confer together most diligently concerning the election; next day they shall summon the other cardinal clergy; and then the rest of the clergy and the people shall approach to give their assent to the new election. (Gratian, Decretum I.23.1).*

The phrase 'clergy and people' is repeated forty-two times within Gratian's *Decretum*, a tribute to the power of a formula that goes back at least to the time of Cyprian, and indirectly to republican ideals. The College of Cardinals attempted to implement Cyprian's principle – that the pope should be chosen by clergy and people – as Gratian reiterated in his *Decretum*(II.7.1.5).In practice, the formula provides little explanation of how the people might exercise that power, except in the acclamation of a pontiff by the assembled crowd.

The first goal of Pope Nicolas II was to remove choice of the pontiff from the control of the holy Roman Emperor. But in creating a College of Cardinals, whatever his intention for involving both clergy and people in the choice of the one who would be their pastor or shepherd, he allowed the original idea to slip from people's minds. Kings and emperors adapted to the reforms by expecting their senior churchmen to become cardinals and represent their interests. And in a society in which the great majority of the population were unable to write Latin, it was a legal fiction to claim that the people could be involved in choosing a pope. A cardinal's role was not to represent a grade of holy orders. His role was to represent different grades of clergy in the church.

The broader reforms of Pope Nicolas II were directed against powerful families securing ecclesiastical positions through simony. While all bishops were in theory meant to be chosen 'by clergy and people', in practice they were chosen by cathedral canons, often belonging to powerful families who wanted to see bishops appointed from their ranks, with their appointment ratified by the pope. These anti-simoniac reforms were enthusiastically supported by upwardly mobile classes, who were unhappy with the way the old nobility controlled senior positions in the Church. Yet it did not take long for these reforms to take a clerical turn by attacking clerical marriage rather than simony. The official rhetoric was always about the importance of maintaining chastity rather than imposing celibacy. In practice, the reforms became a campaign against clerical wives, often labelled as concubines, with very little said about the abuse of minors, which (from occasional reports) was certainly a problem within single-sex communities. By the twelfth century, popes enthusiastically supported churches being run by canons regular, committed to following the Rule of Augustine.

Unlike the Rule of Benedict, the Rule of Augustine recognised the importance of both pastoral care and contemplation. Such Augustinian houses could, however, quickly become wealthy, and could be seen as paying lip service to the Gospel. While they introduced more rational ways of thinking about the Bible and theology, they also served to reinforce rather than challenge clericalism within society.

The reforming vision of the Cistercians and Joachim of Fiore

This reforming vision led to the dramatic growth of the Cistercian Order, established in 1098 as a radical reform of traditional Benedictine monasticism. Its ideals of simplicity and service to the community through promoting a space for contemplation was embraced by female religious communities (like that of Heloise at the Paraclete), even if they did not become part of the established Order, with its institutional requirements of an annual General Chapter.[12] While senior secular clergy were often as wealthy as the families from which they came, monks like Bernard of Clairvaux (1090-1153) – from a knightly class, but not of noble birth – seemed to promote (at least to those from his social class) a more collective vision of religious life. The Cistercian constitution was called 'The Charter of Love' (*carta caritatis*). Like the apostles, their movement expanded through the support of powerful patrons, female as well as male. They saw the Order as offering a vision of the Church as driven by ideals of simplicity and authenticity, and opposing a privileged secular clergy, whose way of life was little different from that of the aristocracy from which they emerged.

In 1163, Joachim of Fiore (c. 1135-1202) was so inspired by Cistercian ideals – of monks retrieving apostolic example – that he quit his position as a lawyer working for the Norman regime in Sicily. Following a visit to the Holy Land, he decided to establish a monastic community in his native Calabria, modelled on that of the Cistercians.[13] He eventually decided to break away from the Cistercian Order so as to pursue his own vision of monastic community. He was also inspired by Greek monasticism, still locally revered in Calabria, although subjugated to Latin authority.

Joachim's hermeneutic genius was to read the Old and New Testaments not in allegorical terms – as about the coming of Christ as an individual, freeing humanity from sin – but as a historical record of the self-revelation of the Father, Son and Holy Spirit in history. Augustine's heavy Christological focus downplayed the role of the Holy Spirit. Joachim (like Hildegard of Bingen, only a generation earlier) gave much more attention to reading scripture, above all the New Testament, as about the working of the Holy Spirit in driving Christ and the apostles. Joachim's triadic vision supplanted the binary tendency of Augustinian (and Pauline) thought, which contrasts flesh and spirit, the Old and New Testaments. Joachim wanted to give equal attention to the three persons of the Holy Trinity in ways he thought accorded with scripture.

He saw history as a series of concordances between different periods of history, for example, between the prophets of the Old Testament and the great monks, like Benedict of Nursia, in the time of the new covenant. For him the unifying element in history was thus the Holy

Spirit. Joachim's reading scripture in terms of the working of the Holy Spirit (rather than focusing purely on Christ) would resonate far beyond the monastic milieu in which they were generated. They would influence more radical groups within the Reformation, and, indirectly, during the twentieth century, in the formulation of Liberation Theology, particularly within the context of Latin America.

Francis of Assisi and Franciscan responses to clericalism

Joachim's awareness of the power of the Holy Spirit was also shared by Francis of Assisi (1181-1226), who broke with centuries of tradition by refusing to become a monk. As the son of a merchant, he realised that the socio-economic structures of Europe were changing, and that religious renewal had to take a different direction from that of previous centuries. Urban prosperity was challenging the traditional social order, under which the nobility used their patronage of wealthy monasteries to legitimise their authority. Whereas monks took vows of stability, changing one's way of life, and obedience, Francis composed a Rule that imposed three vows: absence of personal property (commonly called poverty), chastity and obedience.[14]

The idea behind these three vows was probably not initially his own. The vows had been formulated a few decades earlier by the Trinitarian Order (canons regular, committed to redeeming captives from slavery). Quite possibly, Francis included them at the suggestion of Cardinal Hugolino de Conti (the future Pope Gregory IX), who recognised the radical originality of Francis' understanding of the Gospel, but wanted to find a way of integrating his movement within the established Church. While Francis had little to say about chastity and obedience, he placed great emphasis on poverty, which he saw as the ideal from which the Church had fallen away. Like Jesus in the New Testament and Carthach in seventh-century Ireland, Francis saw lepers as the true children of God, because they had been rejected by society.

The process of establishing cohesion within the movement Francis inspired was not easy, any more than it had been for the movement associated with Jesus. The Order of Friars Minor grew rapidly, in large part because of the charismatic personality of Francis, who always remained a layman, and never took holy orders. He had more difficulty in holding his movement together than did Dominic Guzman, an Augustinian canon, who established the Order of Preachers at about the same time. Dominic promoted values of poverty, humility and love, but did not turn them into specific vows. Both Francis and Dominic promoted the mendicant way of life as more authentically following the Gospel than that of the monks, who pursued a spiritual path without necessarily engaging in pastoral care. The bishops were able to control both religious orders, however, by the power of ordaining friars to the priesthood, and expecting them to be exemplars of chastity and obedience, even if they differed from other clergy in not being able to possess personal property on their own. While both Francis and Clare of Assisi promoted involvement of both women and as men in their Order, they were still perceived as pursuing a quasi-monastic ideal. Only in the later middle ages, with the development of what became called 'the third order', were married men and women considered able to engage in the apostolic mission promoted by both Dominican and Franciscan orders.

The Protestant Reformation

In many ways the fifteenth century was an age of optimism in the Church. Humanists hoped that the Popes would acknowledge the authority of Church Councils as the best way of bringing together the wisdom of the ecclesial community. The failure of the papacy to heed voices calling for reform led Luther and others to abandon hope that Rome could or would engage in meaningful reform. The Protestant Reformation of the sixteenth century was more successful and wide ranging than any previous reform; it harnessed the invention of printing and the expanding literacy of the laity. It also benefited from one of the long-term consequences of the plague endemic in Europe between the mid fourteenth and mid seventeenth centuries. Religious orders were seen as wealthy landowners with few committed members able to preach the Gospel. In consequence, at least in the British Isles, their enormous landholdings were confiscated by the State.

On the continent, the Catholic Church was obliged to introduce its own reforms at the Council of Trent, and recognise the different world that was emerging. It refused to acknowledge or value, however, alternative models of ecclesiastical organisation, such as those offered by establishing presbyters, or convocations that involved laity as well as clergy and bishops. The Roman Church insisted on establishing itself as a clerical institution around a papal court, which could rival those of any princely or royal court. Popes continued to be chosen from a small group of cardinals, who tended to have little communication with the outside world. These were totally male assemblies, attracting clerics who had little interest in marriage. They were entering a large and powerful institution, in which clerics could complain about the ambitions of wider secular society, without engaging in genuine debate about the best way to promote the Gospel.

This is not the place to survey the wide range of directions taken by religious reform since the sixteenth century. In many ways, the American and French Revolutions, each with their own way of reframing the relationship between religion and the state, opened up new opportunities for religious reform movements to prosper. The age of Constantine was finally over. Christianity no longer had any claim to a privileged position of political influence within the State. Industrialisation and mass migration created a new situation, in which religious reform could prosper. Missionaries and religious orders identified new forms of injustice and social division deserving of a Christian response, with a new formulation of what the kingdom of God might mean. Yet there were many who still hankered after an older time, when they saw religion as a stabilising force on the social order.

This is still the case. On both sides of the Atlantic there are those who view new social, cultural and intellectual developments in a negative light, and look to the Bible and an authoritarian Church to resist these changes. In a sense, they espouse an exclusivist vision of the Church, not unlike that of Novatian, rejecting all compromise with the world. While this exclusivist vision may offer security to those who fear the outside world, it is not part of Catholic *tradition*, in the broadest sense of the word.

Conclusion

Movements of reform within Christianity are as multiple and as varied as the stories that were told about Jesus in the first century (only some of which made their way into writing). The situation in the twenty-first century is quite different from that of the thirteenth or sixteenth centuries. Equal opportunity now applies to women as much as men. Sexual diversity is a recognised element of society, creating social conditions very different from those of the time in which Jesus was alive. The message of the *basileia* of God crossing the boundaries of the kingdom of men can now be reframed very differently. The teachings of the New Testament need to be reinterpreted in a host of new ways, as we realise that what we call Christian teachings are the responses of particular communities to the way they understand the teaching of Jesus. This is never a static process. Just as Paul realised that he had to reinterpret the message of Jesus in a Hellenistic environment, so there will be more ways of reframing what Jesus has to say to us within different cultural contexts, shaped by different religious and philosophical traditions.

Within the Catholic Church, the principles formulated by Cyprian in the third century – that the bishop of Rome should be chosen with the support of both clergy and people – continued to be articulated in canon law throughout the medieval and early modern periods, even though no mechanisms were ever implemented to put these principles into practice. The formation of the College of Cardinals in 1059 was a bold attempt by Pope Nicolas II to remove the papacy from undue control by the ambitious families who competed to hold the position of Holy Roman Emperor. In practice, however, Nicholas's initiative only reinforced the development of the papal court (*curia*) as a clerical institution.

The terminology of 'clergy and people', re-asserted by Gratian in the twelfth century, would remain largely ignored within the Church, especially when it polemicised against the evils of democracy in the wake of the French Revolution. It would disappear until the first major reform of medieval canon law was implemented, in 1917, by Cardinal Gasparri. But not in Pius XII's reform, nor in a further reform implemented by 1983 by Pope John Paul II, would there be any acknowledgment of lay participation in the government of the Church.

There is an urgent need for the College of Cardinals to recognise the antiquity of the tradition that requires the bishop of Rome, like any bishop, to be chosen by clergy and people. Involvement of the laity in a plenary council is no more than a return to the oldest traditions of the Church. There is no canonical reason why cardinals, both women and men, cannot be appointed to represent lay people, who are central to the survival of the Church as a community. There is a similar historical blindness with respect to the vows of poverty, chastity and obedience, often assumed to be conditions of all in religious life. In fact, this particular triad of vows was first widely adopted only in the thirteenth century.

Just as the mendicant movement rejected the monastic emphasis on stability, so new vows are needed to formulate religious community in the twenty-first century. Chastity, typified in the image of the Virgin Mary's avoiding all sexual intercourse, needs to be redefined in terms of dignity and respect. Celibacy is not a moral virtue, but a state of being, one that has allowed clerical abuse of minors to flourish, and be covered up by episcopal authorities. To forbid divorcees from receiving communion, as still happens across the Catholic world, is a travesty of the message of the Gospel and Catholic tradition. If Cyprian taught that those who sacrificed to pagan gods, out of fear for their lives, should be allowed to return to communion, how should not the same generosity apply to those whose marriages have failed? One suspects that liturgical rules, as they did in the time of Novatian, are being used politically, as instruments to preserve clerical exclusivism.

Catholicism needs to be awakened to a fresh awareness of its traditions, and a going back to the New Testament. Just as medieval thought was transformed in the thirteenth century by the rediscovery of new perspectives, put forward by Aristotle, so also is contemporary theology shaped by newer ways of understanding the search for wisdom. Changing social and political assumptions will force the Church to reconsider how it defines religious life. We are all called to re-read our traditions afresh, whether those of the New Testament or those of subsequent centuries.

Endnotes

1. For a useful introduction to key documents relating to the early Church, see J. Stevenson (ed.), *A New Eusebius* (London: SPCK, 1957), and for a rich overview, Robin Lane Fox, *Pagans and Christians in the Mediterranean World from the Second Century AD to the Conversion of Constantine* (London: Viking, 1986).
2. Novatian, *On the Trinity*, available at http://www.newadvent.org/fathers/0511.htm.
3. Cyprian, *On the Mortality*, available at http://www.newadvent.org/fathers/050707.htm.
4. There is an excellent YouTube lecture (no author identified), 'The Plague of Cyprian (249 to 262 A.D)' in the History of the Papacy podcast, in the series 'The Study of Antiquity and the Middle Ages'.

5   Cyprian, Letter 51.8 (55.8 in Latin edition) http://www.newadvent.org/fathers/050651.htm and Letter 66.2 (68.2 in Latin edition) http://www.newadvent.org/fathers/050666.htm.

6   For a rich guide to these issues, see for example Peter Brown, *Through the Eye of a Needle: Wealth, the Fall of Rome, and the Making of Christianity in the West, 350-550 AD* (Princeton: Princeton University Press, 2012).

7   Book 2 of Gregory's *Dialogues* is entirely about Benedict as a charismatic figure in sixth-century Italy, available in translation at https://osb.org/gen/greg/tocalt.html.

8   An English translation by Patrick Power of the Life of Mochuda is available at http://www.storyofasoul.com/resources/mochuda.html; for a fuller study of his context, see my study, 'The flight of Carthach (Mochuda) from Rahan to Lismore: Lineage and Identity in Early Medieval Ireland', *Early Medieval Europe* 21/1 (2013), 1-26.

9   Daibhi O'Croinin, who has edited the Latin text of Cummian's letter on Easter, explains its larger significance in https://www.rte.ie/brainstorm/2018/0329/950886-how-the-irish-helped-to-create-easter-sunday/.

10 A critical edition and translation of the *De XII abusivis saeculi*, initially produced by the late Aidan Breen in his (1988) PhD thesis from Trinity College, Dublin, is currently being completed by the author, working with Stephen Joyce.

11 The best guide to this complex history, as indeed anything to do with the popes, is offered by J. N. D.

Kelly, *The Oxford Dictionary of Popes* (Oxford: Oxford University Press, 1986).

12 A useful introductory guide to key sources relating to Cistercians is Pauline Matarasso (ed. and trans.), *The Cistercian World: Monastic Writings of the Twelfth Century* (London: Penguin, 1993).

13 Only certain of Joachim's writings are available in translation; excerpts from various writings are translated by Bernard McGinn, *Apocalyptic Spirituality: Treatises and Letters of Lactantius, Adso of Montier-en-Der, Joachim of Fiore, the Spiritual Franciscans, Savanarola* (New York: Paulist Press, 1979), pp. 97-148, and *Visions of the End: Apocalyptic Traditions in the Middle Ages* (New York: Columbia University Press, 1998), pp. 158-74.

14 For a collected translation of the writings of Francis, see Regis J. Armstrong, *St. Francis of Assisi: Writings for a Gospel Life* (New York: Crossroad, 1994). For more detail on Franciscan vows, see my chapter, 'Apostolic Ideals in the Mendicant Transformation of the Thirteenth Century: From *sine proprio* to Holy Poverty', in *Poverty and Devotion in Mendicant Cultures 1200-1450*, ed. Constant J. Mews and Anna Welch (London: Routledge 2016), pp. 13-31.

Chapter 10

Evangelisation, Ecology and Australian Catholicism

Paul Collins

Everyone agrees that evangelisation is at the heart of the church's mission. Jesus' last message to his followers was 'Go and teach all nations' (Matthew 28:19). In tune with this, the 2021-22 Plenary Council says that the church's primary focus should be 'missionary and evangelising'. The primary task of a missionary church is to be out-going, open to all. To achieve this, Australian Catholics need the facility to speak and relate in ways that make sense of belief in terms of contemporary culture and language. A New Testament example of this is what happened to the crowd of diaspora Jews listening to Peter's first sermon after Pentecost as he proclaimed Christ's resurrection (Acts 2:5-6). Each heard the message in their own native language, even though Peter was probably monolingual. In other words, these 'devout

Jews' heard Peter's message in a way that made sense to them personally.

But this approach was quickly challenged, even within the New Testament church itself, leading to a deep cleavage between the out-going Pauline faction, which didn't subject gentile converts to Jewish practices, and the inward-looking Jerusalem-based James faction. This division was semi-resolved at the Council of Jerusalem in 49 AD (Acts 15), but it is clear that Judeo-Christianity remained the predominant faction and that the Jerusalem council didn't really resolve the problem. Judeo-Christians maintained Jewish observance, lived a kind of sectarian, apocalyptic life style and were connected with the anti-Roman agitation of the Zealots, even after Titus' destruction of Jerusalem in 70 AD.

I have referred to this early church crisis because I think that it has genuine resonance for us today. We have inherited an out-going model of church which is especially reflected in Vatican II's *Gaudium et Spes*, the document on the church in the modern world. This emphasises the need for the church to present revelation in a way that relates and speaks to the needs and aspirations of contemporary culture. But there is always the temptation to embrace the James-sectarian model, and this danger has not been entirely avoided by the Plenary Council, which seems to exist in a kind of church-created vacuum, something like the 'perfect society', the self-sufficient model of church of nineteenth-century Catholic ideology. Despite the Plenary's claims to be 'missionary and evangelising', there seems to be little or nothing, either theologically or sociologically, about mission and how Australian culture and society are to be evangelised. The whole feel is inward-looking.

The problem is that both the Plenary's open-ended primary question ('What is God asking of the Australian church?') and the widespread consultation in which 220,000 people participated, produced a plethora of discordant or semi-connected issues. While these were reduced by the Plenary organisers into six rather bland 'national themes for discernment', there seems to be no coherent process of teasing out the underlying ecclesiological, cultural and sociological issues. Even though the bishops and Plenary administrators have refused to release the 17,457 individual and group submissions they received, we do know that many were focused on aspects of ecclesial governance and structure, which is partly reflected in the second summary topic that the church be 'inclusive, participatory and synodal'.

The most that can be said for the other four topics – including that the church be prayerful, eucharistic, humble, healing, merciful, joyful, hope-filled, open to conversion, renewal and reform – is that they are so nebulous, pietistic and vague as to render them useless for any coherent discussion. They represent sentiments with which everyone agrees, but they are certainly not the basis for a serious discussion leading to reform and renewal.

What I want to do here is to take the topic on evangelisation and analyse it from both a theological and sociological perspective, and then try to articulate some practical conclusions and methodologies for the actual renewal of Australian Catholicism, which I believe will emerge through a serious engagement with the contemporary emphasis on ecology.

Evangelisation was core business for the apostles and early disciples of Jesus. The key operative words were *kerygma*, or the proclamation of the risen Christ, and *catechesis*, which referred to the formation and deepening of faith in Jesus to build up the body of Christ. These words are really two aspects of the same process. Peter's post-Pentecost sermon in Acts 2:14-42 is *kerygma*, the proclamation of the resurrection of Christ. The 'devout Jews' who heard Peter's message ask the apostles 'Brothers what shall we do?' Peter calls them to repentance and baptism, and then 'they devoted themselves to the apostles' teaching and fellowship, to the breaking of bread and the prayers' (2:42). This last verse describes a kind of catechesis, formation in faith in the risen Christ.

But it is Paul who sets the primary pattern for evangelisation in the New Testament. For him everyone is called to salvation. He tells the Galatians: 'There is no longer Jew or Greek, there is no longer slave or free, there is no longer male and female; for all of you are one in Christ Jesus' (3:28). He repeats this for the Colossians: 'There is no longer Jew and Greek, circumcised and uncircumcised, barbarians, Scythian, slave and free; but Christ is all in all' (3:11). In Christ, God is no longer the exclusive possession of one race or nation. To be a Christian is not about abandoning cultural differences, but of transcending 'the ethno-centric sense of the exclusiveness of [one's own] particular group'.[1]

Certainly, for Paul, evangelisation involves taking culture seriously. In Athens, after preaching in the synagogue, he went to the agora every day and engaged 'with those who happened to be there' (Acts 17:17-34). He dialogued with Stoic and Epicurean philosophers with some calling him a 'babbler', while others took him seriously. With them he establishes a relationship at least on a rational level. He was certainly not shy: 'Then Paul stood in front of the Areopagus and said, "Athenians, I see how extremely religious you are in every way. For as I went through the city and looked carefully at the objects of your worship, I found among them an altar with the inscription, 'To an unknown god'. What therefore you worship as unknown, this I proclaim to you. The God who made the world and everything in it, he who is Lord of heaven and earth, does not live in shrines made by human hands, nor is he served by human hands, as though he needed anything, since he himself gives to all mortals life and breath and all things' (Acts 17:22-25). Essentially, this is the kind of apologetic already developed by Jewish thinkers, but, as Marta Sordi says, 'it was by no means foreign to Athenian thinking, especially that of the Epicurean school'.[2]

But then Paul introduces the Christian-apocalyptic challenge. If you are God's off-spring, then you must repent and prepare 'for a day on which [God] will have the world judged in righteousness by a man whom he has appointed, and of this he has given assurance to all by raising him from the dead' (Acts 17:31). Needless to say, 'some scoffed' at this end-of-the-world vision and its reference to resurrection, but others 'joined him and became believers', including Dionysius the Areopagite and the woman Damaris (17:34). Paul's reaction to the Athenians' rejection of the resurrection is interesting. 'He made no attempt to rationalise it or to transform it into a symbolic representation of Christ's moral survival through his teachings, or the lives of his disciples', when this would have been acceptable to his hearers. Rather, he 'simply accepted the decision of the majority of his hearers', but continued to work with those who had faith.[3]

As Christianity emerged from its original Jewish matrix and as apocalyptic expectation ebbed away, how did the church break down barriers to evangelise the broader Roman society? There is no simple answer to this question, although we can discern some of the key issues. Its growth was slow at first, with many of the converts being Hellenised Jews, but by the third century there were increasing numbers of convert pagans. Conversion was facilitated by the stability of Greco-Roman culture, the imperial road system and a reasonably good shipping infrastructure. From about one million in 250 AD, the Christian community grew to more than six million in a total population of around 44 million by 300 AD. Most Christians were concentrated in the eastern provinces of the empire.

Although it was a grassroots movement, what is striking is that Christians were to be found in every class, from the imperial court to slaves. Most conversions occurred through personal contact. People were impressed by the strict moral code of Christians, by the security they experienced from a close-knit church community and by their care for those in need. Tertullian says that pagans commented on 'how [Christians] love one another and how they are ready to die for each other'.[4] The faith appealed particularly to women in a world in which women's role was largely limited to home and family in households dominated by men. Girls were often married at an early age. Infanticide of female offspring was common and abortion widespread. The result was an imbalance in the population; by 300 AD there were 2.5 men to every woman. Homosexuality among men was common.

Christianity offered a different vision. It condemned infanticide and abortion; it discouraged early marriage and giving young girls to older men as brides. Christian women particularly appreciated the support they received from the church community, and they embraced the strong spiritual dimension of faith.

Christianity also offered salvation, but with the price tag of life-long, exclusive commitment to one God, which might eventually involve martyrdom. Paganism, in contrast, was polytheistic; the gods were there to be called on as required. Mention of martyrdom is important because decent people were also impressed by Christian courage in the face of what was often a horrible death. Jesus told his followers that 'If they persecuted me, they will persecute you' (John 15:20), and Paul challenged the Galatians 'to be crucified with Christ' (2:20). Martyrs were witnesses who represented Christ and through whom the Holy Spirit worked. Their faith and refusal to compromise was seen as prophetic, akin to that of the Old Testament prophets. It was the courage that Christians showed and their refusal to compromise, that cut-through to their pagan neighbours; decent people admired their integrity.

But evangelisation was not just limited to personal contact. The early church also mounted a public apologetic defending Christian belief, beginning with Justin Martyr (c.100-c.165). He was followed by several second-century writers who were seen as philosophers and who mounted an explanation of Christian belief in terms that attempted to make sense to their thinking contemporaries. It was 'faith seeking reason', Christian belief explaining itself in terms of Greco-Roman culture. The late-second and early-third centuries were the high point for Christian apologetics. This was the era of Clement of Alexandria (c.150-c.215), Origen (c.184-c.253) and the catechetical school of Alexandria's attempt to meld theology with the dominant Neo-Platonic philosophy and in this way to speak to the culture. It was also a period of syncretistic religious pluralism and tolerance during which 'Christian theology suddenly became fashionable'.[5]

Christianity remained an urban religion until the mid-fourth century. The very word 'pagan' is derived from *paganus* meaning 'countryman'. In the period after Constantine and the Edict of Milan (313), which granted religious toleration to Christians, the evangelisation of rural areas began and Christian landholders were told that they should make sure their slaves and peasants converted.

After the collapse of the Western Roman Empire in the early fifth century, the work of converting the barbarian tribes began. The task lasted for 700 years, and serious questions are now being asked as to the depth of that evangelisation. Some historians claim that it was just the replacement of pagan superstitions by a Christian overlay, perhaps understandable when mass baptisms followed the conversion of the local ruler, or when people like the Saxons under Charlemagne were faced with the choice of either baptism or death. It was in this age that 'christendom' evolved, as the whole of European society, both church and state, conformed to Christianity, which dominated people's lives from baptism to burial.

Sure, there were many Europeans for whom Christianity was culturally liberating and spiritually transforming, for example the erudite monks and nuns in post-Patrick Ireland, but, as Jean Delumeau says, as late as the seventeenth century in Europe, 'the intellectual and psychological climate of the people was characterised by a profound unfamiliarity with the basics of Christianity, and by a persistent pagan mentality with the occasional vestiges of pre-Christian ceremonial'.[6] It is now seriously questioned as to whether rural Europe was ever genuinely evangelised. While on the surface christendom reigned supreme, there was a thriving underworld in which sub-Christian beliefs and pagan folk practices flourished.

Christendom was swept away by the Enlightenment and the French Revolution, but a kind of 'Christendom' survived in pre-Vatican II Catholicism. For instance, in Catholic countries like post-Famine Ireland, the church dominated culture, and, after liberation from the British in 1921, politics and society. The result was that clerics like John Charles McQuaid, archbishop of Dublin from 1940 to 1972, whom John Cooney describes as 'ruler of Catholic Ireland', effectively controlled not only the church, but to a considerable extent even the government of the republic.[7] Reflecting on his own country, Austria, in 1962, theologian and liturgist Josef Jungmann says that in countries where Catholicism was the 'traditional confession' many people felt social pressure to observe religious externalities, but they 'had never given the slightest thought as to what that means'.[8] He distinguished 'conscious' faith from 'unconscious' belief. Unconscious Christians conformed externally and passively. Essentially, their engagement focused around ill-assimilated doctrines from catechisms and strict moral demands, especially in the sexual sphere. In contrast, conscious Christians understood that the externalities were signs and symbols of a genuine interior commitment to relationship with the person of Christ within the community of believers.

In pluralist countries where Catholics were a significant minority, like Australia, there was a kind of private form of 'Christendom' that we called the 'Catholic ghetto'. Dominated by clericalism and under powerful bishops like Daniel Mannix and Norman Gilroy, a kind of external conformity was encouraged rather than a serious and conscientious commitment. Catholicism involved strong identification with the church community, an identification often encouraged by sectarianism.

In a sense, Vatican II was about recovering conscious commitment to faith within the church. Meaningless rules, obscure liturgical forms and historical accretions were jettisoned and Catholics were challenged to recover conscious and committed faith through hearing the Word of God, participatory worship and a spirituality focused on Jesus. The gradual decline in Mass attendance and active participation in the church in Australia shows that, since Vatican II, the reality is that Jungmann's 'unconscious Catholics' have gradually dropped away to become at best 'cultural Catholics'. Unfortunately, the failure of church leadership to implement Vatican II has also led to a large-scale departure of more conscious Catholics, disappointed and frustrated by the destructive clericalism of popes like John Paul II, and of local bishops and other hierarchs.

The process of alienation from the church has been exacerbated by developments in Western society since the 1960s. Fundamentally, what we are seeing is a culture increasingly detaching itself from its Christian roots, even actively repudiating those roots. This manifests, in part, in the way many have turned inward, feeling that they owe nothing to the *res publica*, the public, the common-wealth, the community. With individualism dominant, many feel the world owes them protection and nurturance, but there is no sense of mutual obligation, no feeling of connection, as we live in our own subjective subcultures. This is reflected in public life by institutions like banks and corporations where the bottom-line is the only governing ethic, and in government where political survival is the only moral norm. We only read, talk to and listen to those who agree with us.

While called a 'global culture', the world of Facebook, Twitter, WhatsApp, WeChat, Instagram, and other apps connect us to millions, but the algorithms always point us toward those who agree with us.

Waleed Aly is right when he says 'the very notion of a "public" started rapidly disintegrating while we were busy staring at our phones'. He maintains that we are no longer 'connected', and 'Despite the propaganda of relentless "connection", what's actually happening is that we're living in separate worlds'. The closest thing to a public space that we have 'is a world of endless subcultures'.[9] While the advent of social media is a key factor in this, our communication systems have been breaking down for decades now. Our atomised, subjective, post-modernist attitudes have created what Theodore Roszak called, as early as 1972, 'the anaesthetised eye and ear'.[10]

Back in the church, there are still Catholics who nostalgically long to recover and re-establish Christendom. They are quick to blame 'secularisation' for all the church's ills and failures in evangelisation. But, as Canadian philosopher Charles Taylor has pointed out, 'secularisation' is a multi-faceted, complex word that can be taken in several senses; it resists easy definition. Taylor says that the first form of secularisation is when religion and God are literally formally expelled from the public square and relegated to the private, as in France's policy of *laïcité*, and more recently in the aggressive secularism embraced by the present government of the Canadian Province of Quebec. Public spaces, Taylor says, have been 'emptied of God, or of any reference to ultimate reality'. In a typically post-modern fashion, civil society and the state retreat from questions of ultimate meaning and value. Nevertheless, Taylor says, this is compatible 'with the majority of people still believing in God, and practising their religion vigorously'.[11]

Taylor's second understanding of secularisation is practical. Referring specifically to Catholics, it is when people either actively or, more likely, passively abandon religious belief, practice and the church to become 'ex-Catholics'. Nevertheless, in Europe particularly, there is still a nostalgia for the (medieval) past, and people still visit the symbols of that past – like cathedrals – as tourists, and there is still remnant public reference to God, for example in prayers before Parliamentary sittings.

Taylor's third form of secularisation focuses 'on the conditions of belief'. We have moved, he says, 'from a society in which it was virtually impossible not to believe in God, to one in which faith, even for the staunchest believer, is one human possibility among others... Belief in God is no longer axiomatic. There are alternatives'.[12] Conscious faith is just one free choice among many. The presumption is that religion is fading away as science explains everything and people search for their own meaning structures and ethical norms. Others look for spiritual inspiration in other faiths. The majority have pretty much abandoned the religious search altogether, with a small but vociferous minority seeing faith as particularly toxic. The popularity of Richard Dawkins and his fellow neo-atheists illustrates this trend.

Dawkins and company notwithstanding, Taylor argues that transcendence of self is at the core of religious belief, and that nowadays Western culture, having abandoned its Christian roots, lives with a flat conception of human existence. By that he means that many people today believe that the only kind of transcendence possible is this-worldly; they believe that there is nothing of significance outside human life and are suspicious of claims about spiritual transformation. He calls this the 'malaise of immanence... In a sense, we could sum up the malaise of immanence in the words of the famous song by Peggy Lee: "Is that all there is?" '[13] He's right when he says that many today ask the same question as Peggy did in her 1960s song:

> Is that all there is?
> If that's all there is my friends, then let's keep
>   dancing,
> Let's break out the booze and have a ball
> If that's all there is.

Taylor says that when people today attempt to answer Peggy Lee's question, they often talk about 'spirituality' rather than 'religion' as they assemble their own personal outlook. He sees this search for spirituality in a positive light, especially as the gamut of beliefs widens.[14] In this context, God is seen more like an impersonal force than as a person. People believe without belonging to a church or community. Taylor sees this as moving from Christendom into what he calls 'an Age of Authenticity', as many abandon any permanent church identification, or group or political affiliation.[15]

In addition to issues like secularisation that create challenges for evangelisation, Australian Catholicism's own reputation is currently at rock-bottom due to the sexual abuse crisis, as well as to the institutional church's unattractive, unwelcoming image. Church leaders seem besotted with a narrow range of issues, focusing on gender, sex and reproduction. Catholicism doesn't project an image of a church with an open door, but rather a hard-nosed, unwelcoming, uncompromising institution. The damage done to the church's reputation by bishops and Catholics with a 'boots-and-all' mentality is terrible. Add to that the fact that the church's utterly inadequate response to the sexual abuse crisis has been appalling and any attempt at evangelisation sits in catastrophic territory.

As Father Hans Zollner, papal advisor on protection of minors says, 'The level of trust [in the church] is below zero, and this is devastating for an institution based on trust and faith'.[16] Mention of trust is extremely important. Pope Francis was blunt when writing to the United States Bishops' Conference: 'The Church's credibility', he said, 'has been seriously undercut and diminished by these sins and crimes, but even more by the efforts made to deny or conceal them. This has led to a growing sense of uncertainty, distrust and vulnerability among the faithful... God's faithful people and the Church's mission continue to suffer greatly as a result of abuses of power, conscience and sexual abuse, and the poor way that they were handled'.[17] Francis told the US bishops that 'credibility is born of trust, and trust is born of sincere, daily, humble and generous service to all'. Trust is not restored by a good public relations policy, or by endless apologies that sound insincere. It is restored by humble ministry and service, by following Jesus who washed feet (John 13:1-7).

Regaining trust and credibility is going to be extraordinarily difficult, but without them any form of evangelisation will be whistling in the wind. The chair of the bishops' own Truth, Justice and Healing Council, Francis Sullivan, says, 'There is now simmering anger within the community about the church and child sexual abuse... The very fact that the church was on trial [at the Royal Commission]... speaks of a profound loss of direction, integrity, purpose and meaning... a spiritual wasteland. People say the Church needs to get its house back in order, but I say we have to rebuild the house'. Sullivan is right: Australian Catholicism needs rebuilding from the bottom up.

In the media nowadays, there's really only one story about Australian Catholicism and that's sexual abuse. No matter how much good Australian Catholics do in society, their deeds will remain unreported. And it's hard to shift established media perceptions. Experienced *New York Times* religion reporter, Peter Steinfels, has highlighted the convergence of the way lawyers frame sexual abuse cases and the way a media story is framed. Cases are framed 'in terms of personal injury and wrongdoing'. Steinfels points out that 'the media thrive on personal drama, shocking events implying a larger trend or crisis, identifiable public figures, familiar settings and straight-forward moral lessons'.[18] Add to this the sheer volume of sexual abuse cases and you have what Steinfels would describe as a perfect storm. This is not to deny the reality of the tragedy, but given the church's recent history of priggish righteousness, you can't blame journalists for the negative focus on Catholicism. Throw in old style, anti-Catholic prejudice, which is never far below the surface in the Anglo world, and it's no wonder the church has an appalling image.

So, here we are facing a monumental task of evangelisation in secular Australia, a challenge that doesn't even seem to have entered the purview of those running the 2021 Plenary. Before the gospel can be proclaimed, let alone formation in faith occur, we have a massive amount of recovery work confronting us.

In the contemporary world, evangelisation begins with *pre*-evangelisation. This idea emerged from the experience of missionaries and catechists from all over the world who gathered at the East Asian Study Week in 1962 in Bangkok. Their conclusion was that God's word only took root and grew in soil that had been prepared. That is, there needs to be preparation before the gospel is proclaimed. Otherwise, as Jesus says, the word falls on hard ground, or rock, or among thorns (Matthew 13:18-23).

It was the theologian Alfonso Nebreda who systematised the notion of pre-evangelisation.[19] Initially, it is the creation of an atmosphere that helps secular society understand that a sense of transcendence and belief in an overarching context for life is an integral part of being human. It is no use barging in and banging people over the head with the Bible, the church, or doctrine without preparation and respect for their convictions and commitments. There are two elements in pre-evangelisation: first we need to understand and be able to speak in terms that make sense to the culture and society within which we are proclaiming Christ. Second, we have to look for bridges and openings through which we can find common ground and enter into dialogue with society generally and individuals specifically. Perhaps the best bridge is service, meeting society's needs through ministry and personal contact, and the Australian church is pretty good at that. As Australia's largest charity, the Saint Vincent de Paul Society is an excellent example.

When we look at Australian culture, we are mainly immersed in Taylor's third form of secularisation. Here conscious faith is just one free choice among many. Surrounded by scepticism about religion generally and Catholicism specifically, the church needs believing people who are able to engage with society's preoccupations and concerns intelligently and sympathetically. We are back with Paul in Athens at the altar of the unknown god. As Taylor says, the contemporary West is not a completely alien place to engage with people's search for meaning, with many asking Peggy Lee's question: is that all there is? Genuine evangelisation is about an ability to articulate the questions that people are asking themselves, but have not yet brought fully to consciousness. It's no use answering questions people are not asking, articulating needs the community doesn't experience. The challenge is being part of the culture so we can discern the issues that stir the community at a deep level.

Certainly, part of our task as believers is to offer a critique of societal and cultural mores. No community is perfect and it is a basic function of the gospel to speak and act critically when societal norms clash with evangelical values. But no one will listen and we will be dismissed if we haven't already established our *bona fides* by being an accepted part of the society we criticise.

The other reality we face is that at best pre-evangelisation might impact some people, but that there will certainly be no mass conversions. Jesus himself was not particularly successful. He finally ended up with a small band of followers who largely abandoned him when the crucifixion threatened. Pentecostals and Charismatics seem particularly fond of mass conversion, which in the end is a deceptive form of triumphalism. A profound faith is the product of deep commitment, not superficial enthusiasm.

I will turn now to practical ways in which we can actualise pre-evangelisation.

One immediate place where we can apply pre-evangelisation is in Catholic schools. Most students come from homes that are either weakly affiliated, or unaffiliated with the church. Only a tiny proportion comes from committed Catholic families. There is also an increasingly higher proportion of non-Catholic students in Catholic schools. In 2018 nationally, 72.5% of students in Catholic schools were at least nominally Catholic, 14.9% came from other Christian churches, 2.6% were non-Christian and 7.8% were non-religious.[20] In this context, the primary task of religious education is not catechesis or formation in faith already assimilated, because so few students have that level of commitment, but rather building a supportive, hope and love-filled community, strongly linked to the Christ-like values of compassion, acceptance and forgiveness. Rather than focusing on a kind of exclusive 'Catholic identity', this pre-evangelical approach takes a more open stance and gradually forms students in that ethos. No one should have Catholicism forced on them. There is anecdotal evidence that this is a more effective way of pre-evangelisation than an upfront 'Catholic' approach.

Catholic schools are often harshly criticised by conservative Catholics because they are not mass-producing Mass-goers and supporters of local parishes. But nowadays that is not their primary task. They will be far more effective as places where gospel values and personal integrity are inculcated. Their experiences of liturgy should give students a feel for the transcendent, a sense that there is more to life than individualism and the selfish pursuit of mammon. As someone with long-term experience in the ecological movement, I am still struck with the number of former Catholic school students who are deeply and selflessly involved in environmental activism. At first, I thought I might be deceiving myself until William Lines, an environmental historian with no religious axe to grind and a deep knowledge of the movement, asked me if I'd noticed how many former Catholic school students were committed to action to protect the natural world. What they had picked up from school, almost by osmosis, was a sense of the deep transcendence embedded in the natural world, as well as an active commitment to social justice.

Talk of ecology leads me to the most important and effective way in which the church can engage in pre-evangelisation by linking Christian belief to the major concerns of our culture. Our society is increasingly preoccupied with the environment, global warming and biodiversity loss. Even before the unprecedented bushfires of 2019-2020, Roy Morgan research found that in early-November 2019 '46% of Australians mentioned some form of environmental concern as the most important problem facing the world – nearly three times as many as the 16% who mentioned economic problems'.[21] This is a decisive shift, and to their credit, the churches generally and Catholics specifically have shown awareness of environmental issues. Sure, they are not at the top of hierarchical preoccupations, but a number of Australian religious orders and many ordinary Catholics and Christian communities have made serious environmental commitments. Catholic religious education has done good work in this area, and a number of Australian theologians have written thoughtfully on ecological theology. In fact, the Catholic record on these issues is closely aligned with broader societal concerns.

The Catholic position on ecology has been enormously strengthened and expanded by Pope Francis' 2015 encyclical, *Laudato Si'*. Francis has been uncompromising in his support for environmentalism, species protection and the overwhelming scientific consensus on global warming. In *Laudato Si'*, Francis articulates what the French philosopher and sociologist Edgar Morin describes as, 'a complex view that is global in the sense that it... takes into account the relationship among all the parts'. In a time of fragmented thought, Morin says the pope takes a very integrated approach and calls us to 'awareness, inciting us to rethink our society, and a call to act'.[22] *Laudato Si'* says simply: 'Rather than a problem to be solved, the world is a joyful mystery to be contemplated with gladness and praise'.

Even more important than Francis' repudiation of much of the politics, economics, technology, capitalist theory and denialist rhetoric of the post-modern world, is the theological and philosophical revolution that he points towards. Few seem to have noticed his radical questioning of human dominance over nature, and the way in which he reintegrates humankind back into the biological matrix from which we first emerged by emphasising the biological connectedness of all reality. 'A good part of our genetic code is shared by many living things', Francis says. He has no sympathy whatsoever for anthropocentrism, saying that 'the Bible has no place for a tyrannical anthropocentrism unconcerned for other creatures'.

The word 'anthropocentrism' crops up regularly in the encyclical, usually in a negative context; he talks of 'distorted anthropocentrism', 'excessive anthropocentrism' and 'misguided anthropocentrism'. He re-enforces negativity to anthropocentrism by saying that 'nowadays, we must forcefully reject the notion that our being created in God's image and given dominion over the earth justifies absolute domination over other creatures... [Rather] this implies a relationship of mutual responsibility between human beings and nature'. This is precisely the way in which modern science views our place in nature. The pope has bridged the religion/

science divide giving us a firm cosmological ground upon which we can enter into dialogue with our culture.

He is particularly critical of the loss of biodiversity: 'The great majority [of plants and animals] become extinct for reasons related to human activity. Because of us, thousands of species will no longer give glory to God by their very existence, nor convey their message to us. We have no such right'. He refuses to see 'different species merely as potential "resources" to be exploited, while overlooking the fact that they have value in themselves'. 'Nature', he says, 'cannot be regarded as something separate from ourselves, or as a mere setting in which we live. We are part of nature'. Leaving out the God-references, we could be reading the Harvard biologist Edward O. Wilson's splendid book *The Future of Life*.[23] 'We are part of nature.' This is a message that runs right through *Laudato Si'*, as Francis radically re-situates and re-roots humankind in the natural world.

What we need to recover within Catholicism is the deep tradition of seeing the natural world and the cosmos as revelation in the full and proper theological sense of the word. On this Saint Thomas Aquinas is unequivocal. He says that the cosmos is revelation because God is the creator of everything. 'You find traces of the Trinity in every creature', he says in the *Summa Theologiae*. 'Every creature... shows forth [something of] the personality of God the Father... and represents the Word [Christ], just as an artistic work represents the creativity of the artist, and reflects the Holy Spirit in so much as She is love.'[24] Essentially, Thomas is saying that everything in the cosmos conjures up a reflection of its Creator and therefore the whole of creation is an icon or sacrament of God. He regularly returns to the notion of God as the *artifex* (artist or craftsperson) of the cosmos: 'God acts just like an artist in creating things, working from an idea conceived in the mind and from a love which bends the will to that work'.[25]

Thus, when we come to dialogue with our contemporaries, we have strong theological grounds on which to find common cause and to base moral obligations to protect nature. Catholicism has already developed a moral theory focusing on social justice calling for equitable treatment of all. Clearly the same applies to natural justice and in *Laudato Si'* Francis attempts to integrate environmental ethics with social justice. Until now, the Catholic emphasis has been almost entirely on social justice. Francis is trying to rebalance this by focusing *equally* on the environment. He sees the two as intimately interconnected. 'There can be no ecology', he says, 'without an adequate anthropology.' Everything is inter-related. This is close to the essence of his message.

Nevertheless, the pope says that 'a misguided anthropocentrism need not necessarily yield to "biocentrism", for that would entail adding yet another imbalance, failing to resolve present problems and adding new ones'. I am not so sure of that. There will always be tension between human beings and the environment, especially when, as now, we face massive world over-population. To protect the natural world, I would argue that *the* primary ethical principle has to be the protection of the earth and nature, because without them we will be homeless. As Francis says, the natural world is not derived from us and, I would add, transcends us. We have to move beyond an anthropocentric to a biocentric ethic. While *Laudato Si'* tries hard to keep ecology and social justice together, I'm not sure that it succeeds. The reason is because I don't think you can, much as I would like to think otherwise. The primary moral emphasis has to be on the earth; the natural world comes first.

All of these issues make sense to our contemporaries. They are questions that are debated in scientific, political, social and economic circles. The church must enter into these discussions, not as an institution with the definitive answers, but simply as a community of believers willing to ask and confront the questions. It is the questions that will give us common ground, so that our fellow citizens are aware and appreciate the fact that we are not afraid to tackle the hard issues with them. It is through this kind of dialogue that human relationships are built and that together we can come to a deeper understanding of the problems confronting us. The gift that we as Christians bring to this discussion is explicit reference to the transcendent aspect of nature, to the way in which the natural world is a symbol and sacrament of that which reaches beyond human experience and which gives a broader context to our lives.

Genuine Catholic faith is always rooted in communication with the material world. 'God so loved the world' that 'the Word became flesh and dwelt among us' (John 3:16 and 1:14). God literally assumed human flesh in Christ and entered intimately into the stuff of the world, into matter. That is what the incarnation means, what Saint Paul means when he says that God 'made him [Jesus] to be sin who knew no sin' (2 Corinthians 5:21). The word 'sin' here refers to the fact that God in Jesus knew our weakness, failures, mistakes, vulnerability, illness, frustration, fear, despair and the frightening knowledge that we will eventually die. The incarnation means that God didn't resile from anything human. What pre-evangelisation demands of us is that we recover ways of speaking to our society about these issues at the heart of our faith. In our world the most effective way of doing this is through connecting ecology with belief and theology, so that we are able to speak to our fellow citizens about what is mutually most important to us all.

This is the real challenge that the Plenary Council faces, and it is the only way in which we will save Catholicism in Australia from degenerating into a sect. And sects are the absolute antithesis of all that is genuinely Catholic.

Endnotes

1. Marta Sordi, *The Christians and the Roman Empire* (London: Groom Helm, Engl. trans., 1983), 157.
2. Sordi, *Christians*, 158.
3. Sordi, *Christians*, 159. Sordi's whole treatment of Christianity and Roman culture is excellent. See 156-170.
4. Tertullian, *Apologeticus*, 39,7.
5. Sordi, *Christians*, 164.
6. Jean Delumeau, *Catholicism Between Luther and Voltaire. A new view of the Counter-Reformation* (London: Burns & Oates, Engl. trans., 1977), 176.
7. John Cooney, *John Charles McQuaid. Ruler of Catholic Ireland* (Dublin: The O'Brien Press, 1999).
8. Josef Andreas Jungmann, *The Good News Yesterday and Today* (New York: Sadlier, Engl. Trans., 1967), 9.
9. Waleed Aly, *The Age*, 3 January 2020.
10. Theodore Roszak, *Where the Wasteland Ends: Politics and Transcendence in Post-Industrial Society* (New York: Doubleday, 1972), 91.
11. Charles Taylor, *A Secular Age* (Cambridge, Mass.: Harvard University Press, 2007), 2.
12. Ibid.
13. Taylor, *Secular Age*, 311.
14. Taylor, *Secular Age*, 507-513.
15. Taylor, *Secular Age*, 514.
16. *The Tablet*, 6 February 2020.
17. Letter of Pope Francis to the United States Conference of Catholic Bishops, 1 January 2019.
18. Peter Steinfels, 'The Media as a Source for the History of Catholic Sexual Abuse in the United States', *Studies*

105 (2017), 434
19 Alfonso Nebreda, *Kerygma in Crisis?* (Chicago: Loyola University Press), 1965.
20 Paul Collins, 'God and Caesar in Australia', *Australian Book Review*, March 2018
21 Roy Morgan, 4 November 2019. Finding No. 8184.
22 *La Croix*, 23 June 2015.
23 Edward O. Wilson, *The Future of Life* (New York: Knopf, 2002).
24 *Summa Theologiae*, I, q 45, a 7. Author translation.
25 *Summa Theologiae*, I, q 45, a 6. Author translation.

Chapter 1.1

Interreligious Relations in Multicultural Australia

John D'Arcy May

Universalism is out: in different parts of the world, politicians are denouncing globalism and espousing nationalism. Supranational organisations are suspect; populists, demagogues and other types of authoritarian leaders are putting national interests first, withdrawing from international trade arrangements and undermining democracies by cynical manipulation of institutions, constitutions and social media. As so often, these developments have parallels in the religious sphere: ecumenists are looked upon as hopelessly out of touch idealists; fundamentalists are rallying support from the credulous faithful. This is true not only in the 'health and wealth' churches of Africa, South America and the Pacific Islands, but also among Christians in Europe, North America and Southeast Asia.

Nor is Australia immune: our prime minister belongs to a Pentecostal church that keeps spiritual experience carefully separate from ethical issues such as the humane treatment of asylum seekers and environmental destruction. And the same tensions are manifest within the Catholic Church: younger clergy seem oblivious of the reform movement initiated by the Second Vatican Council and their congregations take refuge in supposedly traditional ritual and narrow interpretations of doctrine. How did it come to this? There is undoubtedly a loss of nerve brought about by the sexual abuse scandals and the public scrutiny to which the church has been subjected, but in what follows I will argue that these are merely symptoms of a crisis that goes much deeper, and is in essence theological.

Anecdotally, one hears of parish priests who have never read Vatican II's Decree on Ecumenism (*Unitatis Redintegratio, UR*) and of seminary students who are shocked to discover its Declaration on the Church and Non-Christian Religions (*Nostra Aetate, NA*). Yet these documents, together with the Declaration on Religious Liberty (*Dignitatis Humanae, DH*), basing themselves on the unprecedented Dogmatic Constitutions on the Church (*Lumen Gentium, LG*) and the Church in the Modern World (*Gaudium et Spes, GS*), were at the cutting edge of what promised to be a root and branch reform of church teaching, structure and practice. As we know, the reform was largely thwarted by revisionist elements in the Curia and the episcopate, encouraged by the hesitancy of Paul VI to approve of artificial contraception, the grim determination of John Paul II not to make concessions to liberationist or pluralist theology, and the ingrained conservatism of Benedict XVI.

This is not the whole picture, as we shall see, but as a preliminary sketch it sets the stage for an assessment of just how 'ecumenical' the Council's heritage has proved to be. If in the 314-page preparatory document for the Plenary Council, *Listen to What the Spirit is Saying to the Churches*, interreligious dialogue is not even mentioned,[1] there is a huge blank in the thinking of a church that is supposed to be engaging with a secular, pluralist, multicultural and multireligious society.

The picture, of course, is not entirely bleak. The Australian Catholic University has conducted successful international conferences on comparative theology, of which more below, and the Archdiocese of Melbourne has produced an impressive program for interreligious dialogue in schools, which references official church documents on the subject.[2] There are a number of local and state-wide Councils of Christians and Jews and wider ecumenical and interfaith bodies. Progress has been made, admittedly from the very low base of pre-conciliar condemnation and rejection of non-Catholics and, inasmuch as they were adverted to at all, other religions. The long-standing policy of mission to convert the Jews was officially abandoned, but otherwise all that was not Catholic was subject to missionary activity on the premise that only the Church possessed saving truth; this mentality has only reluctantly been complemented by interreligious dialogue.

Polite conversation and theological curiosity are immeasurably preferable to the condescension and hostility of former years. Yet I cannot forget how Robin Eames, the former Archbishop of Armagh and (Anglican) Primate of All Ireland, called these polite exchanges 'teacup ecumenism': one socialises, but one makes no concessions. Keeping one's identity intact takes priority over all else. Eventually, professional ecumenists – those who travel the world sitting on interdenominational and interfaith commissions – begin to talk of 'sharpening one's confessional profile', just as their political counterparts speak of reasserting national identity, often coupled with a Christian (or Hindu, or Buddhist, or Muslim) inheritance which must be defended against pluralism and multiculturalism. This is all very understandable, from a sociological point of view if nothing else; but it conveniently sidesteps the deeper issues thrown up by the differences – at times open conflicts – between Christian and other religious traditions at a time when the persecution of Christians is more widespread and intense than at any other period since the first Christian centuries.

Part of this failure of nerve goes back to the compromises that had to be reached in order to promulgate the Vatican Council documents at all. This is not the place to rehearse the history of the Council once again, but a few points need to be made. One of the most controversial issues as preparations for the Council began was the Church's relations with the Jews. The proposal, put forward by Cardinal Bea, to draw up a document on the Church's relations with other Christians was difficult enough, and in any case the Council was not the place to address the Church's part in the tragic history of the Jews in Europe. This was close to John XXIII's heart as a result of his wartime experience and his conversation with the French Jewish scholar Jules Isaac, whose family were victims of the Holocaust. On the other hand, a separate document on Judaism would have caused anxiety among bishops from the Middle East, who had to deal with tensions between their countries and the State of Israel. Arab governments were also alarmed: was the Vatican indirectly legitimising the State of Israel? After much acrimonious debate, culminating in the 'October crisis' in 1964 when the conservatives attempted to wrest control of the document from Cardinal Bea, the solution was to formulate two separate documents, one dealing with Christian ecumenism (UR) and another on relations with other religions *including* Judaism (NA).[3]

The problem with that was that Judaism, as the 'root' that supports the 'branches' grafted on as the Christian movement spread among the gentiles (Romans 11:17-18), is not simply one of the 'other religions' for Christians. In the words made famous by Pius XI, we are 'spiritually Semites': the Jewish tradition of prophets, poets and lawmakers is an integral part of our heritage, so that we venture to call the Hebrew Bible, the literature of the Jewish people, *our* 'Old Testament'. For centuries Christian theology proclaimed that the Church had *replaced* unfaithful Israel as the bringer of God's salvation ('supersessionism'). It was central to Pope John's and Cardinal Bea's intention, not only to get rid of the 'teaching of contempt' that had blighted the Catholic liturgy for so long and helped maintain the anti-Jewishness which gave legitimacy to persecutions and eventually the Holocaust, but to assert the continuing legitimacy of the Jewish religion. In the words of St Paul: 'I ask, then, has God rejected [God's] people? By no means!' (Romans 11:1).

The Council's statement on the Jews (NA 4) thus sits among the unprecedented and initially unintended positive assessments of a selection of the world's religions. Here the Church 'acknowledges that, according to the mystery of God's saving design, the beginnings of her faith and her election are already found among the patriarchs, Moses, and the prophets... The Church, therefore, cannot forget that she received the revelation of the Old Testament through the people with whom God in [God's] inexpressible mercy deigned to establish the Ancient Covenant' (NA 4, quoting Romans 11:17-24). Stated more baldly, this implies that Christianity receives its revelation through a non-Christian religion and stems from a non-Christian, the Jew, Jesus of Nazareth.

Despite the transformations it went through in its subsequent history, Christianity is Jewish to its roots.[4] The doctrine of incarnation states not simply that the Word was made flesh, but that God became a Jew.[5] The American Catholic scholar of Jewish-Christian relations, John Pawlikowski, draws the conclusion: 'The theological about-face on the Jews at Vatican II represents one of the central theological developments at the Vatican Council. Unfortunately its full significance has not yet been realised'.[6] It calls for a revision of Christian theology and a reassessment of Christian identity. Pawlikowski develops his argument by drawing three further conclusions: '1) that the Christ Event did not invalidate the faith of Israel; 2) that Christianity is not the fulfillment of Judaism as is traditionally claimed; and 3) that Christianity must re-incorporate dimensions of its original Jewish matrix in its contemporary expression of faith'.[7] He points to the 'profound Christological implications' of the abandonment of missionary outreach to Jews, and he continues:

> *The extent to which we create theological space for Jewish faith, against which Christianity had defined its identity, to that extent we moderate, albeit implicitly, the absolute claim of Christian faith... recognizing that the New Testament is not as totally 'new' or as fully 'complete' as we once glibly proclaimed, is to moderate, however implicitly, the classical Christological vision.*[8]

'*Nostra aetate*', he concludes, 'obliges Christian theologians to rethink their ecclesiology... to recognise the lack of fullness in the Church and the incompleteness of the order of redemption'.[9] One might add: Christology itself will be in need of reconceptualisation if the centrality of Judaism is taken seriously. Not many have taken up the challenge.

It is easy to overlook the implications Pawlikowski has discerned, because *Nostra aetate* is embedded in a matrix established by *Lumen gentium*, the Constitution on the Church. This takes the form of concentric circles, with the Catholic Church at the centre as the mediator of divine revelation and the indispensable means of salvation, though the concession was made after heated debate that *the* Church 'subsists in' rather than 'is' the visible institutional church (*LG* 8). This tiny crack of light opened up the possibility of acknowledging the ecclesial reality of other churches in the Decree on Ecumenism, for 'some, even very many, of the most significant elements or endowments which together go to build up and give life to the Church herself can exist outside the visible boundaries of the Catholic Church' (*UR* 3). The Council then moves on to evaluate the ecclesial traditions of the Orthodox East and the Protestant West according to their approximation to the Roman Catholic norm (*UR* 13-23). The same pattern applies to the Constitution on the Church (*LG* 15-16). Thus it is no surprise that *Nostra Aetate* is structured in exactly the same way: the search of humankind in every age to find spiritual meaning is acknowledged, more explicitly in the case of Hindus and Buddhists. Muslims, as heirs of Abraham, are given special recognition (*NA* 2-3), issuing in the landmark statement: 'The Catholic Church rejects nothing which is true and holy in these religions' (*NA* 2).

The fact remains, however, that this same Catholic Church is presented as the ultimate and, in the end, the *only* fully endowed means of salvation. In terms proposed by the Anglican theologian Alan Race in 1983,[10] this amounts to a progression from the 'exclusivism' of Catholic teaching up to this point to a position of 'inclusivism', for inasmuch as these religions 'reflect a ray of that Truth which enlightens all men' (*NA* 2) they are not *ipso facto* excluded from the possibility of salvation but may be included within the scope of the Church's saving presence. In short: they are salvific to the extent that they participate in Catholic fulness. Even before the Council, Karl Rahner had referred to members of other faiths as 'anonymous Christians'. At the time, this was a bold move, and because of it the Council was ahead of the World Council of Churches, which was still seeking a basis for interreligious dialogue that would not affront its more conservative, and therefore exclusivist constituents. But it was also felt by many to undermine the basis of mission, and from today's perspective it is obvious that it was merely a starting point, more likely to offend adherents of other religions than to foster relationships with them.

The further step identified by Alan Race was to acknowledge a genuine *pluralism* of religions and their theologies, such that no single one of them is uniquely true and thus superior to all the rest. As the American Catholic theologian Paul Knitter pointed out, 'truly' does not necessarily mean 'only', and he called on his fellow-theologians to 'cross the Rubicon' and move beyond the safe haven of inclusivism to the further shore where a multitude of religious traditions, *including one's own*, may be complementary and commensurable.[11] Many theologians, such as Hans Küng and Jürgen Moltmann, were reluctant to take this step, and it goes without saying that the guardians of orthodoxy in the churches rejected it out of hand as 'relativism'. Josef Ratzinger, as president of the Vatican's Congregation for the Doctrine of the Faith and later as Benedict XVI, was particularly exercised by what he saw as the 'dictatorship of relativism' spreading throughout the post-modern West and corroding the certainties enshrined in the Church's teaching. Addressing an audience of Latin American bishops, he said that, having dealt with the liberation theologians, it was now time to turn their attention to the pluralists, mentioning Knitter by name. The Declaration of the CDF *Dominus Iesus* (2000) reinforced this position by asserting the 'unicity' of the Church as the 'unique' mediator of revelation and saving faith, what a German Catholic commentator called 'meliorism' (from Latin *melior quam*, 'better than').[12] In the eyes of many respondents, such a stance would spell the end of both ecumenical and interreligious dialogue.

In a way analogous to the encounter of persons, there needs to be a recognition of the inalienable autonomy of the Other as the basis for recognising one's own autonomy, in the expectation that this recognition will be reciprocated. In other words, the encounter has an ethical dimension, and this carries over to the encounter of religious traditions. Each bears witness in its institutional, scriptural or cultural 'face' to the uniqueness of its 'personality', a uniqueness that needs to be acknowledged if real communication is to take place.[13] Each Christian tradition has its 'confessional inhibitions', its own particular reasons for being wary of the commitment to its Others in interreligious dialogue, especially if such commitment seems to acknowledge not just diversity but a religious and spiritual validity of the other tradition *equivalent to our own*. This, of course, underlines the continuing need for ecumenical dialogue among Christians, which could reveal unsuspected resources to be shared with others as they confront the diversity of the religions together. In practice, of course, many of the same inhibitions bedevil relations among Christians themselves. Given this context, it is not surprising that the Catholic Church's involvement in relations with other religions has definite limits: whatever gestures of recognition are made, nothing must endanger the uniqueness *and superiority* of Catholic identity.

The question to be asked at this point is: is this caution justified? It is certainly understandable in view of the centuries-long history of distrust and hostility among religions, especially but not exclusively those of the so-called 'Abrahamic' monotheistic traditions (Judaism, Christianity and Islam). But in a world in which globalisation of various kinds has opened the religions up to one another, so that members of virtually all religious traditions are aware of most of the others and have immediate experience of them, it is becoming downright dangerous for *any* tradition to claim superiority because of its possession of ultimate truth. Let us be under no misapprehension: they – we – *all* do this in one way or another. But in a number of cases this meliorism has been reinforced by doctrinal or structural or ethical fundamentalism, a failure of imagination that clings to particular scriptures, authority structures or practices as alone valid and normative.

When we think of the Christian manifestations of this, whether in the distant past (persecution of the Jews, crusades against Muslims, execution of heretics) or in the present (denial of science, intrusive proselytism); when we are astonished at the vehemence of religiously fuelled Hindu or Buddhist nationalism (India, Sri Lanka, Myanmar); when we watch the spread of Wahhabi Islamic rigorism in countries formerly as tolerant as Indonesia, and its apotheosis in the misguided violence of Islamic State, then we realise that interreligious dialogue is much more than a polite exchange at a discreet distance. It is an engagement with difficult but fundamental issues of meaning, truth and ethics whose outcomes could affect human and ecological survival. If this is the case globally, it is even more so in a multicultural country like Australia, a settler society where the unresolved relationship with the original inhabitants and the land itself uneasily underlies all other ecumenical efforts. This relationship is analogous to the unresolved relationship to the Jews as an unacknowledged brake on ecumenical openness.

The inclusivist teaching of Vatican II left the Catholic Church stranded at the threshold of true universality, which is to say: catholicity (from Greek *kath'holon*, 'orientated to the whole'), the dimension in which its unity and unicity are fulfilled by becoming open to the whole of human and cosmic reality, including and especially the religions.[14] The Council's biblical language sometimes approaches this threshold:

> *So it is that this messianic people, although it does not actually include all men [sic]... is nonetheless a lasting and sure seed of unity, hope and salvation for the whole human race... While she transcends all limits of time and of race, the Church is destined to extend to all regions of the earth and so to enter into the history of mankind.*
> (LG 9)

Beautiful as it is, this language is fundamentally ambivalent. The 'new People of God', to which all are called to belong, blurs the boundaries of what would formerly have been called the Catholic Church as hierarchically, sacramentally and juridically constituted: 'among all the nations of the earth there is but one People of God, which takes its citizens from every race, making them citizens of a kingdom which is of a heavenly and not an earthly nature'. 'This characteristic of universality (*universalitatis character*)' or 'catholicity' (*huius catholicitatis*) is 'a gift from the Lord', and 'All men [sic] are called to be part of this catholic unity (*catholicam… unitatem*) of the People of God, a unity which is a harbinger of the universal peace it promotes' (*LG* 13).

Let us not minimise the impact of this entirely fresh way of speaking about the Church. It was generous and outward-looking, an offer of hospitality to those who were disposed to be open to the divine Word made visible in Christ. But what it was really saying was that 'the Catholic Church strives energetically and constantly to bring all humanity with all its riches *back to Christ its Head*' (LG 13, my italics). In the background of this language is the relationship of the Church to the people of Israel from which it stems, and underlying that is the tribal language of a people struggling to assert itself in the hostile environment of rival tribes and nations, each claiming to belong to the most powerful god of all. The way from polytheism (many gods) through henotheism (there are many gods, but ours is the first, *henos*, 'number one') to arrive at monotheism (the true God – our God – can only be One, *monos*, 'one alone'), which leads through the historical books and the psalms to the prophets, is long and torturous. It has bequeathed to Christianity and Islam a universalism that encompasses the whole of creation, surely an asset in a time of ecological crisis, but it is symbolised in the figure of a jealous God who brooks no rivals.

Pluralism, however, has its own problems, not necessarily the ones that make church authorities uneasy, but problems to be taken seriously nonetheless. Unlike the other two categories, exclusivism and inclusivism, which may fairly be called descriptive, pluralism has been presented as a *theory* of interreligious relations, indeed as the only logically coherent account of them. We owe a debt of gratitude to the British philosopher-theologian John Hick, who – to borrow Kant's phrase acknowledging the influence of David Hume – 'awakened us from our dogmatic slumber' by proposing his 'Copernican revolution' in the theology of religions. It is not that the other religions revolve around Christianity as their centre (the concentric circles model of Vatican II): rather, *all* the religions revolve around the one God, or, in the terminology he deployed later in his career, religion consists in the journey from the unreal to the Real.

This involves some huge assumptions, however, about the nature and knowability of this Real, which is modelled on the inaccessible *noumenon* of Kant's metaphysics.[15] The result is an extremely abstract conception that does not seem to correspond to what any religion regards as the object of worship and celebration. Believers in any given tradition are asked to transpose, as it were, the content of their faith onto this meta-level before they can deduce what they might have in common with others. Ground-breaking as it was, this approach does not seem to do justice to the way religion actually works in historical and social contexts: theory has gone well ahead of religious sensibility and practice. Paul Knitter has acknowledged the value inherent in each of the three categories, modifying them and adding a fourth to accommodate the wealth of religious experience, while Gavin D'Costa, vigorously defending inclusivism as a valid position for Catholic and other theologies, accuses the pluralists themselves of being exclusivist in the way they insist on the superiority of their theory.[16]

Most recently, Perry Schmidt-Leukel has introduced a new perspective into the debate by utilising the theory of 'fractals' developed by the mathematician Benoît Mandelbrot to describe apparently irregular repetitive patterns in nature. In geometry such patterns may be repeated with strict exactitude, but in nature they are found everywhere in somewhat looser form, in the shape of leaves, the contours of coastlines, the structure of ice crystals and so on. Schmidt-Leukel proposes that something similar applies to the religions. Quite independently of one another, historically they have evolved comparable forms of belief, such as faith and works in Christian theology and 'other-help' (*tariki*) and 'self-help' (*jiriki*) in Amida Buddhism.

All the major traditions have internal 'confessional' divisions roughly corresponding to those of Christianity: Sunni and Shi'a in Islam, Theravada and Mahayana in Buddhism, Shaivism and Vaishnavism in Hinduism, to name only a few obvious ones. The patterns Schmidt-Leukel identifies hold good interreligiously, intrareligiously and intrasubjectively for individual believers. More fundamentally, Schmidt-Leukel suggests that the central conceptions of enlightenment, incarnation and prophecy may be found, though in quite different forms, in *all* the major religions. This means that the Buddha, the Son and the Prophet, the central figures of Buddhism, Christianity and Islam, each contain aspects of the others. There is thus no need to construct abstract theories of pluralism; we can explore the interrelationships of these and other religions by sifting through the empirical evidence available to us.[17]

This would seem to approximate to the other recent innovation in the field of interreligious relations (though it has a previous history going back to around 1700): the 'comparative theology' practised and inspired by Francis Clooney SJ. Clooney's meticulous examinations of Hindu and Christian texts cautiously identify themes and formulations which may be equivalent, but he refrains from drawing general conclusions that would amount to a theory of religious pluralism.[18] Schmidt-Leukel, on the other hand, insists on moving beyond the texts and other evidences of religious diversity to formulate a comprehensive account of their interrelationships. His 'fractal' theory is no doubt an important step forward, but it is not yet clear how it deals with the immense variety of human religious reality, in particular the 'primal' religion of indigenous peoples, which invariably forms the matrix in which the religiosity of the 'universal' traditions, with their scriptures and philosophies, develops and diversifies.

These are not deliberations which one would expect to find in the documents of an ecumenical council, much less at the plenary council of a national church. Yet they touch on questions of fundamental importance, as another key document of Vatican II attests. The Declaration on Religious Liberty, *Dignitatis Humanae(DH)*, which like *Nostra Aetate* began life as a chapter of the Decree on Ecumenism but was eventually voted on as a separate document, gave rise to more controversy than any other Council text. Although, as it says itself, 'Religious freedom has already been declared to be a civil right in most constitutions, and it is solemnly recognised in international documents' (*DH* 15), the Catholic Church had combated and condemned this principle throughout the modern period. Where the Church was in the minority, as in Australia or the USA, it demanded the right to maintain its own schools and determine the ethical policies of its hospitals; but where it was in the majority, as in some of the Latin countries and Ireland, it arrogated to itself a leading role in political life and made only grudging concessions to minority religions.

The prospect of a Council document affirming the dignity of the human person and the primacy of freedom in matters of religion, both private and public, met strong resistance from those who were at home in the old order. The crux of their opposition was that such a teaching would represent a departure from traditional theology and practice, in other words, a development of doctrine, which the document itself explicitly confirms: 'in taking up the matter of religious freedom this sacred Synod intends to develop the doctrine of recent Popes on the inviolable rights of the human person and on the constitutional order of society' (*DH* 1). The Declaration, in fact, takes further the rather general statement on freedom as an exceptional sign of the divine image within man [sic]' in the Constitution on the Church in the Modern World (*GS* 17). *GS* notes that 'It is highly important, *especially in pluralistic societies* (*ubi societas pluralistica viget*), that a proper view exist of the relation between the political community and the Church' (*GS* 76, my emphasis).

As a prelude to developing this line of thought, the Declaration states a simple but fundamental principle: 'This Vatican Synod declares that the human person has a right to religious freedom', which implies that all 'are to be immune from coercion' in matters of religion (*DH* 2). The affirmation of religious freedom as a right inherent in the dignity of the human person, of course, opens up a Pandora's box of complicated issues, as the present controversies about proposed legislation in Australia testify. Nor does the Council shy away from the relationship of freedom and truth. Though 'every man [sic] has the duty, and therefore the right, to seek the truth in matters religious', it is 'to be sought after in a manner proper to the dignity of the human person and his [sic] social nature', which in turn implies that 'he [sic] is not to be forced to act in a manner contrary to his [sic] conscience' (*DH* 3). Significantly, as critics such as Hans Küng and Paul Collins have frequently pointed out, there is no mention of freedom and rights *within* the Church, but to accept that these exist in pluralist societies is an enormous advance on previous teaching.

Though the document does not explicitly do this, it is here that we rejoin the discussion of religious pluralism. By 'truth' *DH* means the truth of divine revelation, entrusted to the Church (*DH* 9). Asserting the right to religious freedom entails acknowledging that there are those who seek truth elsewhere, and their right to do so; that is, that there *is* indeed truth in other religious and non-religious traditions (see *GS* 20-21 on atheism, culminating in the important statement: 'All this [i.e. the restoration of the divine likeness in humankind through Christ's paschal mystery] holds true not only for Christians, but for all men [sic] of good will in whose hearts grace works in an unseen way', *GS* 22). This is in fact an ancient teaching going back to the Church Fathers, based on the universal salvific will of God to lead all creation, including humankind with its religions, to salvation. But it has always stood in an uneasy balance with the equally ancient teaching that this salvation can only come about through the Church, which is the repository of revelation and the universal means of grace (*extra ecclesiam nulla salus*). It is precisely this uneasy balance that runs through the Council and problematises the role of mission and evangelism, to reappear here in the context of civil and religious liberty.

A fundamental reason for the Church's unease with modernity is its failure to come to terms with the Enlightenment. Johann Baptist Metz rightly said that the only way to do this is to *go through the Enlightenment*, to take seriously the civil and human rights, the commitment to social justice and democracy, in short: the freedoms that the Enlightenment sought to incorporate in the structures of national and global civil society.[19] In the twentieth century, the Catholic Church went a long way towards promoting these values in the social and political spheres after overcoming its traditional reservations about them. But in its own internal structures they are still largely absent, and there has always been a disconnect between Catholic social teaching and the dogmatic theology that is supposed to support it.

Both at the Council and in its aftermath, there was a strong consensus that ecumenism must never imply the relativising or relinquishing of what has been handed down as truth; in the Catholic interpretation, *the* truth of faith. But as Metz also insisted on many occasions, this conception of doctrinal truth with its implications of absolutism and meliorism was intrinsically sectarian, notwithstanding the size and extent of the Church as institution.[20] At an even deeper level, this doctrinal solidity has been fatally compromised by the centuries of Catholic anti-Judaism which prepared the ground for the Holocaust, and by the positions taken or not taken by German Catholics and their leaders as the Nazis set out to exterminate Europe's Jews on an industrial scale.

The tragic inadequacy of Pius XII's response, which saw in the Nazis a bulwark against the 'godless communism' of

Russia, highlights once again the strange mixture of theology and diplomacy that characterises the Vatican's political role: *ipso facto* political, but in intention pastoral. The absence of the Jews from traditional Catholic theology comes into focus once more. One does not offer one's victims a dialogue: one listens in humility and repentance.[21] Only then, when the relationship to the Jews has been clarified both historically and theologically, can any ecumenical or interreligious initiatives by Christians stand on firm ground. For many years after Vatican II 'ecumenism' was regarded as a purely internal Christian strategy for bringing divided churches closer; what Hans Hermann Henrix calls 'the presence of Judaism in Christian theology' was completely overlooked.[22] More recently, this has been corrected to a certain extent, but the fundamental significance of Christianity's Jewishness is still not fully appreciated.

Ecumenism is not simply tolerance, though this, an important part of the Enlightenment heritage, is the kindergarten of democracy, the indispensable first step towards responsible pluralism. Full acceptance of the liberal political and moral order established in our democracies is the next step, but the encounter of the religions goes well beyond mere liberalism. Though they seem increasingly irrelevant, as what the Catholic philosopher Charles Taylor calls 'exclusive humanism' becomes the taken for granted coinage of civil and ethical discourse, the religions and their interrelationships tap into the deepest levels of human experience, the search for meaning which drives people to pose the fundamental questions and cling to hope in the face of political oppression, gratuitous warfare and ecological destruction. The religions dare not abandon their own search for mutual understanding and reciprocal witness, but first they must all teach one another how to overcome their deep-seated reservations about really opening themselves to their respective Others.

We may envisage, not the abstract pluralism of liberalism, but an *interactive* pluralism which would lay bare the sources of religious truth in human suffering, confrontation with death and the celebration of life and beauty. Doctrinal orthodoxy has its part in preserving the testimony to revealed truth handed down by tradition, but only lived commitment, *praxis*, can validate it and make it accessible to others whose doctrinal, legal and ethical categories are different from ours. The matrix of the dialogue of religions is not liberalism but liberation; it does not compel us to abandon or relativise truth but to deepen it as we engage with others. To repudiate this and choose the alternative of fundamentalism is to start down the path to violence, and the complicity of the religions in violence is perhaps the major objection of our contemporaries to religion in any form.

Prime minister Scott Morrison, parroting the views of Donald Trump, recently declared that national interests now take priority over globalism, and the former treasurer and ambassador to the United States Joe Hockey casually announced that 'The US has basically torn up the whole multinational framework... Relationships now are overwhelmingly bilateral, not multilateral'.[23] In the light of the global crisis visited upon us by the corona virus COVID-19, this and the US Republican nostrum 'government is not the solution to our problems, government is the problem' seem cruelly ironic. Even if it is national governments that must now fight off the threat, viruses do not respect national boundaries – or sensitivities.

The multinational organisations set up after the Second World War, especially the UN and the EU, are now more necessary than ever, but they are widely regarded as obsolete and marginal, and the high-minded philosophies of justice and peace that inspired them are also being abandoned. This sorry situation has nothing directly to do with ecumenism, but its acceptance is a sign of the times. Interreligious dialogue seems irrelevant in such a framework, a marginal activity without any impact on human and ecological wellbeing, which themselves are relegated to secondary importance in favour of commerce and competition. Celebrating diversity seems a futile exercise when the shocking depths of global poverty and inequality are being revealed and democratic freedoms are being compromised. Just as Australia itself faces the challenge of avoiding crude nationalism and isolationism by remaining committed to an international order based on cosmopolitanism and cooperation, so the Catholic Church is challenged to live up to its ancient name and embrace, in doctrine and practice, the *oikoumene*, the 'household' (*oikos*) of men and women of all ethnicities and faiths over the whole inhabited earth.

The Vatican Council confronted the Church for the first time with the full implications of religious and political pluralism. The Church can only offer a theology wounded by Auschwitz, the atrocities of its absolutistic past and the abuses of its shameful present, but for this very reason it should be fully aware of the dangers of religious intolerance and its potential for violence. The others, including both Judaism and Islam and even Hinduism and Buddhism as well as traditions such as Shintoism and Confucianism, are invited to confront their own complicity in violence and oppression. Here they would have to face the shadow side of their spiritualities and doctrines, which could become the *real* common ground of humility and repentance.

What has variously been called the 'authority of the poor' or the 'consensus of the suffering' underlies and in a sense relativises all the certainties of doctrine, as we have seen in the exposure of clerical sexual abuse. But on this basis a more honest church and a stronger society could be built. Hardly any other member of civil society in Australia is better placed to contribute to this than the Catholic Church. If the Plenary Council takes up and develops the legacy of Vatican II, there is a fair chance that these deeper relationships could be achieved. But it is a very big 'if'.

Endnotes

1. Patrick McInerney, Editorial, *Bridges* No. 85, December 2019.
2. *Welcoming Each Other: Guidelines for Interfaith Education in the Schools of the Archdiocese of Melbourne*, Ecumenical and Interfaith Commission of the Catholic Archdiocese of Melbourne, 2018. The Commission has also produced brief but comprehensive guidelines on *Promoting Interfaith Relations* which quote the more positive statements of recent popes.
3. The most recent detailed account of these debates is to be found in Hans Hermann Henrix, *Irael trägt die Kirche. Zur Theologie der Beziehung von Kirche und Judentum* (Münster-Berlin: LIT Verlag, 2019), 17-27. Henrix also documents the abandonment of the 'mission to the Jews', 161-173.
4. Rabbi Fred Morgan remarked during a discussion in the focus group on comparative theology at Australian Catholic University that the Lord's Prayer is the New Testament text most easily translated into Hebrew, because it is entirely Jewish.
5. On the theological significance of Jesus' Jewishness, see Henrix, *Israel trägt die Kirche*, 177-200.
6. John Pawlikowski, 'Vatican II's Theological About-face on the Jews: Not yet fully recognised', *The Ecumenist* 37/1 (2000), 4-6, 4.
7. Pawlikowski, 'About-face', 5.
8. *Ibid.* Here Pawlikowski recapitulates arguments developed more fully in his *Christ in the Light of Christian-Jewish Dialogue* (New York: Paulist Press,

1982), and *Jesus and the Theology of Israel* (Wilmington, DE: Michael Glazier, 1989).

9 Pawlikowski, 'About-face', 6.

10 Alan Race, *Christians and Religious Pluralism: Patterns in the Christian Theology of Religions* (London: SCM, 1983; rev. ed. 1993).

11 Paul F. Knitter, *Jesus and the Other Names: Christian Mission and Global Responsibility* (Maryknoll: Orbis Books, 1996), 72-83. See also the papers from the 'Rubicon conference', John Hick and Paul Knitter, eds., *The Myth of Christian Uniqueness: Toward a Pluralistic Theology of Religions* (Maryknoll: Orbis Books, 1987).

12 Ottmar Fuchs, Plädoyer für eine ebenso dissensfähige wie ebenbürtige Ökumene', Michael Rainer, ed., *'Dominus Iesus': Anstößige Wahrheit oder anstößige Kirche? Dokumente, Hintergründe, Standpunkte und Folerungen* (Münster-Hamburg-London: LIT Verlag, 2001), 169-195. Fuchs uses the somewhat inelegant term *Meliorität*, which he distinguishes from straight-out *Superiorität*, 173. See also John D'Arcy May, 'Catholic Fundamentalism? Some Implications of *Dominus Iesus* for Dialogue and Peacemaking', Rainer, *'Dominus Iesus'*, 112-133, and the Australian study by Patricia Madigan, *Women and Fundamentalism in Islam and Catholicism: Negotiating Modernity in a Globalized World* (Oxford et al.: Peter Lang, 2011), especially chapter 3 and the testimonies of Muslim and Catholic women, chapter 6.

13 The analogy is with the philosophy of the Jewish thinker Emmanuel Levinas, that the face of the other person immediately confronts us with the

imperative 'Thou shalt not kill', thereby awakening us to our own uniqueness.

14 I developed this further in John D'Arcy May, 'Realised Catholicity: The Incarnational Dimension of Multiculturalism', *The Australasian Catholic Record* 76/4 (1999), 419-429.

15 Hick, from an Evangelical background, early in his career wrote *Christianity at the Centre* (London: SCM, 1968), but his appointment to the University of Birmingham in one of Britain's most multicultural cities prompted him to reappraise his view of the status of Christianity in *God and the Universe of Faiths* (New York: St Martin's Press, 1973), and in his Gifford Lectures, *An Interpretation of Religion* (New Haven: Yale University Press, 1989) he embraced a full-blown and radical pluralism.

16 Paul F. Knitter, *Introducing Theologies of Religions* (Maryknoll: Orbis Books, 2002) gives an even-handed and innovative treatment of the various theologies, classifying them as 'replacement', 'fulfilment', 'mutuality' and 'acceptance' theologies, while in Gavin D'Costa, Paul Knitter and Daniel Strange, *Only One Way? Three Christian Responses to the Uniqueness of Christ in a Religiously Plural World* (London: SCM, 2011) we find a lively debate about the merits of different approaches.

17 We can follow the discussion that Schmidt-Leukel's Gifford Lectures, *Religious Pluralism and Interreligious Theology: The Gifford Lectures – An Extended Edition* (Maryknoll: Orbis Books, 2017), initiated in the volume edited by Alan Race and Paul Knitter, *New Paths in Interreligious Theology: Perry Schmidt-*

Leukel's *Fractal Interpretation of Religious Diversity* (Maryknoll: Orbis Books, 2019). The full scope of Schmidt-Leukel's thought is to be found in his *God Beyond Boundaries: A Christian and Pluralist Theology of Religions* (Münster: Waxman, 2017).

18 A good introduction to Clooney's thought, before tackling his detailed comparative studies, is his *Comparative Theology: Deep Learning Across Religious Borders* (Chichester: Wiley-Blackwell, 2010); he engages with Schmidt-Leukel in Race and Knitter, *New Paths*.

19 Johann Baptist Metz, ‚Kirchliche Autorität im Anspruch der Freiheitsgeschichte', Johann Baptist Metz, Jürgen Moltmann, Willi Oelmüller, *Kirche im Prozeß der Aufklärung. Aspekte einer neuen ‚politischen Theologie'* (München-Mainz, Kaiser-Grünewald, 1970), 53-90.

20 Metz, Kirchliche Autorität', 80-81.

21 Johann Baptist Metz, ‚Christen und Juden nach Auschwitz. Auch eine Betrachtung über das Ende bürgerlicher Religion', *Jenseits bürgerlicher Religion. Reden über die Zukunft des Christentums* (München-Mainz: Kaiser Grünewald, 1980), 29-50, 33-35.

22 Henrix, *Israel trägt die Kirche*, 127-139.

23 *The Age*, 17 January 2020.

Conclusion

From Clericalism And Hierarchicalism Towards Regeneration And Reform

A Change of Paradigm

Berise Heasly

Clericalism is a stance seemingly popular among its adherents for its rigidity, absolute certainty, reluctance to distinguish between ideology and faith, and resistance to regeneration and reform – even in the face of the 2018 Royal Commission findings into scandalous clerical sexual abuse in Australia, findings echoed around the Catholic world. The rigidity of stance has been particularly noticeable among some clergy, and even some laity, since the Second Vatican Council ended in 1965. It partly derives from the rigidity of the doctrine of 'ontological change', that is, an altered state 'bestowed' upon the ordinand by the sacrament of ordination, and before *he* is assigned a parish or other missionary responsibility. And after ordination, *he* is expected to be immediately able to minister, and be equipped with all manner of expertise in areas pertaining to the care of the faithful, those whom we call the laity – *us*!

Clericalism has a number of elements: a belief in the pre-eminence of those who have received the sacrament of ordination (but who may, nonetheless, be unable to read 'the signs of the times'); a stress on dogma rather than listening to human distress; a resort to simplistic piety rather than walking with the persons (the laity) called the People of God, and a tendency to intervene rather than respect those who are pursuing a personal relationship with Jesus through the gospel stories and good exegetical development and study – those I have called 'People in the Pews' (see Heasly, *Call No One Father*, 2019). It is important, in the interests of inclusiveness, to recognise that the term 'People in the Pews' includes those who have hung on to the practice of their faith even in the face of the betrayal and distress caused by clerical sex abuse and appalling cover-up behaviours. However, the term also embraces those who have been so traumatised by that same pain and destruction of the soul that they have walked away.

In countering clericalism, we need to distinguish between traditionalism and Tradition, a distinction carefully drawn by Brother Mark O'Connor FMS (*Catholic Outlook*, 14 February 2020). He reminds us that an educator 'can never be an ideologue, for ideologues can never "instruct the ignorant", or "educate in faith" since they do not dialogue with learners but talk "at" them'. Expanding his theme, he identifies the need to give people 'a healthy sense of their Catholic identity or imagination... to help us all live in a postmodern relativistic culture and understand that there is a rationality to Christian faith'. O'Connor cites Pope John XXIII as a model teacher, one who 'opened the windows' of the Church, a Christian educator who 'instructed the ignorant'. O'Connor's last comment is a telling one: he stresses that Pope John was 'not a humourless ideologue who alienated and frightened people away from Christ, the Merciful One'. O'Connor follows and expands then on the concept of 'ideologicalisation' that Massimo Faggioli (e-book, *The Church in a Change of Era*, 2019) has introduced.

The 2019 Amazonia Synod was attended by 185 bishops and other significant clerics. They gathered to discuss the difficulties facing the Church in the various cultures of the Amazonian countries. At issue was the vexed question of the dearth of sacraments available for the peoples of each of those countries. There was also much focused discussion of the degradation of the forests of the Amazon River Basin, and the effects of rapid biological decline and manipulation of forest ecologies – a matter that seemed to be central to Pope Francis' response, and fittingly so. However, discussion did not satisfactorily address the evangelisation of those vulnerable First Peoples, or consider an updating of priestly formation to make it fit to serve the real-life needs of the People of God in the twentieth century.

We are aware, of course, that Francis is emphasising the importance of decision-making at the level of synodal gatherings, but when a request is made for increased diversity in the priesthood, and consideration of inclusion of women priests and married priests, then to refuse to address that request is suspect, and unsustainable (see Beattie, T. and Pepinster, C., both in *The Tablet*, 22/2/20). Furthermore, the pope's response, couched in terms of wishing to avoid 'clericalising' women, seems a clear example of an admission that men priests *are* 'clericalised'. Marie Naudascher, ('*La Croix International*', 17/2/20) is reported as accepting that Pope Francis has allowed 'the faithful to dream'! By contrast, the Wijngaards Institute for Catholic Research (12 February 2020, press release), analyses the stance of Pope Francis on women deacons in the following sharp terms: 'The Pope's refusal to consider the ordination of women rejects the explicit recommendation of the Synod on the Amazon'.

When Francis justified his unilateral decision by saying that he did not wish to 'clericalise women', my first reaction, I have to say, was that his reply was a dereliction of duty. 'His position cannot be justified unless and until the Pope also declares that no more men should be recruited for the ministry so as not to "clericalise" them', declared the Wijngaards writers (17/2/20). And I agree. However, it will be interesting to watch developments as requests come in to Rome for the establishment of a new commission, comprised of scholars from outside the realms of the Curia, chosen for their diversity, their expertise and their knowledge rather than their hostility to women. I shall wait to see whether we have no choice but to agree with the final statement of the Wijngaards news release: 'Pope Francis' decision perpetuates gender discrimination that denies women the dignity and respect to live out their vocations and be recognised as critical to the equal leadership of Church communities as the peers of, not servants of men'. (I was reminded, after reading that statement, of theologian Uta Ranke-Heinemann's harsh treatment for her independence of mind, and her published history of women's treatment by the Catholic Church. But that is a story for another time and place.)

In fairness, though, we (and I) should concede the possibility that we have misread the thrust of *Querida Amazonia* and the subtlety, or diplomacy, of Francis' style of writing. Perhaps he is resisting binary thinking patterns by not favouring one side or other of the debate over priestly celebration of Eucharist and delivery of the Sacraments. If so, he may be being cagey enough to allow space for an historic opportunity for participants of the Bishops' Conference – all 185 of them – to take up their responsibility in servant leadership, the consequence of which would be that they *themselves* would have to make the decisions regarding married priesthood and women deacons and women priests. A first in the history of the Catholic Church in Synodality mode! And the decisions would have to apply for the dioceses within their governance boundaries!

That would require personal courage, advanced trilectic thinking patterns (that is, using and prioritising options at all times as the foundation of decision-making – see Heasly, *Towards an Architecture for Teaching of Virtues, Values and Ethics*, 2015), considerable debating and discussion skills, and wide knowledge of the gospel, where we meet the Jesus message. It would require exegetes to be at the centre of this crusade, attending to the Cry of the Poor. To be 'married' to the Cry of the Earth carries with it the responsibility to attend also to the Cry of the Poor. The Amazonian Bishops' Conference must accept their leadership opportunity as a given and as a gift. This gift is from the Will of Sophia-Spirit, who wishes us to be as co-creators of the Will of the Holy Trinity and living in twenty-first century.

In *Catholic Outlook* (29 February 2020), Daniel Palmer made a point that had escaped me previously. Palmer notes that Pope Francis, as the first pope from the Americas (born 1936 in Buenos Aires), is only too aware of what 'our brothers and sisters in the Amazon are *actually* experiencing: political exploitation, hunger, marginalisation, and ecological disaster'. In fact, Palmer comments, Francis understands that what these peoples need is food! Palmer then identifies something we should all recognise: 'a rather odd form of clericalism that affects many progressive Catholics, one that allows us to chime in with Francis about the problems of a clericalist Church, yet still believe that the main solution to the problems in the Amazon is ordination (to priesthood) of more people'. This recognition contains its own challenge because Francis is emphasising the Cry of the Poor and the Cry of the Earth as equal in weight for the People of God, those I have called the 'People in the Pews'. Francis has provoked me to see a distinction here, a priority that is a direct consequence of his preference for the poor and their *real* needs, as well as a priority for the careful listening required when we try to understand cultures so different from our own. And a further priority: we can no longer turn a blind eye to the raging misogyny in early Christianity (see it laid out for us by Chris Geraghty in his book *Virgins and Jezebels*, 2020) because still we experience it, and in such a pronounced fashion today.

Hierarchicalism is a stance marked by an almost cultic emphasis among the clergy, and particularly among young seminarians, and ambitious priests and bishops who have consciously chosen careers (or who have been earmarked by ordained men further up the ladder of importance within the organisation of the Catholic Church) for the sake of the power, control and deference that comes with position. This can be seen in some episcopal appointments. The Catholic Church structure is such that it can offer ambitious men authority, deference, prominence, political acceptance and a luxurious lifestyle. Elevation can quickly become the goal, rather than the careful study and practice of the elements of pastoral care, administrative transparency, and efficiency, all of which are the right and expectation of the 'People in the Pews', in other words – *us*! An emphasis on pomp and ceremony, accompanied by external show of holiness and an assertion of ontological exclusiveness can then take precedence over proper knowledge and understanding of how life is lived in twenty-first-century communities all over the globe. How can one reconcile the church's obsession with saints – attaining sainthood, having it conferred etcetera – in a world of such need? I am reminded that Richard Rohr (2013), in one of his 'Underlying Themes' for daily meditations, is reputed to have written that: 'there is only one Reality. Any distinction between natural and supernatural, sacred and profane, is a bogus one' (Meditation 33 of 49). I would add a parallel: the distinction between the status of Holy Orders and Baptism is unreal and bogus too.

Hierarchicalism becomes toxic when it translates into the power of men, centrally chosen, who direct the lives of the laity in culturally diverse dioceses all over the world. This power to rule has become divorced from the real-life needs and lives of the twenty-first century laity. Even the use of the term 'laity' is suspect: it is a convenient label that allows for the glossing over of contentious issues like diversity of gender in church governance. And no great show of mercy (called for so urgently by Pope Francis) is evident in the exercise of the power over the laity.

The emphasis on the power to rule also isolates the hierarchical church from another phenomenon of recent centuries: that of cumulative and universalised education and specialisation in the many humanities disciplines, as well as the remarkable research and scientific discoveries of our world. New knowledge can be overwhelming in its scope, depth and impact; the laity however have no choice but to explore, discern, reflect, absorb, and where necessary, change, if they are to live full and productive lives in their own times. But in episcopal circles? In episcopal circles all talk and no action is still well entrenched.

This is so very evident in the information that the Polish hierarchy wish to appoint John Paul ll a Doctor of the Church. In his *Love and Responsibility* (1982) we find the following: 'For the purposes of the sexual act, it is enough for her to be passive and unresisting so much so that it can even take place without her volition, whilst she is in a state in which she has no awareness at all of what is happening, for instance when she is asleep or unconscious.' (Wojtyla, 1982, p. 271). The interpretation of 'responsibility' in these writings of John Paul ll in this volume is insulting to women, and appallingly unaware of woman as a being created in God's image by a loving Creator. One wonders also at the obsessive emphasis on the apparent cult of personality. We are better served by Federico Lombardi SJ, whose paper in *La Civiltà Cattolica* (10 March 2020), titled 'Women and Men in the Church', draws attention to the writings of Anne-Marie Pelletier. Lombardi alerts us to her focus on relationships between men and women in the Church, referring in particular to *Pacem in terris* (John XXlll's 1963 encyclical): 'John XXlll has rightly identified the new awareness of the dignity and responsibility *of women* and men [my emphasis] as one of the main issues' of Vatican Council ll.

Hierarchicalism is on full display in the nature of preparations being made for the Australian Bishops' Plenary Council (originally to be held in Adelaide in October, 2020, now postponed). Small, specially selected groups are preparing material to be discussed under six topic headings (six distilled from the thousands of submissions). Each of the six discussion groups is to be led by a bishop. Elimination of many of the pressing issues raised by the laity in their submissions has been achieved by a small group subject to the Bishops' authority. This procedural high-handedness shows disdain for, if not ignorance of, proper process. It also spotlights a fear many have that some very significant and complex topics are apparently beyond the ken of the reigning Bishops and their confreres. The hierarchy might be controlling the process, but they seem to be bypassing much that is of real anxiety for the 'People in the Pews'.

Regeneration will depend on growth and development of better understanding, theological precision, general knowledge and wide learning, especially through the contribution of science in recent centuries. Regeneration is intrinsic to the message of Jesus: we are tasked through our Cosmic Sophia-Spirit with the responsibility of renewal consistent with the various balances of virtues, values and ethical behaviours relevant to the communities in which the 'People in the Pews' live their daily lives (see Heasly, *op. cit.* 2019). Again, we must not forget that the concept of 'People in the Pews' is deliberately broad, covering those who grit their teeth and try to be loyal in practice, but also those who, for painful reasons, have walked away or disengaged from the present practices in parish life.

Regeneration is built on growth in understanding and an acceptance of a paradigm change that does not subvert the message of Jesus, but re-interprets the way his message is to be lived out. If it is to be thorough, regeneration will take into account the remarkable contributions in various fields of science over the last one hundred and fifty years. We must carefully absorb, critique and learn from disciplines like neuroscience, nuclear medicine and other medical technologies; we must be aware of developments in psychiatry, psychology, environmental ecology, quantum physics, cosmology, archaeology, artificial intelligence, and robotics; we must take note of the work of theologians like Karl Rahner and Denis Edwards, and be alert to the presence of the Spirit in Vatican Council ll.

Regeneration will entail our finding ways to confront the ethical implications of some new industrial developments – the effects of hydro fluorocarbons for example. It will require us to find ethical ways to manage the transition from fossil fuel industries, and assist in the development of ethical, sustainable alternatives. We must not sit by and endorse a current tendency to allow every kind of innovation without regard for environmental consequences. This means that our church leadership must be fully *involved*, learning along with those who research and innovate, and being alive to the possibility of risk and mistake, confident in the will of Sophia-Spirit. A new paradigm will emerge as new knowledge from all fields of the secular domain is brought to the service of faith in the message of Jesus. This should not cause confrontation, rather an expansion, a breadth in trilectic thinking terms (Heasly, 2019, p. 117, describing decision-making) and a move away from binary thinking that chooses one 'side' of a contentious question and outlaws the opposing stance ('heresy' is the term we have used). The acceleration of this evolution is the work of Sophia-Spirit, readying us to become co-creators in the next stage of the history of the evolution of our planetary home and our progress towards our Cosmic Creator God, through Jesus, by the Will of Sophia-Spirit.

We must not forget, either, that the superiority implicit in rigid church teaching, with its insistence on being 'right', has done appalling damage to all First Peoples. In *Dark Emu* (2019 edition), writer Bruce Pascoe, echoing many other revelatory Indigenous and settler authors, illustrates the extent of damage done to Australian Aborigines and their way of life all over this island continent. In Pascoe's account, tribes and clans managed industries, built homes, used art and craft, interacted with other tribes and clans all over the land, and practised a version of a federation of states and territories, boundaried by song-lines, for thousands of years before the advent of men from the Northern Hemisphere, who thought they could subdue any Indigenous civilisation, in the belief that they (and we?) were superior beings. No wonder the suffering of many Aboriginal people of today is so entrenched. We ruined their management practices all over this continent, and we have the gall to throw money at them, provided they are sufficiently far from us, and we add to the insult by telling ourselves we only need to make a public apology. Our regeneration as humans must include a righting of this wrong, because it is part of our legacy too.

Gerald Arbuckle, in *Abuse and Cover-Up* (2019), has provided a detailed analysis of a church and its people in trauma. Bishops' Conferences don't seem to be conscious of the extent of trauma experienced around the world by Catholic laity – the 'People in the Pews'. That trauma is too often dismissed, or denied, even as abuse and cover-ups are brought to light. Arbuckle talks of 'refounding' the Church in twenty-first century terms. He has developed a complete set of Action Plans, addressing and analysing cultural dynamics (seemingly unknown to episcopal figures, especially in the Curia). He identifies the grief that is at the seat of the trauma, and apparent in every culture of our globalised church. It has led him to explore leadership for the church, focusing on servant leadership, but also identifying other leadership styles. Trauma dismissed is an evil that the Church must address, urgently. And the address must extend to human tragedies in the form of priestly or ministerial mental and emotional illnesses that lead to cessation of ministry and eventual death. Only then can regeneration flower according to the will of Cosmic Sophia-Spirit in this, our third millennium.

Reform in this context will require us to identify the areas where canon law, dogma, doctrine, and the various practices of liturgy and faith have failed to take account of the new knowledge and disciplines that should inform transparency, accountability and good governance for the Catholic Church and make it relevant in twenty-first-century terms. The necessary reform measures are ably and succinctly developed in *Getting Back on Mission* (2019) put together by the Council of Catholics for Renewal. From a different, but equally important perspective, Gerald Arbuckle (in *Abuse and Cover-Up*) provides us with his action plans, which allow us to explore that important area of adult learning success – process. He insists there must be space and time to investigate, to test, and to do the work of real, not false, discernment. Arbuckle shows courage and clarity, respect and responsibility in his naming of the very wide-ranging challenges that we must address. In collaboration with our few remaining priests and the administrative arm of our church, we must proceed with careful understanding of cultural elements within liturgical reform. We must *not* subside into adversarialism, because such stances do little to promote mercy and understanding.

It is urgent that transparent and radical care of the planet (the 'Cry of the Earth') be shared by every follower of Jesus through deliberate changes in our daily lives. That urgency must be demonstrated in our immediate remedial care of the various areas of our dying planet that are in such desperate need of rejuvenation. It must be accompanied by wholehearted acknowledgment of the presence of the will of our Cosmic Creator God in the evolution of human life over the last one hundred and fifty years. Transformed by new knowledge, we must contest the deliberate use of power over peoples by despots, secular and sacred (the 'Cry of the Poor'). We must accept our responsibility for the predatory destruction of so much of our planet. It is time to de-emphasise the 'dominion' angle and substitute the conservation and development of our world, including the use of what is today so disdainfully termed 'waste'.

Discussion: This paper is an overview in auto-ethnographical style (see Heasly, *Towards an architecture for the Teaching of Virtues, Values and Ethics*, 2015, chapter 5) of some ways in which we as the laity can address, compare, discern, test, develop, adjust, recognise, and acknowledge the condition of our church today, drawing from the deep wells of mature wisdom that arise out of our lived experience of the message of Jesus. We live in a secular twenty-first century world; we acknowledge changes and progress; we see God's hand as we stand in wonder and awe of what we find in the realms of digital technology, artificial intelligence, cosmology, quantum mechanics and quantum physics. The false dichotomy between the secular and the sacred, so beloved of earlier clerics, must be reconciled in a parallel movement towards regeneration and reform of our church life. Leadership today must comprehend innovation. Innovation is not evil! Changes of emphasis are not evil! Faith in our Cosmic Creator requires our ethical appreciation in the beauty and usefulness of much that is now available for the benefit of humankind. We are tasked with being proactive in the defence of that beauty and mystery (so ably highlighted in the work of teams like the one headed by Professor Brian Cox in his *Wonders of the Universe* BBC television series, 2011).

Response means finding our own Response-ability (the various knowledges and skills of discernment, and the caution that accompanies such reflections). *Response-ability* means we must *not* rely only on social, intellectual and spiritual resources that were already worn out centuries ago. We must accept *Responsibility* for ourselves and our planet before our Cosmic Creator God (Heasly, 2015, chapter 9). Reading the signs of the times today, as John XXIII asked us to do when he called for an ecumenical Vatican Council II, we must follow the sweep of interpretation of trends abroad in society and in our church. In this we can be ably assisted by Massimo Faggioli's 2019 book, *The Church in a Change of Era*, which, among other considerations, highlights the 'ideologicalisation' of what we see around us. Ideology is not always evil! But if it is mistakenly used in place of Faith, it wreaks havoc among the unwary, the lazy, and the confused among us.

The use of trilectic thinking patterns can help provide an alternative to the polarisation that infects our civilisation today. Their use may allow our Church to profit from the Plenary Councils, from the experience of synodality, and from a new respect for the wisdom of the various levels of the faithful today. I have outlined (see Heasly, *op. cit.*) how trilectic thinking can also serve our needs in a democratic scenario, by building on difference, diversity and development. Exploring the writings of Tom Roberts, James Keenan and Thomas Doyle (in the *National Catholic Reporter*, 1 January 2020), and their concept of vulnerability, can help shift us further towards a necessary change of paradigm. We must reserve the time and space to listen to the impetus of our Cosmic Sophia-Spirit, with whom we are called to partner, as co-creators with our Creator God and Cosmic Christ as Holy Trinity, in promoting regeneration of the communion of followers who saw Jesus lighting a breakfast fire on that Lake in Galilee so long ago; we can recall what Jesus told the daughter of Jairus: '*Talitha, cum*' (come, little one, arise!) (Mark 5:41).

Even though it was a challenge to read *Damascus*, the 2019 novel about St Paul by Australian writer Christos Tsiolkas, I welcomed its uncompromising realism. Tsiolkas shocks us out of our complacency and into a realisation that living in the time of Jesus would have been – for most of us at least – utterly different from living in today's world. Stark as the content of *Damascus* is, and as unblinking as Tsiolkas is in his depiction of degradation, the text challenges us to awake and arise too!

This may be a long-term process, but one with huge benefits: in our *Response* we can revisit the wonder and beauty of the world in which we live; we can change our lives, and change ecological conditions; we can find careful and kind ways to value and reorganise the way we treat our planet (*Response-ability*). We are custodians, we are stewards, and we need to tread lightly on the earth that our Cosmic God created, trusting in the many diverse ways available to us to deepen our relationship with ourselves, our planet and our God (*Responsibility*). Australia's Aboriginal peoples have already modelled – over millennia – how to have a relationship with ourselves, our Earth and our God. We can learn.

We *must* respond to the parlous state of our world today or there will be no possibility of leaving a God-given legacy to future generations. This became more urgent in the face of the pandemic raging at Easter 2020 as this book was being written. But our response must be a God-given approach, as we shift the emphasis towards care for the planet on which we live, and dare to explore what a change of paradigm might mean. We need to read the 'signs of our times' as John XXIII exhorted. There is no more time for dithering, for comfort zones, for personal preferences, for blocking the impulse to link the past, the present and the future in one harmonious process. Our Cosmic Creator God gave us personal intelligence so that we can make sense of the world around us, and reason carefully about how the world was, how the world is, but also how the world will inevitably be if we don't intervene on behalf of our suffering Creator God. A change of paradigm! And is that not another way of viewing what conversion of the heart is all about?

Vulnerability, transparency and inclusivity: we will need to be alive to all three states as we strive to consult, to learn, to respect, and to embrace areas of knowledge that at the moment seem outside the ken or experience of many of the clericalised figures in our church. We will need to discover the vulnerability of Jesus, as a child, as a prophet, as a misread leader of his time. We must recognise *our own vulnerability*, and truthfully, patiently accept it. We must consult, respect, and acknowledge those figures in the present hierarchy who don't seem to realise or acknowledge how vulnerable they are themselves (we can sometimes see this in the way they revert to doing what they have always done). We must recognise that the transparency that Jesus modelled by his living, his friendships, his teachings, his passion, death, resurrection – all this must be ours too. In personal living, in communal living, in governance of our church, we must confront the challenges and complexities of our twenty-first century with all the skills we can muster. That *transparency* must be seen, and be seen to be seen! In particular, it must be a requirement of all decision-making structures of the church. Anything less will be dumbing-down and dishonouring. Is that respect for the message of Jesus?

Inclusivity seems problematic for our church at present. Denis Edwards, in *Deep incarnation, God's Redemptive Suffering with Creatures* (2019), helps us to recognise what *real inclusivity* means. Not only are we tasked by our Cosmic Sophia-Spirit in the third millennium to repair the church itself, but we must also address our disastrous exploitation of the earth's resources. *Inclusivity* must not be just a lazy interest in allowing others to be: it must be an active, keenly conscious approach to diversity and difference.

We are at a stepping-off point. We must move forward, and use strategies like trilectic thinking rather than doggedly remaining within old binary patterns. We were put on this planet as custodians – to care for and replenish the earth we call home. Harmonious response therefore must rely on response-ability – our ability to respond. War and devastation will be our lot if we ignore the importance of honing our knowledge, our skills and our lived experience – our response-ability. We must also accept our personal responsibility to leave a gentle imprint on this beloved earth we share. That will also entail accepting our communal responsibility to work with those around us, sharing our knowledge and skills so we leave a gentler imprint of *each* community on this beloved earth.

The HUG/BUG (see Heasly, 'Uncertainty Grid', 2015) is one way of addressing this aim, because an application of the decision-making skills described there can harmonise life experience with the message of Jesus. Combined with Arbuckle's careful Action Plans and the recommendations contained in *Getting Back on Mission* (2019), the Heasly Thinking Skills system can assist us in addressing vulnerability and reaching for inclusivity. The great Communicator, Jesus, as Second Person of our Cosmic Trinity, has spoken to us through the medium of scripture, theology, philosophy and science, and the Cosmic Sophia-Spirit has invited us to be collaborators in the project of inclusivity in the third millennium. We ignore that invitation at our peril.

Inclusivity will operate in a myriad of ways, allowing us to live as much of the message of Jesus as we can safely understand without slipping into rigid uniformity or colourless piety. We make decisions, good or not-good, daily. Inclusivity will require us to carefully test our virtues, values and ethical decisions on a regular basis. Wide and fearless research and education will be essential. We already know, in this third millennium, just how vital education is for the wellbeing of us all – especially now when we need science and ethics to find our way through and past the crisis caused by the corona virus.

We will contribute as we accumulate information, knowledge and skills. And our contribution must be meant to be generous and outgoing, as Jesus modelled for us. We will find new resources in digital technology, artificial intelligence, quantum mechanics, quantum physics, neuroscience including knowledge of the human body and advances in medical know-how. We will acknowledge the past even as we look forward, and recall Isaac Newton's words (in his 1675 letter to his rival Robert Hook): 'If I have seen further, it is by standing on the shoulders of Giants'.

Being generous and outgoing is an inclusive activity as well as a personal disposition. It is clear, then, that prejudice against women can no longer go unaddressed. We should note the research of Chris Geraghty (*Virgins and Jezebels*, 2020, p. 1), where he examines the long-standing misogyny of the hierarchy. He notes that a misogynist slant can be found even in Paul, Augustine, Jerome, Chrysostom, Bonaventure, Aquinas, many popes including Innocent lll and John Paul ll, and theologians, who have used 'theological nonsense dreamed up and preached to keep women in their place, to undermine the fundamental and foundational values of Jesus' kingdom – to keep the keys of that kingdom safely in clerical hands'. Geraghty highlights also the lingering echoes of Aristotle's assumptions about women's biology: and his discussion of Tertullian's writings (pp. 215 & 334) is hilarious but devastating nonetheless.

And now we must recognise the importance of *vulnerability*. In doing so we must think about the various teachers, lecturers, parents and other people around us from whom we can discover what is to count as learning. This means identifying how we teach and how we learn to make the decisions that we must make as responsible prophets who dispense the message of Jesus to coming generations. We need therefore to remember the question-starters that broaden our responses and add to our burgeoning knowledge and wonder at the diversity surrounding us: how/ when/ where/ why/ what/what else/which/ what if? Questioning helps us to broaden our understanding, and that eternal push to know more leads us towards trust in the Lord. It follows that it could also lead to trust in the teachers, the liturgists, the dispensers of sacraments, the leaders and models – were they not so hierarchical, clericalised and hidebound. If modelling of good governance, transparency and inclusiveness is absent within the structure of the present church, we can turn to what Matthew told his people: that they were to be comfortable rather than anxious because they had brought the Scriptures and their daily practice of prayer with them to the struggling new community of Jesus himself.

Perhaps part of what our Cosmic Sophia-Spirit is asking us to collaborate in is the task of re-educating the hierarchical figures of today, expecting them to put aside the constraints of yesteryear and address – fearlessly – the needs of today. Vulnerability comes into the picture when each one of us is faced with the recognition of how and where we have made mistakes. We are called by our Cosmic Communicator, Jesus, to accept the responsibility to remedy, generously, the hurts we have caused, and to find ways to save one another from devastation, distress and extinction – along with our degraded planet. Jesus taught us how to concentrate on love and care, how to be faithful without extremism and rigidity. We can restore meaning to our lives, by building, in the manner of Jesus, a belief system, and a good life, not just a good career. We are tasked by our Cosmic Sophia-Spirit to lead in the integration of self, family and community with the Cosmic Creator and all humanity in its extraordinary, exciting diversity. It is also our task, every day, to remedy the hurts, the trauma, and to meet the needs of those around us

– just as Jesus did so long ago at the water's edge of the Sea of Galilee.

My discussion now circles back to the imperative implicit in this chapter heading: we require a change of paradigm. Again, Massimo Faggioli (in *Commonweal*, 18 February 2020) is pertinent. He observes that 'Francis' post-synodal exhortation *Querida Amazonia* is unique in more ways than one. It throws his one major structural reform into considerable turmoil'. In Faggioli's analysis, the whole church must now face 'both/and' choices rather than 'either/or' choices. But he also identifies that this 'one major reform – the Bishops' Synod and synodality itself – now shows a systemic weakness', claiming that: 'The moment is a crossroads for the Francis pontificate'. So how do we, in the Great South Land of the Holy Spirit, fashion our contribution? We see the gaping space between the two systems of thinking, and we realise, with some foreboding, that it is to this gap that our Cosmic Sophia-Spirit is pointing. The gap is demanding of us that we take the steps needed to signal clear progress towards paradigm change. We can take some comfort from Austin Ivereigh (*Tablet*, 22 February 2020), when he discerns that Francis, in *Querida Amazonia*, is taking steps to direct us toward a third way, a possible new route to alleviating the suffering and deprivation of his beloved Amazonian First Peoples. Ivereigh here shows us that the practice of trilectic thinking may open the door to more options than we realised.

Cynthia Bourgeault (in *Wisdom Jesus*, 2008) illustrates for her readers a method for transforming heart and mind, calling this a new perspective on Christ and His message. Her helpful reflections include a description of a 'Centring Prayer' she calls 'deeper wisdom knowing', and the value of transforming the way we think. 'Meditation is the tool you use to "upgrade your operating system", to move from that "either/or" thinking of the binary mind into the more spacious heart awareness that sustains the wisdom way of knowing', she writes.

Andrew Hamilton (in *Eureka Street*, 20 February 2020) spells out clearly what a change of paradigm requires of us all: 'Catholic reflection on social justice has been supercharged by Pope Francis, who in his encyclical *Laudato Si'* declared the Cry of the Poor and the Cry of the Earth to be central to faith. He insisted that neither could be addressed simply by technological fixes but required personal conversion to see the world as gift to be respected, a home, and not as a prison or a mine'.

So to analysis: change of paradigm means change of content by degree; it means change of some emphases, adding or dismissing elements that no longer have significance or relevance. The process of change may require a shift in the starting point of deliberations about a contentious topic; it may also mean accepting a change in direction as we delve deeper into the recesses of meaning. Change may also include assigning different weight to the various issues under analysis; new ways of reviewing the whole may bring surprises, or highlight factors hidden prior to the reviewing process. Of crucial importance, then, will be the way we calibrate our *response* and *response-ability*, how we address and manage our further *responsibility* in the light of a bigger picture. Obviously, change must be tested, through a rigorous process that allows for nuances not previously taken into account. It will be a challenge to integrate all into a more authentic whole, but we know well that this is the lived experience of partnership with our Cosmic Sophia-Spirit.

In acknowledging the new, we may not necessarily

– or not yet – want to dismiss the old. It may take at least two full years to test the change of paradigm, and probe its consequences within our lived experience, especially in matters of faith. Too much in today's world speaks of pain and trauma, and we are aware that in this century our church has brought its own pain and trauma to the 'People in the Pews' – all of them. If the aim is to change, it must be a change that builds towards a deeper relationship with our Cosmic Communicator, the 'Wisdom Jesus' of Bourgeault. That way we can expand our understanding of the wonder of this universe given to us under the aegis of our Cosmic Holy Trinity, and be confident that we have not changed any tenet of our faith, but have responded in faith and love to the invitation of our God: Cosmic Creator and Communicator and Collaborator – Father, Son and Holy Spirit of yore.

Quentin De La Bedoyere, in *Autonomy and Obedience in the Catholic Church* (2002) is encouraging: we can deepen this exploration on our journey towards this Cosmic God, conscious that humankind must immediately begin, seriously, to repair. No more prevarication! It is decision-making time. Working together we can balance autonomy and obedience. But we will be working out these virtues, values and ethics in communities facing massive disruption and misrule. De La Bedoyere lays bare the truth of our troubled church as he details the remarkable and alarming decline of the Church, and the maturity of the laity. He argues that the blind obedience of the past is now replaced by the responsibility of personal autonomy. He surveys the changes wrought during the pontificate of John Paul II, where primacy of conscience was downgraded, and moral concepts and reasoning became less important than obedience to laws, papal authority and control. I would argue that we need the freedom to integrate love and law as a means of attaining moral maturity. My HUG/BUG process (Heasly, 2015, p. 120) shows at least one way in which this can be done with integrity.

In this process of change of paradigm, it is possible to take what De La Bedoyere highlights as newer or less familiar virtues, values and ethics into our daily lives. He lists *Self-esteem*, in which we give due emphasis to the personal dignity of each of us as a child of our Cosmic God. This is followed by *Empathy*, in which the spiritual realm is not ignored, but the community aspect is included in our efforts to follow the message of Jesus. (The 'ME' diagram, p. 114 in my Thinking Skills System, addresses this element fully.) The third virtue is also a skill: that of *Listening*. In De La Bedoyere's account, it is central to our growing maturity that we learn all of its elements: hearing, attending, accuracy in interpretation of meaning, reading body language – or the absence of it. Only by listening fully are we able to recognise the gap, that space in which mistaken expectations arise. In the case of Popes and the Curia, this phenomenon is now called by many 'Reception Theology'.

The partner of Reception Theology is perhaps Trauma Theology, so named because of the material unearthed in the research of Ute Ranke-Heinemann (1990), Gianluigi Nuzzi (2015), Frederic Martel (2019), and the various Commissions and Inquiries worldwide into the abuse of children. A burning community anger is the natural concomitant of these abuses and their systematic cover-ups. We need humility, and careful, open investigation as we face the full implication of such behaviours, in our church, and also in the treatment of Australia's Indigenous people over hundreds of years.

De La Bedoyere makes a virtue and value of the skill of *Recognising Qualities of Self and Others*: we must look for the good qualities in those with whom we work and live; we must reject misrepresentation and cover-up; we must choose the generous way of acting and require sincere response rather than the fakery and deliberate lies served up as truth by manipulators in both the secular and the religious domains. These 'new' virtues encourage the development of personal autonomy of each of God's creatures, all sentient beings, and the elements of the world around us. They are pointers to the change of paradigm that is emerging.

Change is natural in the evolution of each created being, allowing for growth – physically, intellectually, socially, emotionally, and spiritually – every day as we journey through life towards maturity, towards partnership with our Cosmic Trinity. Meditation in the Bourgeault way offers a channel for this to happen. Our culture of immediacy, of instant everything, of a theory of everything, tends to make us forget matters central to our challenge to be part of the future, not a remnant of the past. We are indebted to De La Bedoyere: no to clericalism with its emphasis on ontological change! No to hierarchicalism with its emphasis on the minutiae of liturgy, on rigid control of power and dismissal of the 'People in the Pews'! We have the privilege of being loved by our Cosmic Trinity as we are, as we become, as we discover, as we strive to leave this earth with the lightest footprint we can achieve, as co-creators with our Cosmic Creator, as co-communicators with our Cosmic Christ, as co-collaborators with our Cosmic Sophia-Spirit! *Talitha, cum*! As Jesus commanded: We, too, awake! To be awake is to be prepared to adjust, to learn, to respond: and this is central to change of paradigm.

So as I awake and arise on a beautiful Melbourne autumnal day, and watch the delicate burnished gold haze herald the sunrise, I am deeply aware of the beauty and refreshment of a new day, and hopeful for a genuine change of paradigm. We should never forget the sudden prompting of Sophia-Spirit, even at a time when a virus changes the way we live our daily lives. We must be awake to the opportunities that have been masked by our way of life, a way ruinous to the planet we call home. We must become aware of, and appreciate anew, the space around us, the intimacies of touch, a smile, a quick affirmation, catching echoes of the presence of Jesus; we must not allow the clamour of daily living to overwhelm the tiny signs of that presence. There is a freshness now, even amid tragedy, that is bringing us close to one other, to the suffering around the globe, and to the chance to offer kindness and compassion on a daily basis in our lives and in a church free of clericalism, of hierarchicalism, treading the path of regeneration and offering possibilities of reform for our suffering, believing 'People in the Pews'.

Further Reading

Arbuckle, Gerald A., *Abuse and Cover-Up* (Maryknoll: Orbis Books, 2019)

Armstrong, Karen, *The Bible – a biography* (Atlanta Monthly Press, 2007)

Armstrong, Karen, *The Case for God* (London: The Bodley Head, 2009)

Barbour, Ian G., *Religion and Science* (New York: HarperOne, 1997)

Baring, Anne, *The Dream of the Cosmos* (Dorset: Archive Publishing, 2013)

Beattie, Mary, *The Quest for Meaning* (Rotterdam: Sense Publishers, 2009)

Beattie, Tina, Opinion piece in *The Tablet*, 22/2/20

New Revised Standard Version (NRSV) Bible (London: Collins Publishers, 1989)

Bourgeault, Cynthia, *Wisdom Jesus* (Colorado: Shambhala Publications, 2008)

Castley, Paul F., *A Time to Hope* (Melbourne: Coventry Press, 2019)

Catholics for Renewal, *Getting Back on Mission* (Mulgrave: Garratt Publishing, 2019)

Clooney, Francis X., *The New Comparative Theology* (New York: T. & T. Clark, 2010)

Collins, Paul, *Absolute Power* (New York: Public Affairs (Hachette), 2018)

Cox, Brian, BBC television series *Wonders of the Universe*, 2011

De La Bedoyere, Quentin, *Autonomy and Obedience in the Catholic Church* (London: T. & T. Clark, 2002)

Delio, Ilia, *Birth of a Dancing Star* (Maryknoll: Orbis Books, 2019)

Dreyer, Elizabeth A, *Earth Crammed with Heaven* (Mahwah, NJ: Paulist Press, 1994)

Edwards, Denis, *Human Experience of God*, (Mahwah, NJ: Paulist Press, 1983)

Edwards, Denis, *Deep Incarnation* (Maryknoll: Orbis Books, 2019)

Faggioli, Massimo, e-book: *The Church in a Change of Era* (La Croix International, 2019)

Faggioli, Massimo, Opinion piece in *Commonweal*, 18/2/20

Geraghty, Chris, *Virgins and Jezebels* (Mulgrave: Garratt Publishing, 2020)

Goosen, Gideon, *Bringing Churches Together* (Geneva: WCC, 1993, 2nd ed.)

Greenfield, Susan, *Tomorrow's People* (London: Penguin, 2003)

Hamilton, Andrew, Opinion piece, *Eureka Street*, 20/2/20

Heasly, Berise Therese, *Towards an Architecture for the Teaching of Virtues, Values and Ethics* (Bern: Peter Lang, 2015)
Heasly, Berise Therese, *Call No One Father* (Melbourne: Coventry Press, 2019)
Hunt, Mary & Diann L. Neu, *New Feminist Christianity* (Woodstock, VT: Skylight Paths Publishing, 2010)
Ivereigh, Austin, Opinion piece in *The Tablet*, 22/2/20
Jacobs, Alan, *The Gnostic Gospels* (London: Watkins, 2006)
Keller, Catherine, *Cloud of the Impossible* (New York: Columbia University Press, 2015)
Leirvik, Oddbjorn, *Interreligious Studies* (New York: Bloomsbury, 2014)
Lohfink, Gerhard, *No Irrelevant Jesus* (Collegeville, Minn.: Liturgical Press, 2014)
Lombardi, Federico SJ, Opinion piece in *La Civiltà Cattolica*, 10/3/20
Martel, Frederic, *In the Closet of the Vatican* (London: Bloomsbury Continuum, 2019)
May, John D'Arcy, *Pluralism and Peace* (Melbourne: Coventry Press, 2019)
Moloney, Francis J., *Broken for You* (Melbourne: Coventry Press, 2018)
Naudascher, Marie, Opinion piece in *La Croix International*, 17/2/20
Noone, Val, *The Priest and the Pill* (Fitzroy: Mary Doyle and Val Noone, 2019)
Nuzzi, Gianluigi, *Merchants in the Temple* (New York: Henry Holt and Co., 2019)
O'Connor, Mark FMS, Opinion piece in *Catholic Outlook*, Parramatta, 14/3/20
Oelrich, Anthony, *A Church Fully Engaged* (Collegeville, Minn.: Liturgical Press, 2011)

Pagola, Jose Antonio, *Jesus: An Historical Approximation* (Miami, 2013, 4th ed.)
Palmer, Daniel, Opinion piece in *Catholic Outlook*, 29/2/20
Pascoe, Bruce, *Dark Emu* (Broome: Magabala Books, 2019)
Pepinster, Catherine, Opinion piece in *The Tablet*, 22/2/20
Pope Francis, *Gaudete et exsultate* (Strathfield: St Paul's, 2018)
Pope Francis, *Laudato Si'* (Strathfield: St Paul's, 2015)
Pope Francis, *Querida Amazonia* (Strathfield: St Paul's, 2020)
Pope John Paul ll, *Love and Responsibility* (London: Harper Collins Fount, 1981)
Rahner, K. & Johann B. Metz, *The Courage to Pray* (New York: Crossroad Publishing, 1981)
Ranke-Heinemann, Uta, *Eunuchs for the Kingdom of Heaven* (New York: Doubleday for Penguin Books, 1991)
Roberts, Keenan and Doyle, Opinion piece in *National Catholic Reporter*, 1/1/20
Rohr, Richard. *Yes, and... Daily Meditations* (Cincinnati: Franciscan Media, 2013)
Tanner, Kathryn, *God and Creation in Christian Theology* (Collegeville, Minn.: Fortress Press, 2005)
Tarnas, Richard, *The Passion of the Western Mind* (New York: Ballantine Books, 1991)
Tsiolkas, Christos, *Damascus* (Crows Nest: Allen and Unwin, 2019)
Vodola, Max *A, Friendly Guide to Vatican ll* (Mulgrave: Garratt Publishing, 2012)
Wijngaards Institute, Opinion piece 17/2/20
Wilson, George B., *Clericalism – The Death of Priesthood* (Collegeville, Minn.: Liturgical Press, 2008)

Epilogue

Berise Heasly

And now, as we review our own project, we begin to appreciate the depth, wisdom, discernment – and genuine distress – emanating from the laity, those 'People in the Pews' – us.

We have lived through the shock, disgust and exhausting experience of the uncovering of sexual abuse of children and vulnerable others, by paedophile priests and their ilk. The Victorian Royal Commission first told us of the emerging scandals, but did not prepare us for the extent of the official cover-ups by hierarchy or the anguish of the victims and their families. The overwhelming truth became apparent when the subsequent *Royal Commission into Institutional Responses to Child Sexual Abuse*, called by then Prime Minister Julia Gillard, began its harrowing investigations and listened to the victims themselves. And the 'People in the Pews' wept with them.

Then we were threatened by climate variations that have resulted in the longest and broadest drought in Australian history. The same 'People in the Pews' did what they could to help in individual ways, feeling helpless and fearful for the farmers eking out a living in such dreadful conditions. The media showed us pictures of dying fish, scrawny livestock and depressed farmers, and we prayed for them, unable to see an effective way to support them.

But overwhelming as all this was, there came deeper trauma as the appalling bushfires took their toll during the 2019-20 summer. Every state in Australia experienced extraordinary heat, and bushfires more fierce than any endured in living memory. And we wept again for the devastation of those people who lost so much. Yes, we began to help as best we could, but the emotional toll was huge, for all.

And then the Plenary Council requirements were upon us! We did our best to address the lack of guidance, the lost trust and the defiance of some in the Australian hierarchy, for whom not even the manifest evil of child abuse was enough to prompt them to acknowledge that change was urgently needed.

Some developments stand out, as dedicated leaders within the ranks of the 'People in the Pews' used their knowledge, their lived experience and their wisdom to lay down what must be done, and what will not ever be acceptable in the future. Catholics for Renewal's volume, *Getting Back on Mission*, is a particular example, but there are many other works of equal value.

But again, some of the hierarchy of Australia chose to control, as they had always done, and the Plenary Council preparations have been developed to suit much of their preferred style. Confronted with the ABC TV revelations, in mid-March, of the disgusting abuses of former priest Vincent Ryan, we ask one question: is there any chance that the changes needed are even being contemplated in episcopal circles?

We know that the Spirit blows where the Spirit wills. We cling to the hope in Jesus who told us to come to Him when we were weary and overburdened. We see the damage perpetrated on our distressed planet as a biting dismissal of our Creator God. As the coronavirus grips our world, we perhaps begin to see that the Holy Cosmic Trinity is pushing us towards change and harmony even if some Australian hierarchs are not in tune.

We can pray! But we must also step up and humbly offer our leadership, our wisdom, our insights, and do the work needed, step by step, as the Spirit guides us. We must remember that, in Isaac Newton's phrase, we stand on the shoulders of those who went before us. Tradition, rather than traditionalism, is a good starting point, but it must be tradition refreshed for twenty-first-century living.

Readers may notice that, even though authors writing here have not consulted one other, there is an harmonious interaction between concepts, issues, concerns, theologies and philosophies in the various papers. All sketch elements of that 'change of paradigm' that points to a determined preference for an encounter with Jesus rather than ritual, righteousness and relentless judgments.

We, too, are indebted to the church leaders of Latin America who gathered in May 2007 near the shrine of Aparecida. Austen Ivereigh, in *Wounded Shepherd*, his beautiful portrait of Pope Francis (p. 153), draws the connection between the outcomes for these peoples and for us. The encyclical *Evangelii Gaudium* was Francis' official response. In it he heralded the demise of 'Christendom' and the initial promotion of what was to count as synodality.

Francis' priorities as pope included: 'First, a discerning, humble response to the change of era that led inevitably to a program of reform. Second, was a new kind of pastoral action that could offer the experience of God's mercy and an alternative modernity – the 'Kingdom of God'. Third, a resolutely missionary refocusing to enable an encounter with Christ, capable of raising up missionary disciples. Fourth, a Church that needed to become a welcoming, warm mother in response to the cold non-belonging of technocracy. Fifth, taking seriously the Church as the people of God, simultaneously evangelising and evangelised'. (Ivereigh, *Wounded Shepherd*, p.161).

We, too, as the laity of the Catholic Church are searchers, regenerating and reforming our experience of Church today, taking account of the new kind of synodality that is the central focus of Vatican Council ll. This goal is advanced in the 'Fundamental Principles' laid out by Ormond Rush, Parish Priest in Townsville, Queensland, and lecturer at Australian Catholic University, Brisbane. In *The Vision of Vatican II* (2019), he lays out in precise detail some twenty-four principles – hermeneutical, theological and ecclesiological – as fundamental to real understanding of the phenomenon we call Vatican ll (2019).

In his final section, 'Receiving the Vision', Rush takes up the significance of Reception Theology. His analysis of how the reception of all the concepts, directions, issues, theologies and philosophies as understood by sections of the Church today is set out in detail: the *official* reception of Vatican ll 'refers to the interpretation, promulgation and implementation of the conciliar vision of popes and local bishops once the council ends'; *theological* reception of Vatican ll 'refers to the work of academic theologians attempting to bring to synthesis the vision of the conciliar decisions and documents, whether as a whole or with regards to particular teachings'; *spiritual* reception of Vatican ll 'refers to appropriation of the council's call for a deeper faith response to God's saving revelation within the daily life and practice of all the faithful' (pp. 539-542). All three are interdependent, of equal importance, and central to the acceptance of the vision of Vatican ll.

Rush promotes the call of Francis for 'a listening church, a synodal church' (p. 545) with dramatic emphasis, highlighting the change of era, the change of paradigm. And 'We, too', the laity, promote the same call, because, as we step into the future, where the 'new normal' becomes the familiar starting point, we heed Pope Francis' concept of *parrhesia*: speaking frankly and forthrightly, but asking forgiveness for any consequent discomfort. Without adversarialism, we discern where our Cosmic Sophia-Spirit is providing the foundation for newness in our relationship with Jesus, for the flourishing of the 'People in the Pews', for the regeneration and reform of our Church, and for a renewed and refreshed care of Planet Earth, given from eternity by our Cosmic Creator God.

Contributors

Michael Elligate AM is Parish Priest of St Carthage's University Parish Parkville in Victoria. A graduate in Social Sciences and Education, he is Chair of Human Ethics Research (Social Sciences) University of Melbourne, and also sits on the Arts Education Committee. He is Deputy Chair of the Research Committee at The Walter and Eliza Hall Institute for Medical Research Ethics Committee.

Hugh McGinlay was born and educated in Scotland. He has post-graduate degrees in Theology (Gregorian University, Rome), Scripture (Biblical Institute, Rome and Jerusalem) and Religious Education (Dundalk, Ireland). He has worked in publishing in UK and Australia, including twenty years with the Uniting Church's publishing house, where he was responsible for that Church's adult education programs and liturgical resources. He currently works as Acquisitions Editor for Coventry Press in Melbourne. Hugh is married to Andrea, and they have two sons and four grandchildren.

Sue Phillips is a member of an international women's missionary congregation, the Franciscan Missionaries of Mary (FMM). She was missioned to Morocco, North Africa, and for nine years was interacting in the daily dialogue of life with those of the Islamic faith. She has been involved for many years in ministries in Australia, accompanying people on the margins of society. In 2002, she was elected to the FMM International Leadership team in Rome and then for a further six years served as the International Leader. She is a founding member of Women's Wisdom in the Church Inc (WWITCH) and is currently involved in prison ministry.

Marilyn Hatton is a woman of faith, a wife, mother and grandmother, and a long-term advocate for full equality for women and all in the Catholic Church. She began this work as the co-coordinator of Ordination of Catholic Women Inc. and continues to work for full equality in the Catholic Church, particularly for women in decision-making at all levels. She pursues this through active membership of a number of reform groups. As a foundation member of both Catholics Speak Out, and Concerned Catholics, she has represented Australia at meetings in London, Paris, Germany, Rome and USA at Women's Ordination Worldwide (WOW) and the International Catholic Reform Network (ICRN) in Limerick and Chicago. She was also former Convener of the Australian Catholic Coalition for Church Reform. Her tertiary background includes R.N., B.App.Sci. MLitt. Gender Studies ANU, and past professional roles, including as ACT Women's Health Adviser, influence her advocacy.

Eleanor Flynn is a medical graduate, recently retired as Associate Professor from the Department of Medical Education at the Melbourne Medical School. There she was involved in student selection and teaching, particularly aged care, communications skills and ethics. Until 2017 she also worked as a Palliative Care specialist in both hospital and community settings. She has published on clinical and philosophical aspects of care of the dying, selection of medical students, professionalism in medical schools, communications skills and supporting the staff who support students. She has studied Theology for more than twenty years and has a B.Theol and an M.Theol which looked at the differences in the beliefs and rituals of death between medieval Christianity and twenty-first century Australia. She is an active member of her parish where she is a member of the child safety team, and a leading member of Women's Wisdom in the Church (WWITCH) group.

Judy Benson has been a barrister at the Victorian Bar for twenty-two years, practising principally in the area of relationships law, within the Children's Court child protection division, the Family Court, and in the guardianship and disability jurisdictions. Prior to that she worked for twenty years in book publishing both in Sydney and in Melbourne, with publishing houses that included Butterworths (now Lexis Nexis), the University of NSW and Allen & Unwin (in the roles of editor and later commissioning editor), and Oxford University Press, Pitman Publishing, and finally at RMIT Press, where she was the publisher. She served for five years (from 1999) on the Archdiocese's Catholic Commission for Justice Development and Peace and for five years as the chair of a Catholic girls' college council in metropolitan Melbourne.

Janette Elliott is a PhD Candidate at the University of Divinity and currently works as Registrar at Yarra Theological Union, Box Hill Victoria. She has been praying and working with the writings of Julian of Norwich – the subject of her PhD thesis – over a thirty year period. She is fascinated by Julian's engagement with Christ in the context of an 'anxious age' not unlike our own, amidst personal struggles and life's great challenges. Originally a teacher, and formed strongly in Benedictine spirituality, Janette seeks through her writing to empower others to trust the divine strength within them – grounded in the God of love, compassion and blessing – as Julian did.

Constant Mews is a specialist in medieval religious history and thought, and Professor and Director of the Centre for Religious Studies at Monash University, Melbourne. He is internationally known as author of *The Lost Love Letters of Heloise and Abelard: Perceptions of Dialogue in Twelfth-Century France* (2nd ed., Palgrave Macmillan, 2008) and of many studies of their contemporaries, including the German visionary and musician, Hildegard of Bingen. He is currently completing a monograph, *The Scholastic Revolution: The Invention of Theology in Medieval Europe 1000-1300*. He is deeply committed to promoting religious literacy in a multi-religious society, and thus to interreligious dialogue. At Monash, he teaches world religions, and religion and society. He also supervises graduate research in a wide range of fields within religious history.

Ian Hamilton is a cradle Catholic who has spent his working career within Catholic secondary education in NSW, South Australia and Queensland. In addition to his work as an English teacher, he has often taught Religion and Ethics and Study of Religion. His leadership roles within schools included being a Director of Spirituality, Director of Mission and Liturgist. Initially completing an Arts degree and Diploma of Education at the University of Newcastle, he later undertook a MA in English literature at Sydney University. Later still he completed the Graduate Diploma in Theological Studies, followed by the Master's degree in Theological Studies at Adelaide College of Divinity (Flinders University).

Paul Collins is a historian, broadcaster and writer. A Catholic priest for thirty-three years, he resigned from the active ministry in 2001 following a dispute with the Vatican over his book *Papal Power* (1997). He is the author of fifteen books. The most recent is *Absolute Power: How the pope became the* *most influential man in the world* (Public Affairs, 2018). A former head of the religion and ethics department in the ABC, he is well known as a commentator on Catholicism and the papacy and also has a strong interest in ethics, environmental and population issues. www.paulcollinswriter.com.au

John D'Arcy May was born in Melbourne, Australia, in 1942. He now lives in retirement near Geelong. He received doctorates from the universities of Münster (Ecumenical Theology, 1975) and Frankfurt (History of Religions, 1983). He taught at the Catholic Ecumenical Institute, University of Münster, 1975-1982, and was Ecumenical Research Officer with the Melanesian Council of Churches, Papua New Guinea, 1983-1987. He was Director of the Irish School of Ecumenics, Trinity College Dublin, 1987-1990 and 1995, where he was Associate Professor of Interfaith Dialogue, 1987-2007. He is a Fellow Emeritus of Trinity College. His most recent book is *Pluralism and Peace: The Religions in Global Civil Society* (Melbourne: Coventry Press, 2019).

Berise Heasly spent thirty-six years as a secondary school humanities teacher, specialising in Religious Studies, and other disciplines, including English, at both junior and senior secondary levels. She holds a PhD from Victoria University, Melbourne, and a Graduate Diploma of Theology from Catholic Theological College, University of Divinity, Melbourne. She is the author of *Call No One Father* (2019). She has research interests in the teaching-learning process within education, and its relevance for the resolution of issues facing the Catholic Church of the twenty-first century. She is an active member of St Carthage's University Parish, Parkville, Melbourne, Australia and a founding member of Women's Wisdom in the Catholic Church (WWITCH).

www.ingramcontent.com/pod-product-compliance
Lightning Source LLC
Chambersburg PA
CBHW010244010526
44107CB00063B/2678